MEASURED
SHOP DRAWINGS
F·O·R
AMERICAN
FURNITURE

MEASURED
SHOP DRAWINGS
F·O·R
AMERICAN
FURNITURE

Thos. Moser

Sterling Publishing Co., Inc.   New York

Other books by Thos. Moser

How To Build Shaker Furniture
Thos. Moser's Windsor Chairmaking

Edited by Michael Cea

Library of Congress Cataloging in Publication Data

Moser, Thomas.
Measured shop drawings for American furniture.

Includes index.
1. Furniture—Drawings. 2. Furniture—United States.
I. Title
TT196.M68 1985   749.214   84-26872
ISBN 0-8069-5712-3

ISBN 0-8069-6792-7 (pbk.)

Copyright © 1985 by Thomas Moser
Published by Sterling Publishing Co., Inc.
 387 Park Avenue South, New York, N.Y. 10016
Distributed in Canada by Sterling Publishing
% Canadian Manda Group, P.O. Box 920, Station U
Toronto, Ontario, Canada M8Z 5P9
Distributed in Great Britain and Europe by Cassell PLC
Artillery House, Artillery Row, London SW1P 1RT, England
Distributed in Australia by Capricorn Ltd.
P.O. Box 665, Lane Cove, NSW 2066
Manufactured in the United States of America

Table of Contents

Dedication

*This book is dedicated to
the craftsmen at
Thos. Moser Cabinetmakers*

Acknowledgments

These designs are the result of a group effort at Thos. Moser Cabinetmakers. Virtually every piece has been perfected through trial and error, through collaboration and refinement, and each has evolved from earlier prototypes. Although as originator of our company I am responsible for the design work, each cabinetmaker contributes his or her ideas to the process of perfecting a piece. Christian Becksvoort, who worked with us from 1974 to 1982, was responsible for developing the table maximus, the 24″ coffee table, the 30″ coffee table, and the stereo components cabinet. Chris and my wife Mary collaborated on the table maximus variation and both étagères, while Mary and I jointly designed the endchests. Bill Huston, who is a master cabinet-maker and more recently our manager, has been a central figure in standardizing all of these designs. Over the past eight years of our association he has been pivotal in developing and maintaining an uncompromising level of excellence in design and workmanship. Working with occasional advice from me and Mary, Bill designed the panel desk, Gates cabinet, file cabinets and bowfront credenza.

The spindle headboard was conceived by Merry Vaeth, who ran the Finishing Department for several years. David Rogers, who was so instrumental in orchestrating our Chair Department and who has worked with me as a builder and designer on and off for ten years, designed the vault table in 1983. His constant design suggestions and unending provocations are deeply valued. These individuals did not work in a vacuum—each depended heavily on all of us at Thos. Moser Cabinetmakers. We are a team working toward a single goal. All of us take great pride in our work and we are all confident that our best efforts will outlive us in the form of well-made and well-designed furniture.

Brian Vanden Brink has been our photographer for the past four years and has been responsible for much of the good success we have had in advertising and selling our work. His patience and keen eye and his technical ability with all things photographic have been instrumental in creating our regional and national persona. Brian's formidable skill is present throughout the book.

The line drawings are the work of Craig Howard who, over the course of almost a full year, committed himself to translating my scribbles and scratches into a single comprehendible set of plans. Working closely with Bill Huston and Lynette Breton, Craig painstakingly brought together hundreds of diverse sketches and details from a dozen sources to produce this set. His efforts are acknowledged and also heartily appreciated.

Credit must also be given to Carolyn Thomas, who reproduced and collated all the drawings and typed the text. In doing this she has all but learned to build the furniture.

Finally, special credit must go to my wife and business partner, Mary Moser. Although I am the designer of record, it always has been on the basis of Mary's urgings and critical judgment that I proceed. Without her, this furniture would not exist.

Thomas F. Moser
New Gloucester, Maine

Introduction

In 1973 we began building furniture in solid wood here in Maine. Since then, we have shipped it all over the country and abroad. It is possible for us to come across a piece of our work in Indiana or Texas and immediately recognize it as ours. I know our style, our workmanship, our design detailing as I know my own hand, yet I cannot quickly or comfortably label it. I have asked others, students of furniture, experts, critics, professional designers and marketeers to give our style a name. The response is usually the same: "Of course, you make . . . Ah, well, it's wooden furniture." It has been described as transitional, American crafted, post-Modern, post-Industrial, Hi-Tech, Lo-Tech, organic, adaptive.

It *is* difficult to label our furniture. Perhaps it should be enough to know that we have created a recognizable style, the enjoyment of which is shared by a small group of kindred spirits. However, my need for order—a need that manifests itself in our work—necessitates that we categorize what we do.

Every form I have ever attempted had its beginning in something I have seen sometime in the past—maybe a fragment, maybe a detail, maybe a complete three-dimensional piece of furniture, maybe not even furniture at all. It might have been something in nature, but most often it was something man-made from the past. I hold no claim to uniqueness in our design for I do not feel strongly about uniqueness since I do not believe that anything fundamentally new can exist in the decorative arts. At its worst and at its best, furniture design is an accumulatory activity—a gradual process of defining and redefining elements that already exist. Unlike most decorative arts and certainly all fine art, furniture design is restricted by the use to which the object itself must be put. It is not enough to design a beautiful chair or a beautiful table. Real beauty is achieved when a chair is sat upon in comfort, and a table is worked off of in comfort and security. Human needs have changed little in the thousands of years since the first wooden chair was fashioned, and utility is as important now as it ever has been in our history. This in no way diminishes the need we feel to express ourselves in our work; it simply says that our self-expression must be disciplined in that along with giving beauty, we must also give function.

Just as use circumscribes form, the material itself restricts the designer's freedom. The designer who commits himself to the use of solid wood must know about its strengths and weaknesses, about the predictable expansion and contraction that it will experience through the cycle of the year, about grain effect, about joint integrity. As an organic material, wood will change from season to season and from climate to climate. The designer/woodworker knows this; this knowledge further limits undisciplined flights of creativity.

The Evolution of Furniture Design . . .

The 1984 Scandinavian Furniture Fair, held in Copenhagen, had as its theme "As Time Goes By." This refrain from an old song describes the evolutionary process of design, the central notion being that a chair, desk or table evolves from designer to designer, from period to period, into an ever-improving—or at least ever-changing—form. This notion of gradualism, of adaptation and re-adaptation, is the very basis of Danish design. World-class designers such as Hans Wegner have shown how an element of design is introduced, germinates for a period of time and blossoms into a finished piece, only to be redefined, improved upon, adapted and redefined some more until it is possible to trace its evolution over a twenty-year period and note the modifications, often subtle, which lead to a more improved piece of furniture. There is no shame in repetition and rediscovery.

This is not to suggest that the evolution of furniture design is characterized by a steady, even line of improvement, for innovation often comes in spurts caused by some technological advancement. The Bauhaus designers of the early 20th century who adapted the trappings of machinery to interior design did so abruptly. New materials and new methods of working old materials fostered revolutionary design changes, but even these forms were adaptations from pre-existing objects which were used out of context. Today, new man-made materials and finishes offer greater freedom, but to those committed to making functional wooden furniture, the pool of design "genes" has remained more or less constant.

Reaching Back for Permanence . . .

I grew up in suburban Chicago, the child of immigrants. My father and mother, like most parents who struggled through the depression, valued all those machine-made products that were often outside their reach. After the War, this urge to acquire the fruits of industrial American life was even stronger. In the 1950's, a decade of conspicuous consumption, we coveted mass-produced items. And while machine-manufactured products were highly sought after, hand-crafted objects were often considered inferior.

This attitude of depreciating hand craftsmanship existed well into the 1970's, but then the gentle revolution began. Young Americans were no longer satisfied with the throw-away culture. They were looking for something of more permanence, and so was I. I found it in early 19th-century America. In the 19th century, the objects Americans used in their daily lives—whether on the farm, at work or in the home—were often of a human scale, designed with integrity and built with care to last for generations. It is this reaching for permanence, this concern with the future and not just the here and now, that drove our forefathers and made the work of their hands so valuable and so cherished by us today.

From a design point of view, there was also a kind of ultimate utility achieved in the early 19th century. Along with an ethic of utility was the ethic of minimalism or economy. "Waste not, want not" was an adage lived by in those days, although there was an abundance of natural material.

It is possible that I am an incorrigible romantic about the 19th century. To be sure, not all the objects made on the farm, in the home and in early factories of America were well-made. Cabinetmakers often cut corners, worked from unsound principles, but by and large craftsmen of the period were preoccupied with permanence. Unlike so much of what has surrounded us in recent years, what could be used by a man and his family in the 19th-century could also be used by his children's family and even their children's family.

This notion of permanence is once again becoming central to our thinking. There exists a new interest in products well-made, especially wooden products. There exists an enormous interest in fine wood-working, not only in terms of acquisitions, but also among people who want to make things of wood. I suppose it's a kind of quality revolution. It has been my good fortune to produce well-crafted furniture in a time when there are people who are fed up with shoddy workmanship and discriminate in their buying habits.

The Beginnings of American Furniture Design . . .

The pieces of furniture contained in this book have their beginnings in the 19th century. These pieces are strongly influenced by Shaker design and what is referred to at times as country Chippendale, country Hepplewhite or country Sheraton forms. This type of furniture, designed in the 17th and 18th centuries, was based upon European design—more particularly, English style.

American furniture design was basically English furniture often designed 20 years late. The first furniture designed and built in the New World was medieval in appearance. The Pilgrims brought with them notions of furniture from the William and Mary and from the Jacobean periods of English history. This was rugged furniture, often built of oak, and certainly built to last.

But 18th-century England was influenced by the Renaissance, and the medieval forms soon gave way to classical Georgian design. Individuals such as Thomas Chippendale and Christopher Wren brought about a sense of sophistication and appreciation for the classical period. Queen Anne furniture, which consisted of unadorned curves, became adorned with Greek and Roman detailing. Even Chinese and Japanese influences were felt in decorative designs.

Towards the end of the 18th century, English designers such as the Adam brothers, Hepplewhite and Sheraton refined the heavy ornament of Georgian furniture into fine lines and delicate detailing. It was this refinement that so influenced what historians today look upon as American Federal design.

In 1800, every small town in America had its cabinetmaker; in the larger towns and cities there were many cabinetmakers working and interacting. They were grounded in English Renaissance design and in the designs of Hepplewhite and Sheraton. Those working in rural areas did not have access to the fine, exotic veneers and tooling necessary for elaborate inlay work and marquetry. The rural cabinetmaker instead used materials that were freely at hand—American hardwoods such as cherry and walnut, birch and maple. Native pine was used as a secondary wood rather than European beech or oak.

These rural cabinetmakers were not given to fancy applied carvings, perhaps not so much because they didn't know those techniques, but more because their clients could not afford to pay for such ornamentation. And so there appeared by 1820 in our country a kind of unornamented, highly utilitarian furniture which, although it had European origins, was strictly American in nature. Each part of the country had its own characteristic detailing. New England furniture tended to be austere and of smaller scale than that which was built in the middle colonies. In the South, classical English forms lingered. Each area of the country developed an imprint based upon local woods. Individual craftsmen also signed their work, not only with pencil and chalk, but with design details. A certain kind of individuality existed among craftsmen of the period even though they worked from the same design books and, in many cases, used the same imported English "irons" for their moulding planes and profiling tools.

This was the state-of-the-art that the Shakers further developed into clean, functional design. The Shakers themselves drew converts from among the general population. They brought with them skills and a design heritage learned in the secular world. The prevalent secular taste and their commitment to unity and utility is what Shaker furniture is all about.

Keeping the 19th-Century Heritage Alive . . .

From this heritage of 19th-century craftsmanship, Thos. Moser Cabinetmakers has developed furniture for 20th-century use. Natural wood and linseed oil take precedence over plastic and petrochemicals.

Even fasteners, when possible, are made of wood. The natural hardwoods we use have a richness unparalleled by imported exotic woods.

The building techniques themselves are reminiscent of 19th-century joinery. The repertoire of joint work, whether mortise and tenon, dovetail or groove and spline, has proven its usefulness over the centuries. There exists today, particularly in New England, an abundance of antique wooden furniture utilizing this vocabulary of joints; and the furniture is as good today as when it was built 100 or 150 years ago.

One wonders what will be around in the year 2100. What of our production will future generations venerate and point to with pride as having achieved great permanence? Will mould-injected plastic be looked upon as heirloom furniture in the year 2100? Will plastic-veneered plywood held together with neoprene knockdown fittings be looked at with the same wonder and joy that we experience when looking at a handcrafted mortise-and-tenon joint of the centuries past? Can the synthetic achieve affection?

I do know that in today's mass furniture market much of what is offered is called Heirloom quality. Though it is supposed that the pieces so advertised somehow or other have a secure future, calling a piece a heirloom does not make it one. However, I would like to think in a nonboastful way that what we have produced this past decade here in Maine will survive the ravages of time and will be looked upon as a unique contribution to the 20th century—and a continuation of a tradition in wood which has been around for so many centuries. And, I would further hope that in the year 2100 other craftsmen will sustain this tradition, moving forward in the use of solid hardwood construction, improving upon our "improvements."

It has been my philosophy from the beginning that our greatest challenge is to imbue utilitarian work with dimensions of artistry. But the pieces must be used, and that is why we've built tables, chairs, cases, cupboards, clocks and other pieces that people use in their daily lives.

Our shop is not an art studio, it is a working shop. It's a labor intensive environment in which a group of craftsmen work together, producing with efficiency and therefore creating affordable furniture. Underlying all of our production activities is the notion that people, not only mega-wealthy people but those of ordinary means, have the same need to enjoy fine craftsmanship and beautiful materials. With efficiency, finely crafted furniture can again be produced and made broadly available.

Our furniture is by and large unornamented. There is a beauty in a totally functional piece that is far subtler than any beauty that could be achieved through applied ornamentation or decoration. The joint work itself is decoration. The exposed dovetails, for example, which appear on almost all outside edges of cases, give evidence of how the piece is made. When the structure is revealed in this way, it adds another dimension, almost a cubistic dimension, for the inside and the outside are one and the same.

I would like to think that the designs contained here are complete and are the result of a certain economy. If anything is added to a piece, it becomes overdone; if anything is subtracted from a piece, it becomes less useful.

This attempt at reaching back into the past to carry forward a lost craft is certainly not unique to Thos. Moser Cabinetmakers, or to the hundreds of cabinetmakers who are now working. Seventy-five years ago there arose both in England and the United States a design trend called the Arts and Crafts Movement. This was an attempt to bring back some of the dignity of wooden furniture that had been lost during the Industrial Revolution. Designers in England, such as William Morris, and in the United States, such as Gustaff Stickley, worked to revive what was felt to be a lost art. And it is as a result of their activities that there reappeared a reverence for the craft that influenced American furniture design for at least several generations.

The efforts of these men were relatively short lived, however, and by the 1930's mass production again overshadowed craftsmanship. It has only been in the past ten years that there has been a strong revival, and one wonders how long this revival will be sustained.

How long will it be before the American market turns its back upon natural materials and production reminiscent of a simpler day? Americans are a fickle people, and tastes and trends are constantly changing, but there exists a fundamental need for color, texture, natural materials and the mark of the human hand. There is a need in our lives to communicate with one another, not only verbally but through the products we have built.

A handmade object with all of its flaws and inconsistencies provides a kind of comfort; whether that object is 100 years old or was made last week, the builder is still communicating. I cannot tell you how often I have seen a person come into the showroom, first look at a chair, then run his hand over the surface to feel the smoothness of the grain, and finally sit in it—and in a sense be clothed by it. There is something in a well-finished piece of wood that speaks to all of us across generations and across cultures.

How Our Designs Evolved . . .

The designs shown in these chapters are the result of an evolution that is at least ten years in the making. When we first started producing furniture here in New Gloucester, we built entirely to order. A customer would come in with a photograph or a sketch and say, "I would like you to make this, but it needs to be only five feet wide and six feet high, and I want it deep enough to hold a stereo system." So we would design on paper, usually in very rough form, and then proceed to build, the design taking place more on the bench than on paper. When finished, the piece was evaluated, and if it stirred our emotions strongly, it was sketched and a second piece was built, and perhaps a third and fourth, until it gradually became part of our repertoire.

But for the first seven years, none of this furniture was ever drawn. Continuity of these designs were based upon an oral tradition. The dimensions and the details of all the furniture were kept in the minds of the cabinetmakers, and I had only to say, "Chris or Ed, build a No. 23," and they would take from their sketch pads, slips of paper or story sticks, remnants of the last time it was made, and then would produce it. Each time it would be produced with greater refinement. It wasn't until 1977 that any of this furniture was ever seriously drawn. But even after 1977 and the first Shaker book, there was still never an attempt at bringing together all of the designs in a drawn form. We then realized that after ten years of making furniture in the oral tradition, it was time to get our designs down on paper.

This book is the result of that effort. The pieces are drawn with sufficient detail so that any skilled cabinetmaker can immediately recognize the parts and how they relate to one another. We are not so naive as to assume that the furniture drawn here is definitive and not subject to change or modification. There has never been a piece built in our shop that could not be built better next time. They will undergo subtle changes as they are reproduced down the years, and I would encourage any cabinetmaker to use the drawings not so much as the last word in construction and proportion, but rather as reference points. These designs are improvements on the designs of the past; they will be improved upon in the future.

This book is organized into six parts. The first one deals with seating. The second treats table construction. Next comes casework (chests, dressers and such), followed by a section on desks and writing tables and one on beds. Lastly, a catch-all section covers miscellaneous furniture. Each piece is shown as it has been built and photographed here in New Gloucester, Maine. The photograph is accompanied by scaled line drawings which show not only the piece in perspective but also dimensions and, in some cases, exploded views and details. The Appendices carry details which in most cases are shared by a number of different pieces.

SEATING

Chairs must follow several rules of design. The most obvious is that since chairs are sat upon, they must accommodate the human body. Another restriction is that chairs have to serve in conjunction with something else—a table, work surface or desk. Legs must have side clearance, and arms must fit under horizontal surfaces.

Chairs, unlike most case furniture, must be readily moveable and, therefore, light. And because of their lightness and the pressure placed on them, the whole chair must flex with the strain.

Chairs vary considerably in width. A standard width of a side chair ranges from 18 to 20 (45.7 to 50.8 cm) inches. The width must be increased for an armchair to allow for those of wider proportions to fit between the posts of the arms; based on my observations, 21 inches (53.3 cm) seems sufficient. Remember, armchairs and side chairs must fit between table legs with enough space so they can be moved about.

A well-designed chair arm has to fit under a tabletop. Since most desk and tabletops are 29 to 30 inches (73.6 to 76.2 cm) from the floor, and since the average top is 1 inch (2.54 cm) thick, then an arm surface that is not more than 27 or 28 inches (68.5 or 71.1 cm) from the floor is appropriate.

Few table aprons or skirts allow less than 24 inches (60.9 cm) between floor and apron. Deeper aprons can play havoc with kneecaps. In almost all cases, the arm cannot be made low enough to pass under the apron. Therefore, an armchair usually cannot be slid under a table for storage nearly as far as a side chair.

The height of most wooden chairs ranges from 32 inches (.81 m) to 42 inches (1.06 m). Overall height is the result of aesthetic judgment based upon the inherent nature of the chair and the room in which it is to be placed. For example, if a table-and-chair combination is to offer a low profile, such as in front of a picture window or open expanse, then chair backs should be kept low.

For those who would like to see more seating designs, my book *Windsor Chairmaking* (Sterling, 1982) offers a comprehensive explanation of designs for chairs, stools, settees, and benches.

Continuous Arm Chair

The continuous arm chair is one of the rarest of antique Windsor chairs because it was and continues to be the most difficult to make. Having its origins in Rhode Island, the continuous arm chair is the most "American" of the Windsors, as well as the most beautiful.

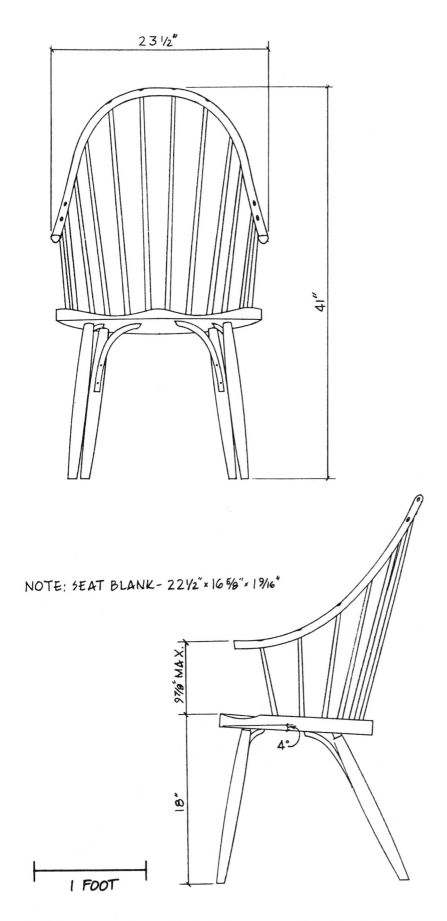

23 1/2"

41"

NOTE: SEAT BLANK- 22 1/2" × 16 5/8" × 1 9/16"

9 7/8" MAX.

18"

4°

1 FOOT

Front and side views of the continuous arm chair. For chair, spindle, leg and stretcher details for this or any other chair see the Appendix on chair details (page 306).

Continuous Arm Rocker

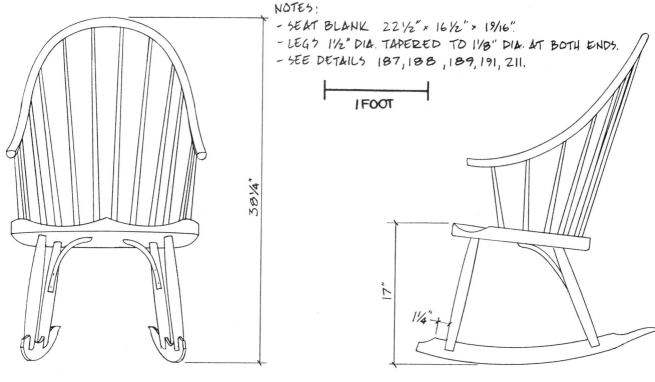

NOTES:
- SEAT BLANK 22½" × 16½" × 1 9/16".
- LEGS 1½" DIA. TAPERED TO 1⅛" DIA. AT BOTH ENDS.
- SEE DETAILS 187, 188, 189, 191, 211.

1 FOOT

38¼"

17"

1¼"

Throughout American history, chairs of all types were cut down and fitted with rockers. The addition of rockers turns this table chair into a comfortable rocking chair.

Continuous Arm Bench

Churches and meeting houses of the past used long benches, usually with rather straight backs, for public seating. This continuous arm bench combines the grace of the continuous arm with the function of the straight-back settee.

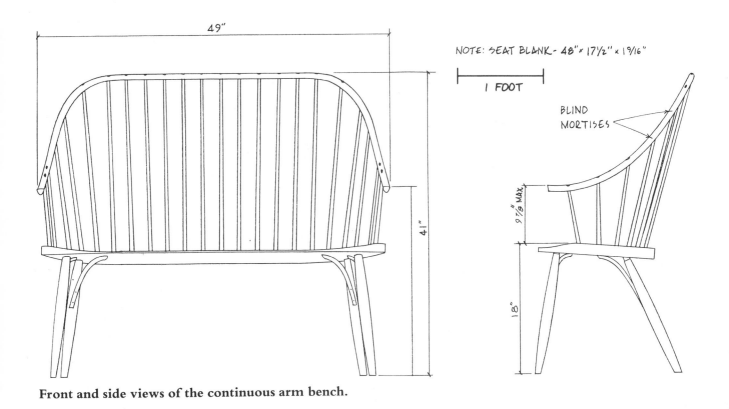

NOTE: SEAT BLANK- 48" x 17½" x 1⁹⁄₁₆"

1 FOOT

BLIND MORTISES

9⅞" MAX.

18"

49"

41"

Front and side views of the continuous arm bench.

Bowback Chair

Slightly smaller than the continuous arm chair, the bowback chair is designed to serve as its side chair. Like the continuous arm chair, the bowback is angled for back support when used at a table or desk.

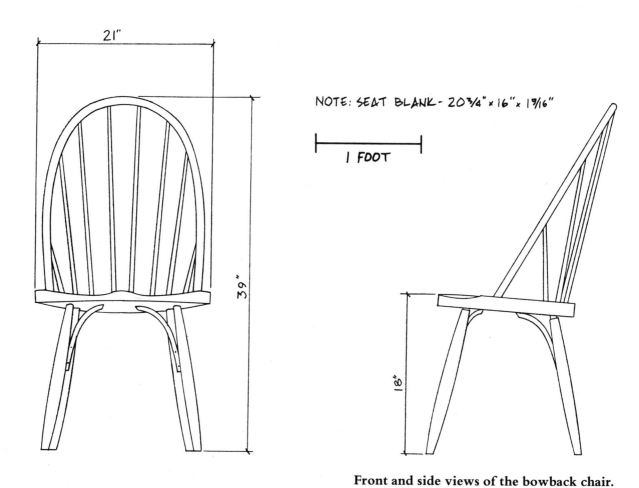

NOTE: SEAT BLANK- 20¾" x 16" x 1⁹⁄₁₆"

21"

39"

18"

1 FOOT

Front and side views of the bowback chair.

Inverted Arm Chair

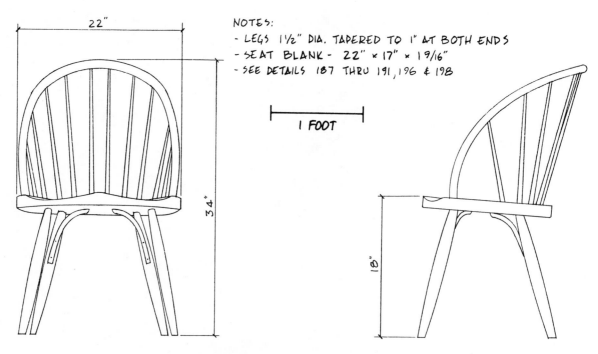

22"

34"

18"

NOTES:
- LEGS 1½" DIA. TAPERED TO 1" AT BOTH ENDS
- SEAT BLANK - 22" x 17" x 1⁹⁄₁₆"
- SEE DETAILS 187 THRU 191, 196 & 198

1 FOOT

In certain rooms, a collection of high-back Windsor chairs offers too much visual activity. The back of the inverted arm chair is lowered to just over table height, offering comfort while maintaining a low profile.

Inverted Arm Bench

The low back and curved stretcher of the inverted arm bench give it a distinct contemporary look. It combines design detailing of the past with the forms of the present.

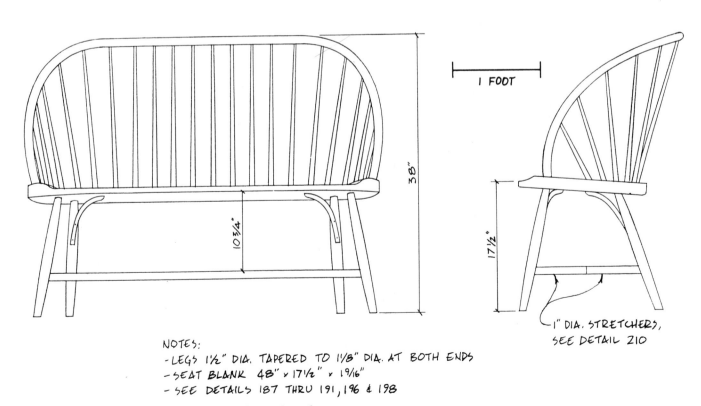

1 FOOT

38"

10¾"

17½"

1" DIA. STRETCHERS, SEE DETAIL 210

NOTES:
- LEGS 1½" DIA. TAPERED TO 1⅛" DIA. AT BOTH ENDS
- SEAT BLANK 48" × 17½" × 1⅞6"
- SEE DETAILS 187 THRU 191, 196 & 198

Front and side views of the inverted arm bench.

Eastward Side Chair

The eastward side chair was first built of walnut and ash. Like the work of George Nakashima, this chair hints of the Orient. It is deceptively comfortable.

NOTES:
- LEGS 1¾" DIA. TAPERED TO 1"
- SEAT BLANK - 16¾" × 17" × 1⁹⁄₁₆" (15" WIDE IN BACK)
- SEE DETAILS 189 THRU 192, 198 & 199

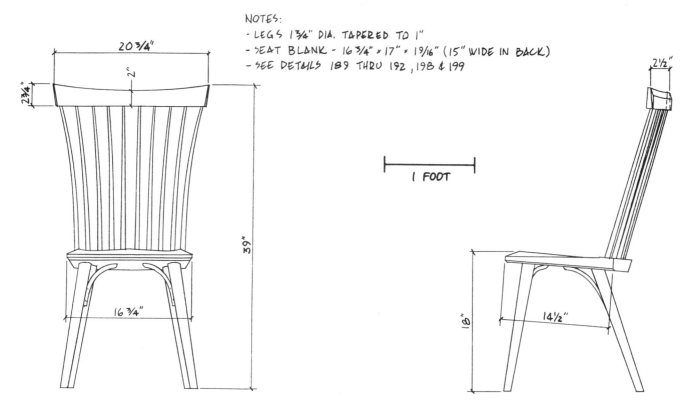

Front and side views of the eastward side chair.

Eastward Arm Chair

Increasing the width of the side chair slightly and adding arms results in the eastward arm chair, which takes its place at the head of the table.

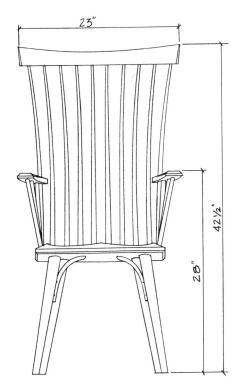

NOTES:
- LEGS ARE 1¾" DIA. TAPERED TO 1" DIA.
- SEAT BLANK 18½" × 18" × 1⁹/₁₆"
- 19⅜" IN BETWEEN ARMS
- SEE DETAILS 189 THRU 192, 198, 199 & 209

I FOOT

Front and side views of the eastward arm chair.

Eastward Settee

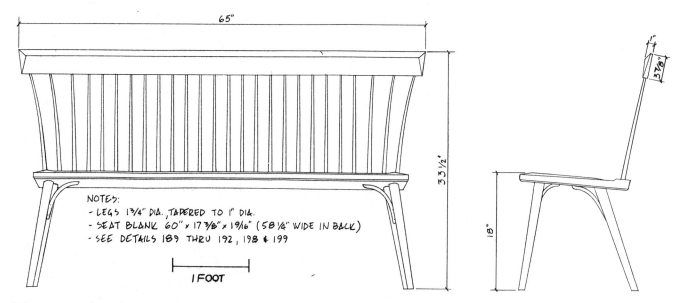

NOTES:
- LEGS 1¾" DIA., TAPERED TO 1" DIA.
- SEAT BLANK 60" x 17⅜" x 19/16" (58¼" WIDE IN BACK)
- SEE DETAILS 189 THRU 192, 198 & 199

65"

33½'

3⅞"

18"

1 FOOT

The eastward settee is an exercise in economy—nothing can be added, nothing can be taken away. Five feet wide, it can seat two people comfortably, and three intimately.

Studio Stool

The studio stool originated as a tractor seat. Depending on its height, the stool can fit at a kitchen counter, bar or under a tall writing desk.

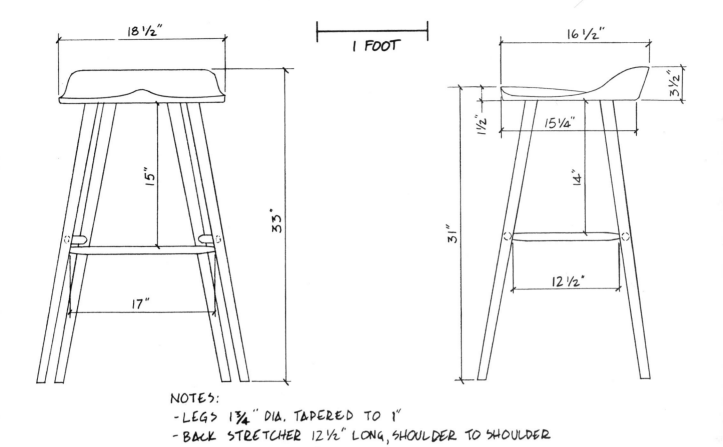

NOTES:
- LEGS 1¾" DIA. TAPERED TO 1"
- BACK STRETCHER 12½" LONG, SHOULDER TO SHOULDER
- SEE DETAILS 192 & 193

Front and side views of the studio stool.

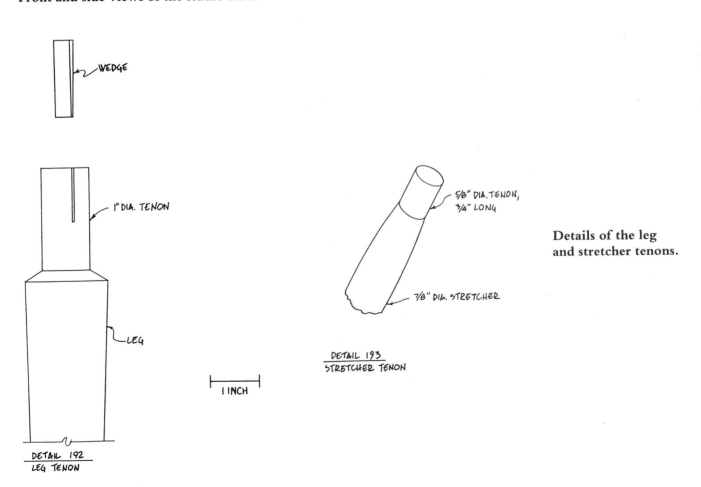

WEDGE

1" DIA. TENON

LEG

DETAIL 192
LEG TENON

1 INCH

5/8" DIA. TENON,
3/4" LONG

7/8" DIA. STRETCHER

DETAIL 193
STRETCHER TENON

Details of the leg and stretcher tenons.

Bowback Stool

The inspiration for the back of this bowback stool was the Harley Davidson motorcycle seat. Those old enough will remember the curved chrome bar at the rear of the saddle, and the white knuckles of the passenger.

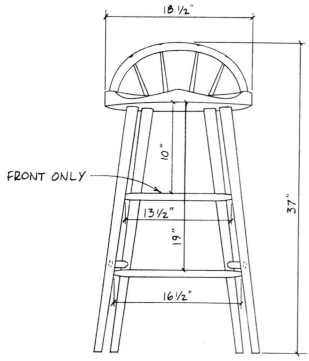

FRONT ONLY

18 1/2"

10"

37"

13 1/2"

19"

16 1/2"

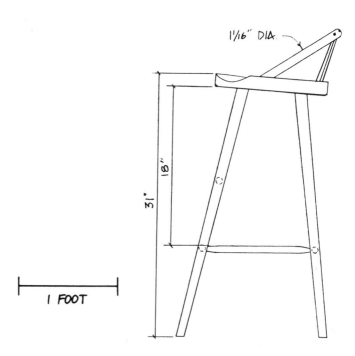

1 1/16" DIA.

31"

18"

1 FOOT

NOTES:
- LEGS 1 3/4" TAPERED TO 1" DIA.
- SEAT BLANK - 18 1/2" × 14" × 1 9/16"
- CAN BE CUT TO A MINIMUM HEIGHT OF 25"
- BACK STRETCHER 13 1/2" LONG, SHOULDER TO SHOULDER
- SEE DETAILS 192 THRU 195

Front and side views of the bowback stool.

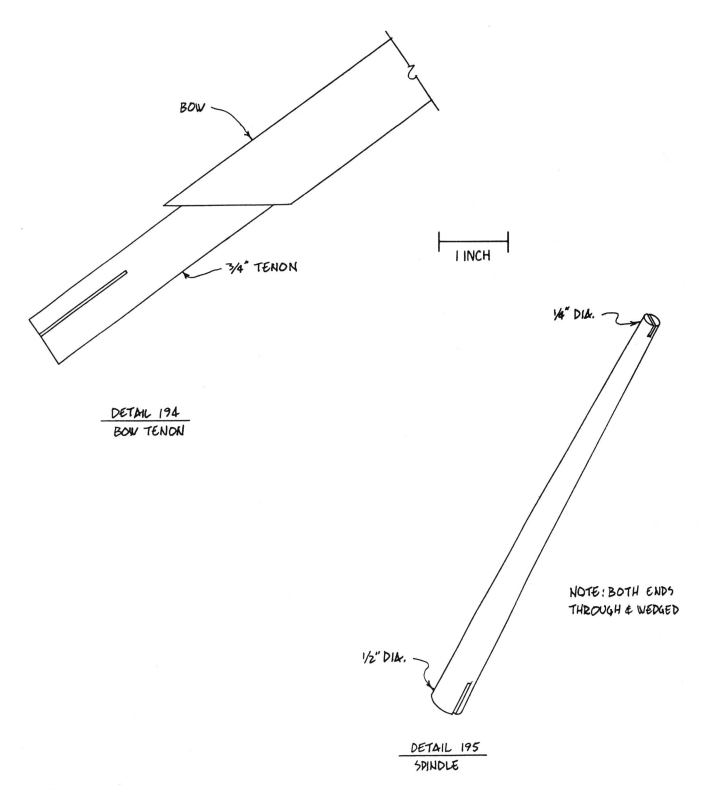

BOW

3/4" TENON

1 INCH

DETAIL 194
BOW TENON

1/4" DIA.

1/2" DIA.

NOTE: BOTH ENDS
THROUGH & WEDGED

DETAIL 195
SPINDLE

Details of the bow tenon and spindle. For details of the leg and stretcher tenons, see page 29.

TABLES

In the early 19th century, the average dining table built in the United States was between 27 and 29 inches (68.5 and 73.6 cm) high. We are considerably taller than our forefathers. Therefore, the tables shown in this volume are 30 inches (76.2 cm) from the floor. Also bear in mind that if a table is to be useful, it must have at least 25 inches (63.5 cm) of free space between the floor and the bottom of the rail or apron. This allows a person seated on a standard chair that is about 18 inches (45.7 cm) from the floor to slide under the table without hitting his knees on the underside of the table.

In the case of a dining table, we view as an absolute minimum 24 inches (60.9 cm) of perimeter space necessary to achieve a place setting, while 30 inches (76.2 cm) would provide a more gracious setting. Remember, too, that a place setting needs 16 to 18 inches (40.6 to 45.7 cm) of depth so that dishes, cups and saucers and water glasses can be placed. When designing a table, it is necessary to think about what's under a table as well as what is on top. Nothing is so aggravating than to be seated at a nice-looking table, only to straddle a leg. Chairs should be storable under a table, although, obviously when an armchair is used, it becomes difficult to have room for the arm to pass under the apron.

Other important considerations of table design have to do with expandability. In many instances a family will seat four or six on an everyday basis, but there comes that special time several times a year when the table will have to accommodate up to 12. During these special occasions it is nice to be able to expand the table. But expandability is almost always achieved at the expense of stability. Leaves, whether they are hinged or external, are difficult to support, so provision must be made to strengthen the table when they are used.

There is one other set of dimensions that should be briefly discussed and that is the overall size of the table relative to the room in which it is to be used. Dining rooms by and large are almost afterthoughts in the design of the average new American home, and often they are very small or so interrupted by windows and doors as to have virtually no undedicated floor space. A fully extended dining table should have a minimum of three feet (.91 m) of floor space between table and wall. Also bear in mind that a large table may not be able to be brought into a room if it requires going up flights of stairs or narrow hallways. Any table measuring six feet in length or less can always be brought into a room tipped on end. But an eight- or ten-foot (2.4- or 3.0-m) table is so massive that it may be impossible to bring it into the room.

Historical Perspectives

Many of the table designs shown in this chapter have interesting origins. The harvest table began in rural early American life, where tables similar to the one shown on page 34 were used at harvest time to accommodate many field hands. The trestle table first used by our Pilgrim forefathers consisted of a long, wide board on a trestle or stand, but gradually evolved into the design you see on page 41.

We based the design for the table maximus (page 48) on the early 19th-century dining table developed by the English. This table could be extended by use of hinged leaves supported by either gate legs or swing legs, and ranged in overall length from a modest eight feet (2.4 m) to 20 or 30 feet (6.1 or 9.1 m), in which many legs and several sections were used. As the name implies, when these table elements are incorporated, a great deal of variety can be used in table design.

The tables shown in this chapter have been tested, and they work. Chairs fit under them, people fit *at* them, and they do indeed perform their function.

Harvest Table (six-foot)

Side, end and top views for the harvest table.

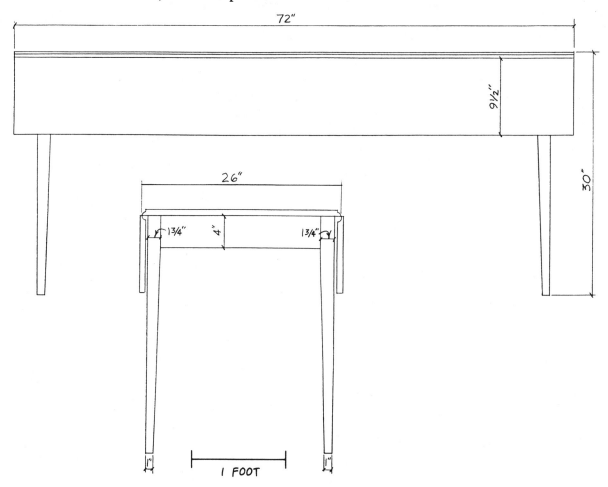

The harvest table can be adapted to a limited space in a dining area, using only 36 inches (.91 m) of floor space with its leaves down. The nine-inch (22.8-cm) leaf allows side chairs to be placed around the table under the leaves when they are down, making this an excellent space for storing unused chairs. Broader leaves, which are more commonly found in drop-leaf tables, offer greater table surface space but do not allow for storing chairs around the table. The leaf supports, called "spinners," work well. The rule joint gives a trim fit when the leaf is down, and also keeps crumbs from falling through when the leaf is up.

Harvest table.

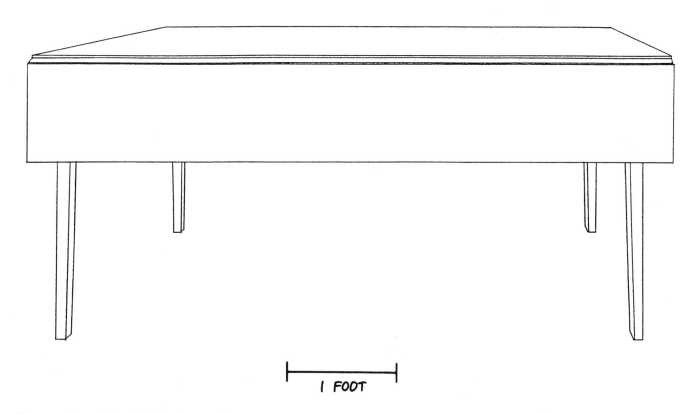

1 FOOT

Perspective of six-foot harvest table.

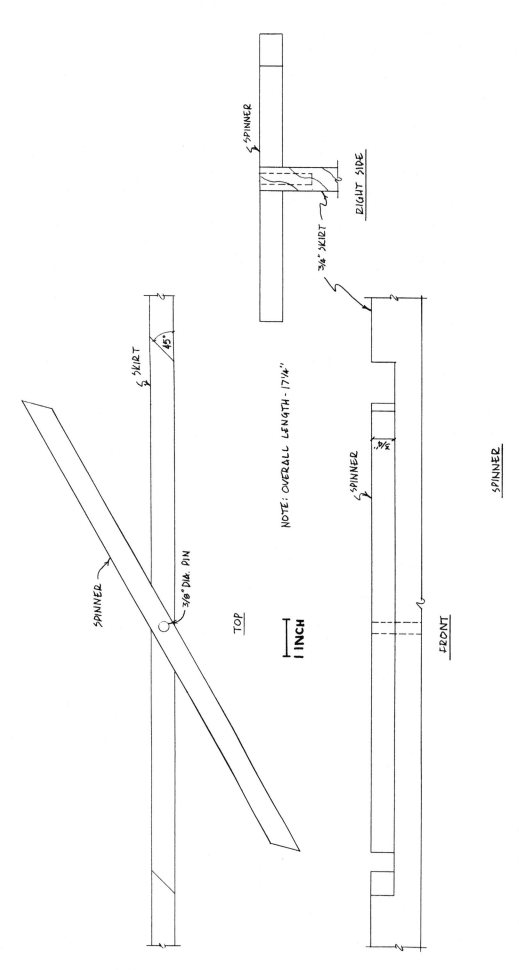

SPINNER

SKIRT

45°

3/8" DIA. PIN

SPINNER

TOP

NOTE: OVERALL LENGTH - 17¼"

1 INCH

SPINNER

3/4" SKIRT

RIGHT SIDE

SPINNER

3/4"

FRONT

SPINNER

Leaf support data for the spinner.

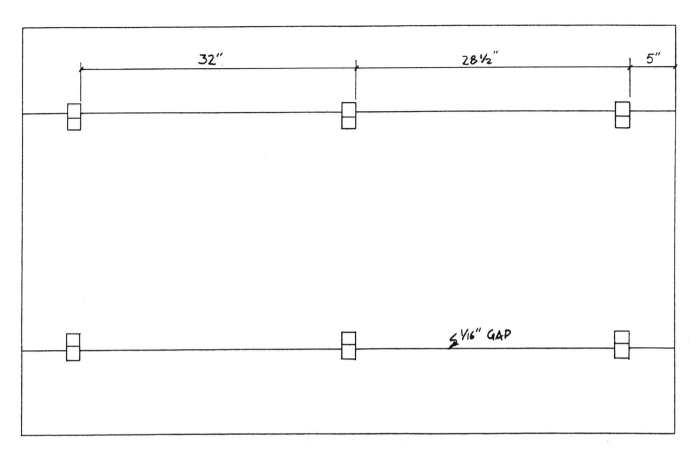

32"   28½"   5"

⟋ 1/16" GAP

HINGE LAYOUT
BOTTOM VIEW

1 FOOT

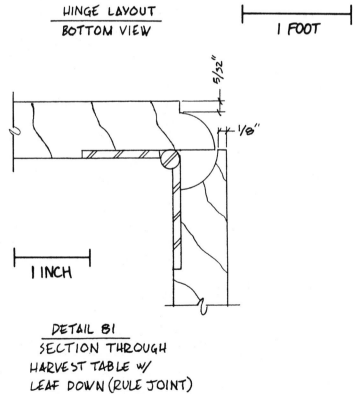

5/32"

1/8"

1 INCH

DETAIL 81
SECTION THROUGH
HARVEST TABLE w/
LEAF DOWN (RULE JOINT)

Hinge layout and Detail 81 for the six-foot harvest table.

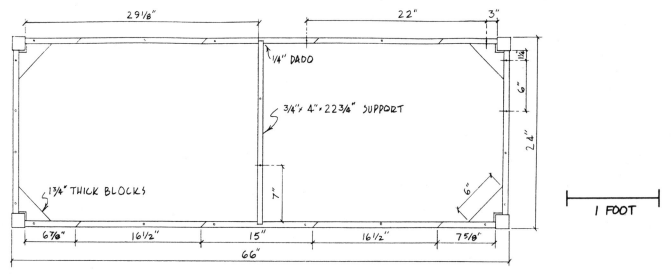

Table frame for the six-foot harvest table.

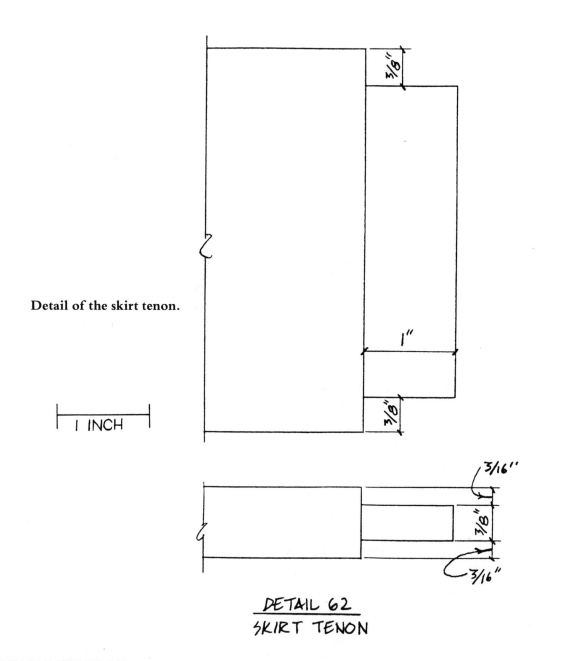

Detail of the skirt tenon.

DETAIL 62
SKIRT TENON

Harvest Table (eight-foot)

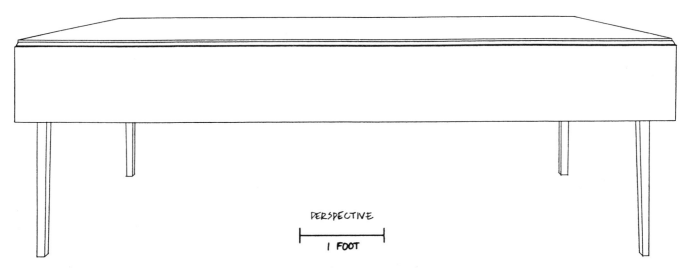

PERSPECTIVE

1 FOOT

The eight-foot harvest table is like the six-foot design except it is 24 inches (69.9 cm) longer and accommodates two additional place settings for a total of eight to ten people. The one outstanding disadvantage is that when you use the table, the leaves have to be extended; otherwise, the table can only be used at its ends.

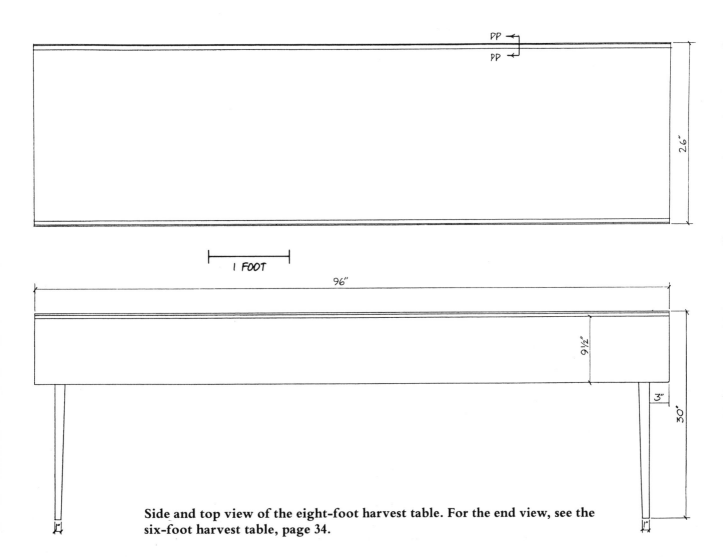

Side and top view of the eight-foot harvest table. For the end view, see the six-foot harvest table, page 34.

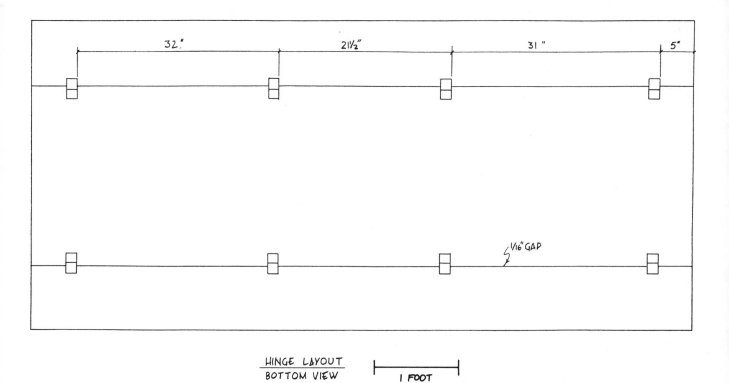

<u>HINGE LAYOUT</u>
<u>BOTTOM VIEW</u>

1 FOOT

32"   21½"   31"   5"

1/16" GAP

Hinge layout of the eight-foot harvest table.

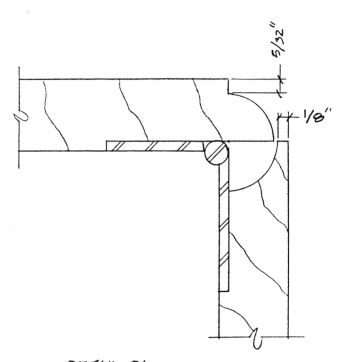

5/32"

1/8"

Detail 81.

DETAIL 81
SECTION THROUGH
HARVEST TABLE W/
LEAF DOWN (RULE JOINT)

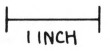

1 INCH

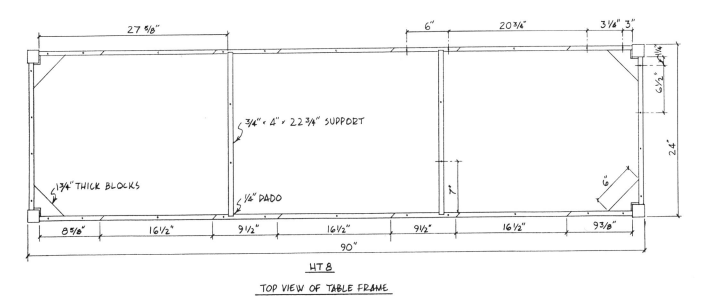

Table frame for the eight-foot harvest table.

Trestle Table (six-foot)

There is considerable room beneath the trestle table for legs and feet. There are no stretchers or perimeter legs to straddle or get in the way, and no perimeter apron to contend with. However, the table has to be very narrow because of the stresses put on the trestle base where it attaches to the top. The narrowest table I've seen is 16 inches (40.6 cm) wide, and the widest is 42 inches (1.06 m). (In order to go beyond 42 inches, one would have to use material other than wood to maintain joint integrity where the leg attaches to the top.) Besides being very narrow, trestle tables are usually fairly long. The six-foot (1.8-m) table accommodates three on a side comfortably, and with a little bit of effort one person can sit at each end, for a total of eight. However, it does not offer much space in the center.

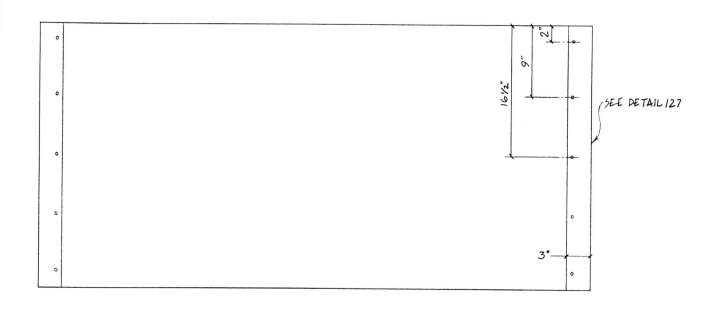

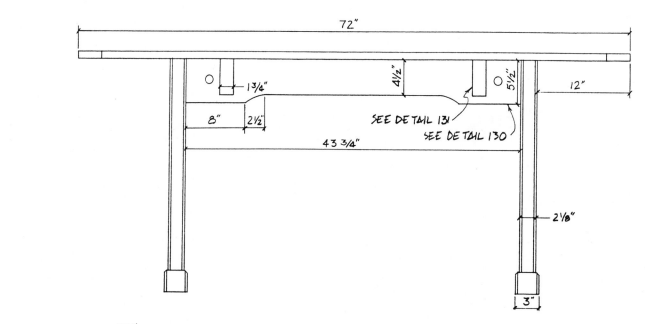

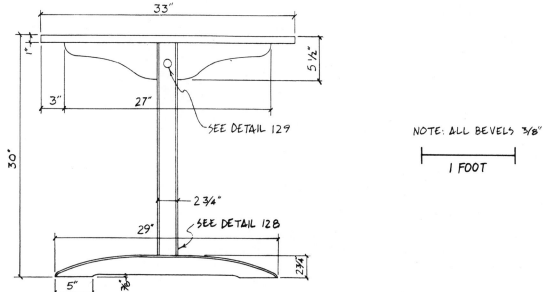

Front, top and end views of the six-foot trestle table.

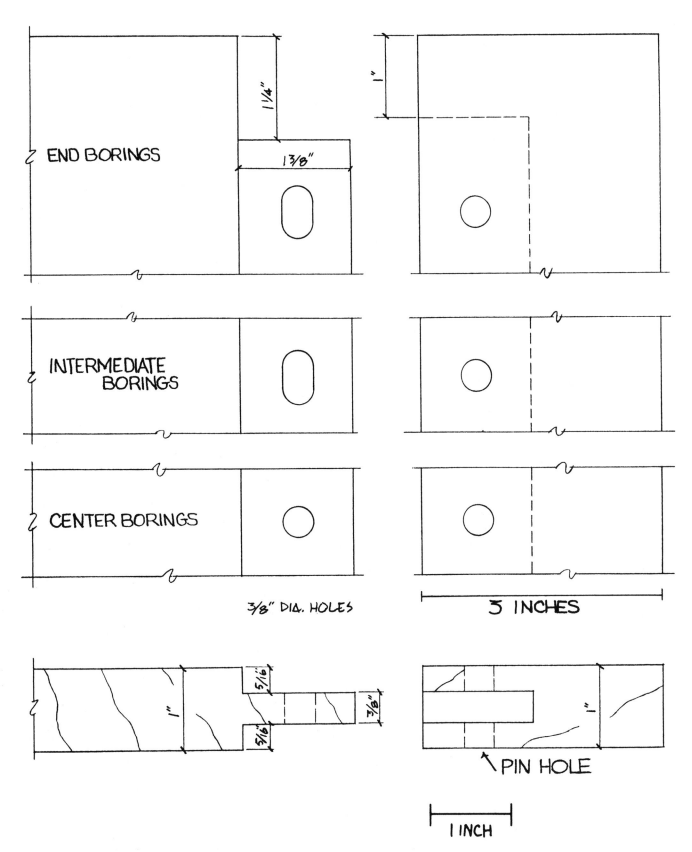

END BORINGS

1 1/4"

1 3/8"

1"

INTERMEDIATE BORINGS

CENTER BORINGS

3/8" DIA. HOLES

5 INCHES

5/16"

1"

3/8"

5/16"

1"

PIN HOLE

1 INCH

Detail 127: Breadboard joint. Borings in the breadboard tenons are ovalized at the ends of the tabletop to allow for seasonal contraction and expansion.

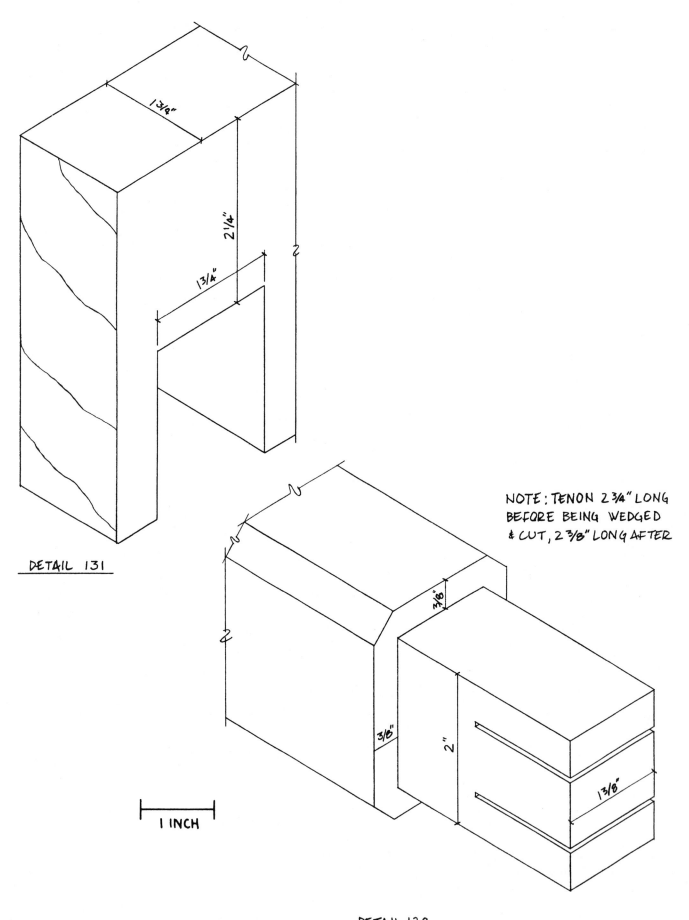

DETAIL 131

1 INCH

NOTE: TENON 2¾" LONG
BEFORE BEING WEDGED
& CUT, 2⅜" LONG AFTER

DETAIL 128
POST TENON

Details 128 and 131: Post tenons.

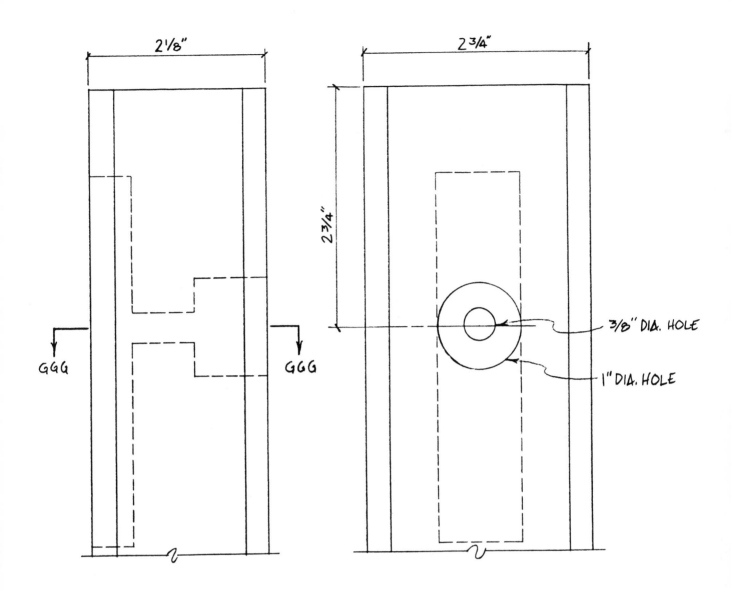

2⅛"

2¾"

2¾"

GGG

GGG

3/8" DIA. HOLE

1" DIA. HOLE

DETAIL 129

1 INCH

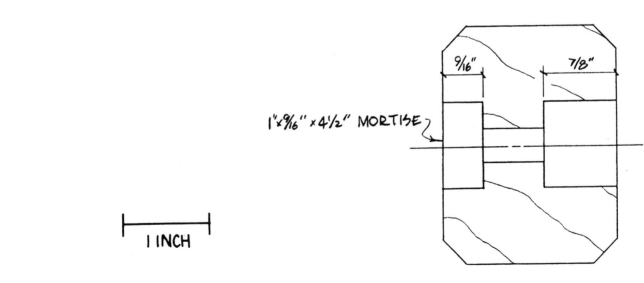

9/16"

7/8"

1"×9/16"×4½" MORTISE

SECTION GGG - GGG

Detail 129: Bolted mortises.

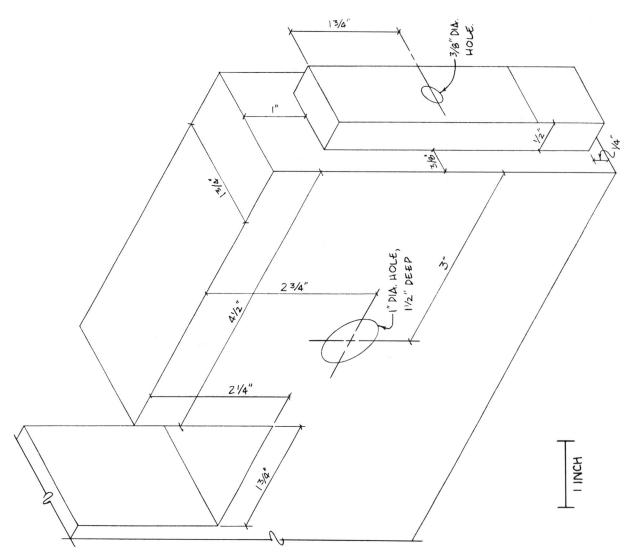

1 3/4"

3/8" DIA. HOLE.

1"

1/2"

1/4"

3/8"

1 3/4"

3"

2 3/4"

1" DIA. HOLE, 1/2" DEEP

4 1/2"

2 1/4"

1 3/4"

1 INCH

Detail 130: Bolted tenon.

Trestle Table (eight-foot)

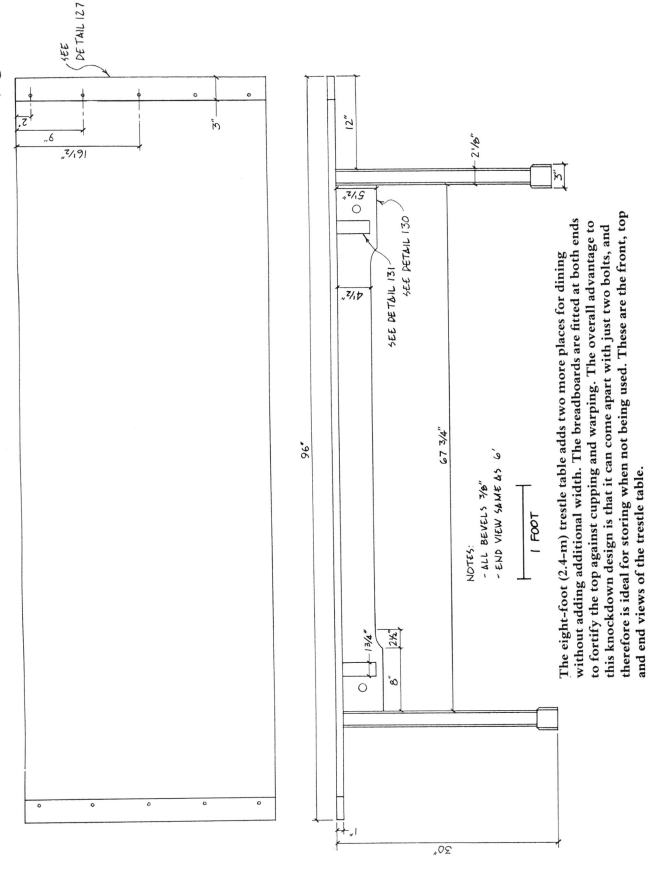

SEE DETAIL 127

2"
9"
16 1/2"
3"

12"
2 1/8"
3"

5 1/2"
4 1/2"

SEE DETAIL 131
SEE DETAIL 130

96"

67 3/4"

NOTES:
- ALL BEVELS 3/8"
- END VIEW SAME AS 6'

1 FOOT

1 3/4"
2 1/2"
8"

1"
30"

The eight-foot (2.4-m) trestle table adds two more places for dining without adding additional width. The breadboards are fitted at both ends to fortify the top against cupping and warping. The overall advantage to this knockdown design is that it can come apart with just two bolts, and therefore is ideal for storing when not being used. These are the front, top and end views of the trestle table.

Table Maximus

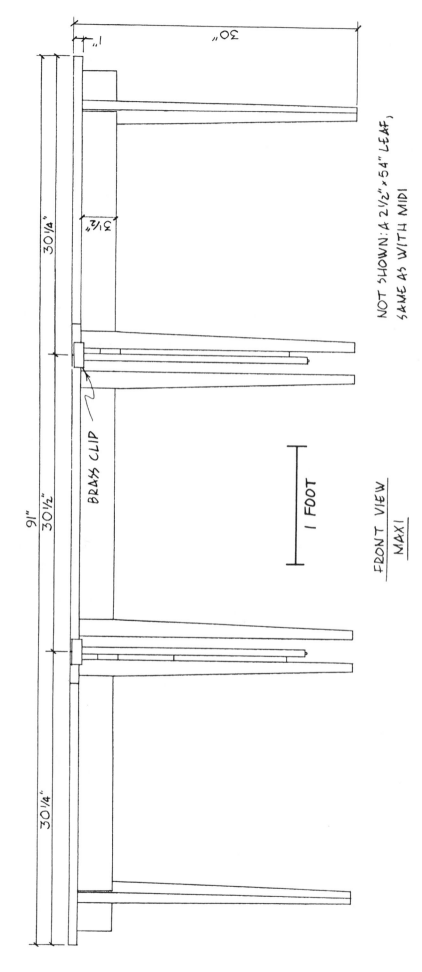

30"

1"

30¼"

3½"

91"

30½"

BRASS CLIP

30¼"

1 FOOT

FRONT VIEW
MAXI

NOT SHOWN: A 2½"×54" LEAF,
SAME AS WITH MIDI

We developed the table maximus on the basis of an early 19th-century
dining table designed by the English. The two end tables can act as side
tables when placed against the wall, while the center section can be used as
a free-standing drop-leaf table. When put together, the three sections can
seat from four in grand style to as many as eight. With the raising of each
leaf, space can be added for two more people. This table also functions well
as a conference table when space is limited and variety in seating is called
for. Here is the front view of the table maximus. See the following page for
a photograph and perspective and page 50 for leaf details.

Table maximus with two center sections.

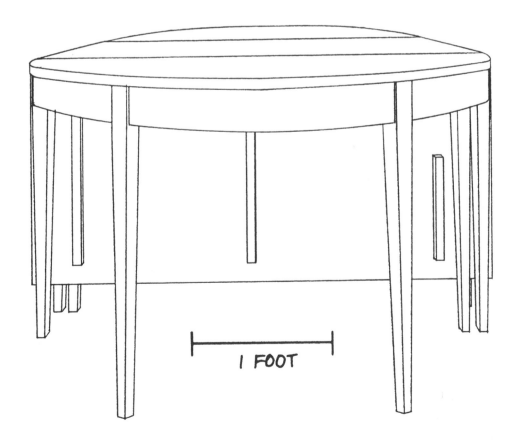

Perspective of table maximus.

1 FOOT

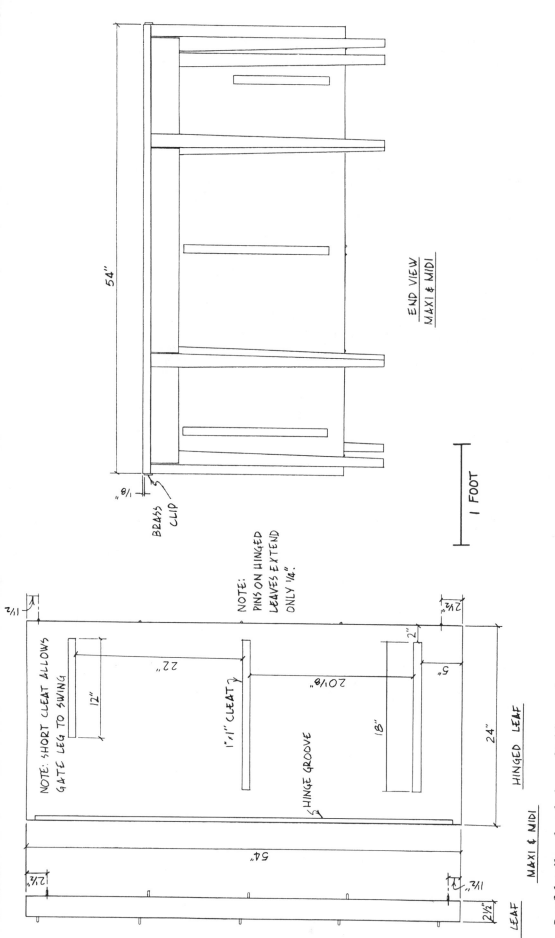

54"

1/8"

BRASS CLIP

END VIEW
MAXI & MIDI

1 FOOT

NOTE:
PINS ON HINGED
LEAVES EXTEND
ONLY 1/4".

NOTE: SHORT CLEAT ALLOWS
GATE LEG TO SWING

12"

22"

1"×1" CLEAT

HINGE GROOVE

20⅛"

18"

5"

2"

2½"

1½"

24"

HINGED LEAF

MAXI & MIDI

54"

2½"

1½"

2½"

LEAF

Leaf detail and end view of table maximus.

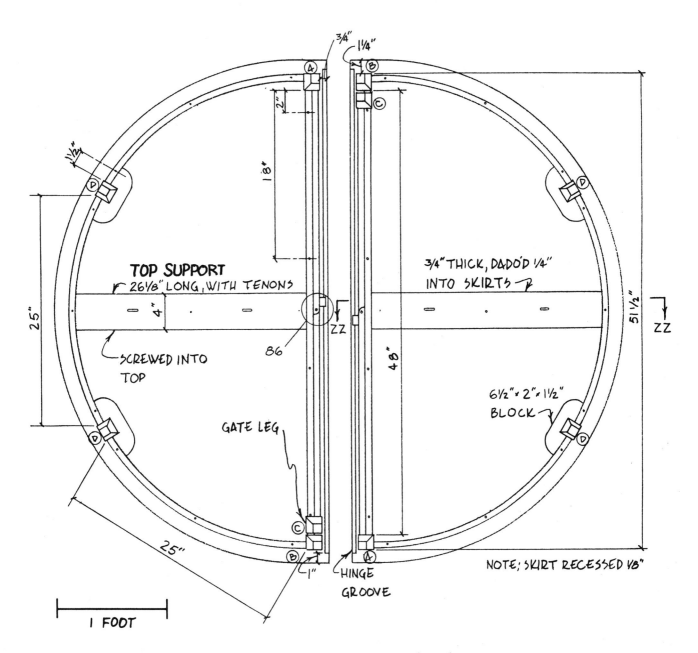

3/4" 1 1/4"

2"

18"

1 1/2"

TOP SUPPORT
26 1/8" LONG, WITH TENONS

3/4" THICK, DADO'D 1/4"
INTO SKIRTS

25"

4"

ZZ

51 1/2"

ZZ

SCREWED INTO
TOP

B6

48"

GATE LEG

6 1/2" x 2" x 1 1/2"
BLOCK

25"

1"

HINGE
GROOVE

NOTE; SKIRT RECESSED 1/8"

1 FOOT

Bottom view of table maximus and table maximus variation without leaves
or center table.

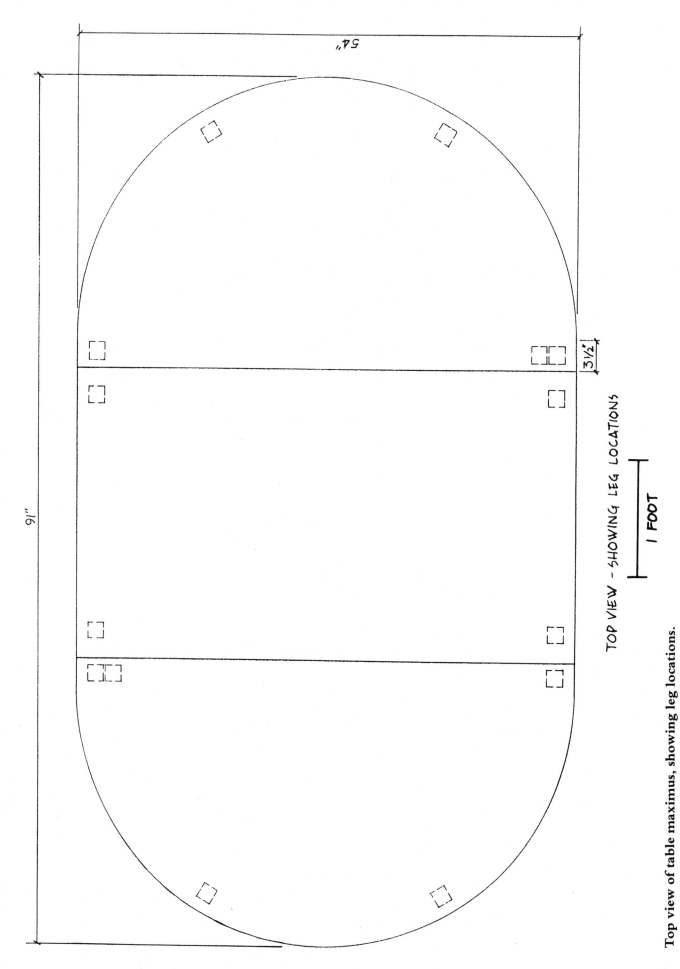

54"

91"

3½"

TOP VIEW - SHOWING LEG LOCATIONS

1 FOOT

Top view of table maximus, showing leg locations.

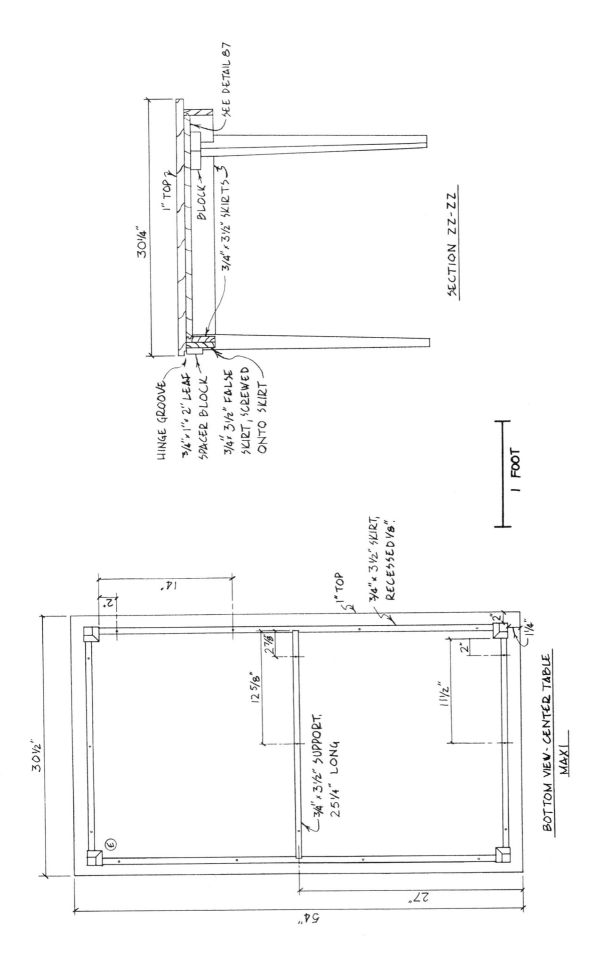

SEE DETAIL 87

1" TOP

30¼"

BLOCK

¾" × 3½" SKIRTS

HINGE GROOVE

¾" × 1" × 2" LEAF SPACER BLOCK

¾" × 3½" FALSE SKIRT, SCREWED ONTO SKIRT

SECTION ZZ-ZZ

1 FOOT

1" TOP

¾" × 3½" SKIRT, RECESSED ⅛".

14"

2"

27⅛"

12⅝"

2"

11½"

2"

1¼"

¾" × 3½" SUPPORT, 25¼" LONG

30½"

27"

54"

E

BOTTOM VIEW - CENTER TABLE
MAXI

Bottom view of table maximus and section ZZ-ZZ.

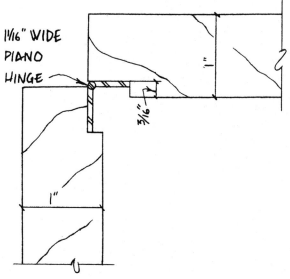

1 1/16" WIDE PIANO HINGE

1"

3/16"

1"

DETAIL 88 -
SECTION THRU PIANO HINGE

NOTES:
- ALL LEGS TAPERED FROM 1 3/4" SQUARE TO 1" SQUARE.
- FRONT & END VIEWS SHOW LEAVES HANGING DOWN.
- MAXI AND MIDI REFER TO TABLE MAXIMUS AND MAXIMUS VARIATION, RESPECTIVELY.
- MAXI & MIDI INCLUDE 4 BRASS CLIPS EACH.
- SEE DETAILS 61, 83 & 86 THRU 89.

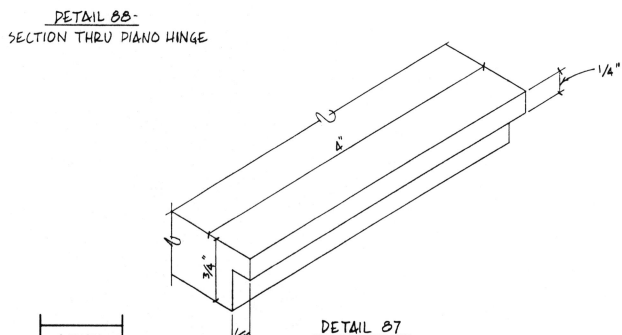

1/4"

4"

3/4"

1/4"

DETAIL 87

1 INCH

Detail 87: Top support. Detail 88: Hinge.

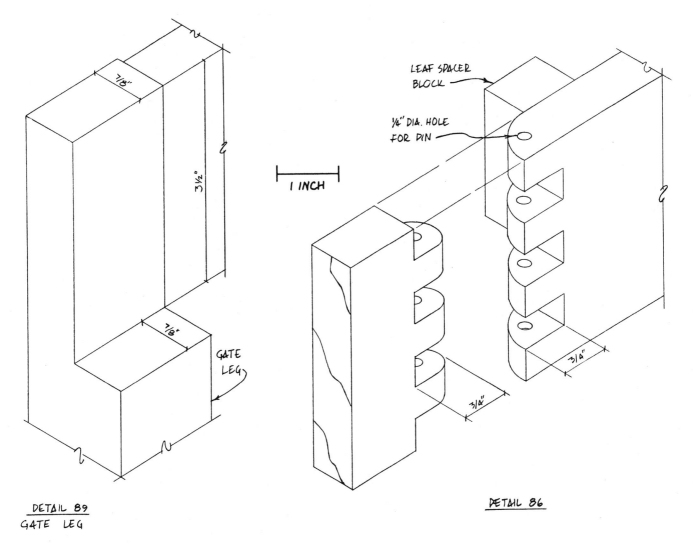

7/8"

3½"

7/8"

GATE
LEG

DETAIL 89
GATE LEG

LEAF SPACER
BLOCK

¼" DIA. HOLE
FOR PIN

1 INCH

3/4"

3/4"

DETAIL 86

Detail 89: Gate leg. Detail 86: Finger joint.

1 INCH

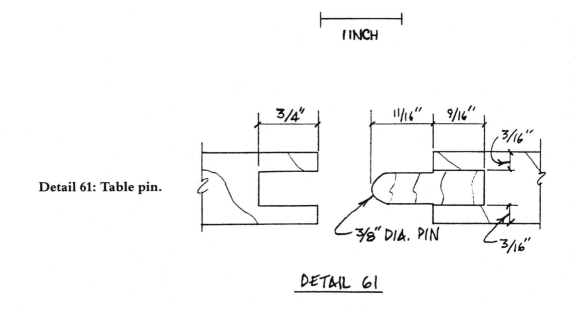

Detail 61: Table pin.

3/4"

11/16"   9/16"

3/16"

3/8" DIA. PIN

3/16"

DETAIL 61

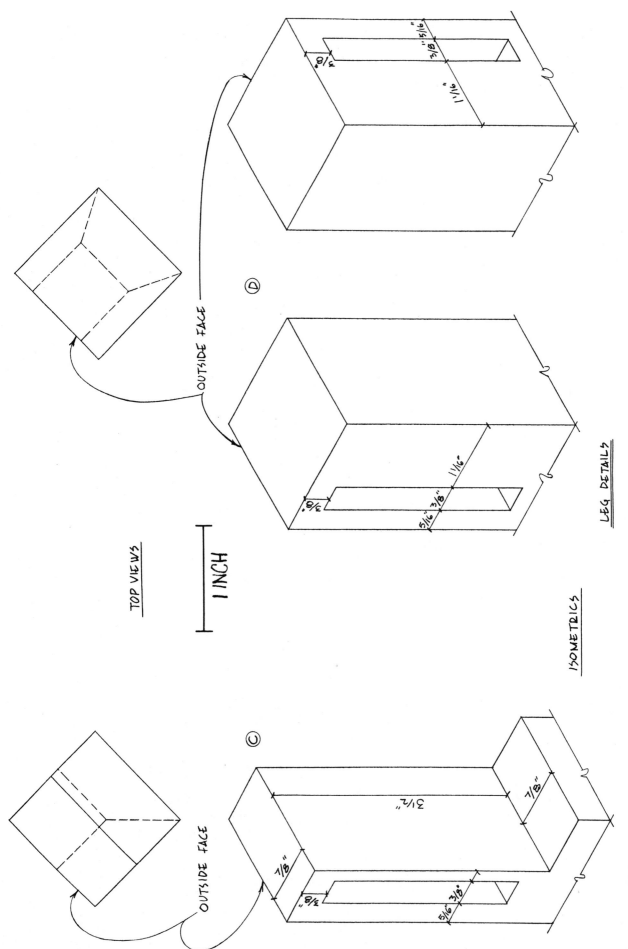

TOP VIEWS

1 INCH

OUTSIDE FACE

OUTSIDE FACE

LEG DETAILS

ISOMETRICS

C

D

3/8"

5/16

1 1/16"

3/8"

3/8"

5/16" 3/8"

1 1/16"

7/8"

7/8"

3 1/2"

3/8"

5/16" 3/8"

Details of leg.

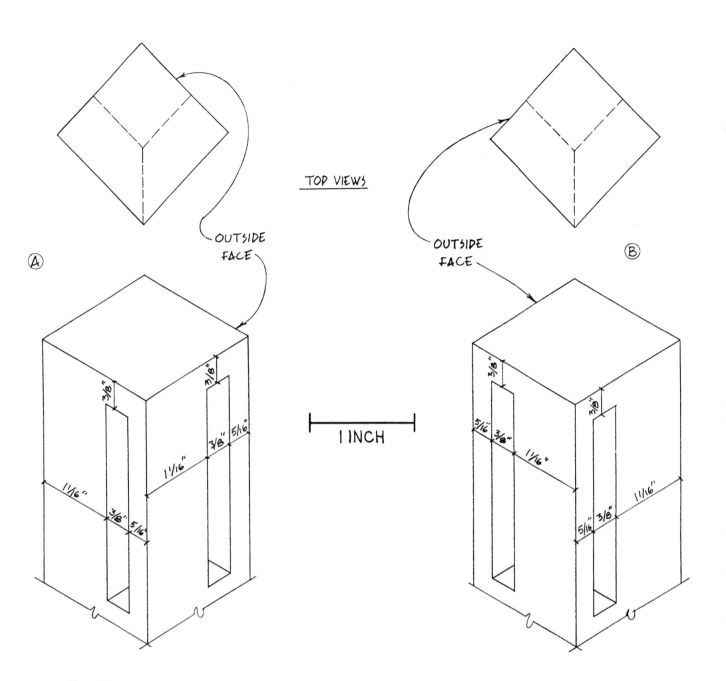

TOP VIEWS

OUTSIDE FACE

OUTSIDE FACE

Ⓐ

Ⓑ

1 INCH

3/8"

3/8"

3/8"

3/8"

3/8" 5/16"

5/16" 3/8"

5/16" 3/8"

5/16" 3/8"

1 1/16"

1 1/16"

1 1/16"

1 1/16"

1 1/16"

Details of leg.

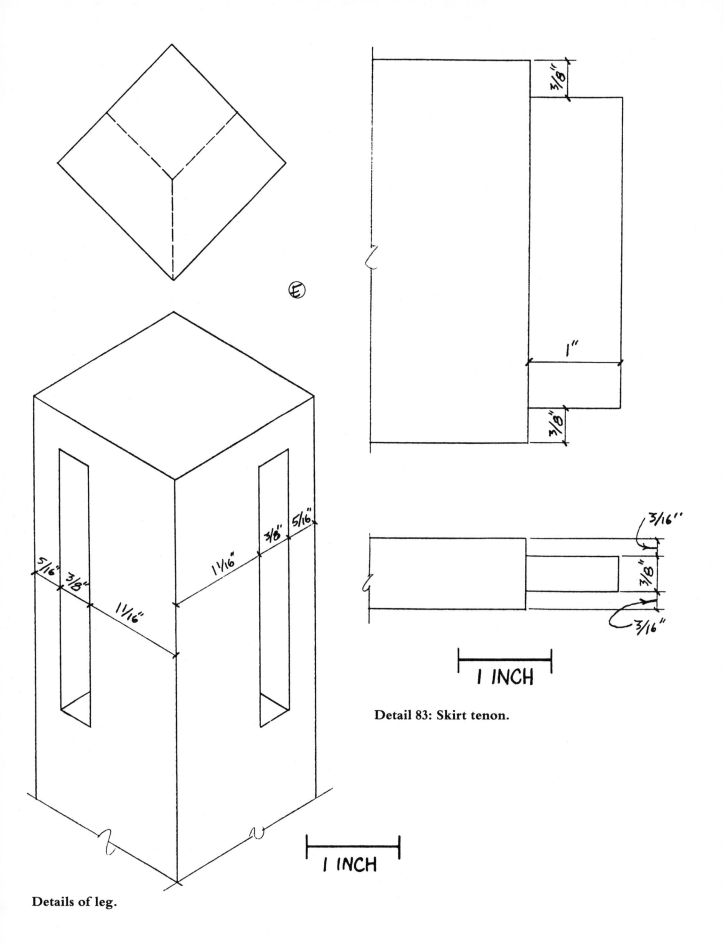

Ⓔ

3/8"

1"

3/8"

5/16" 3/8" 5/16"

1 1/16"

5/16" 3/8"

1 1/16"

3/16"

3/8"

3/16"

1 INCH

Detail 83: Skirt tenon.

Details of leg.

1 INCH

Table Maximus Variation

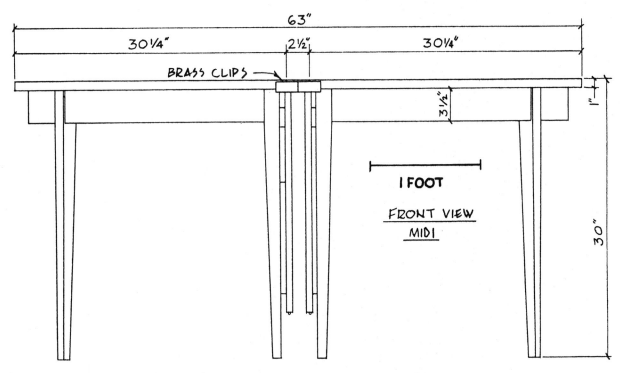

BRASS CLIPS

63"

30 1/4"   2 1/2"   30 1/4"

3 1/2"   1"

30"

1 FOOT

FRONT VIEW
MIDI

This variation of the table maximus offers all of the advantages of the maximus, but it is slightly scaled down to seat fewer people. The width remains the same in order to accommodate three chairs at each end.

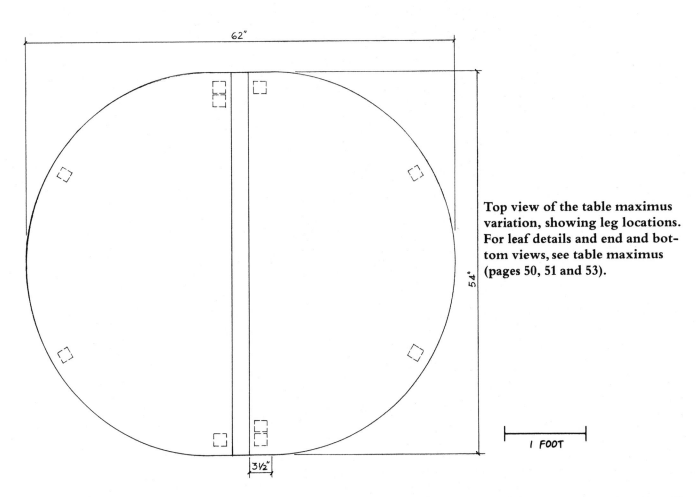

62"

54"

3 1/2"

1 FOOT

Top view of the table maximus variation, showing leg locations. For leaf details and end and bottom views, see table maximus (pages 50, 51 and 53).

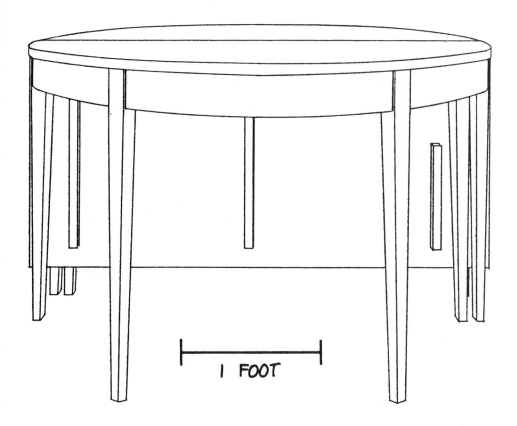

Perspective of the table maximus variation. For more details, see pages 54 to 58.

I FOOT

Round Extension Table

This small, round table is ideal where space is at a premium. It is excellent for seating four, makes a good game table and has maximum space underneath the top. With the leaf in place, it expands to seat six. The disadvantage of this table is that one has to keep track of the leaf, as it can be scratched or, in some cases, even lost. However, it's a price worth paying in order to achieve flexibility.

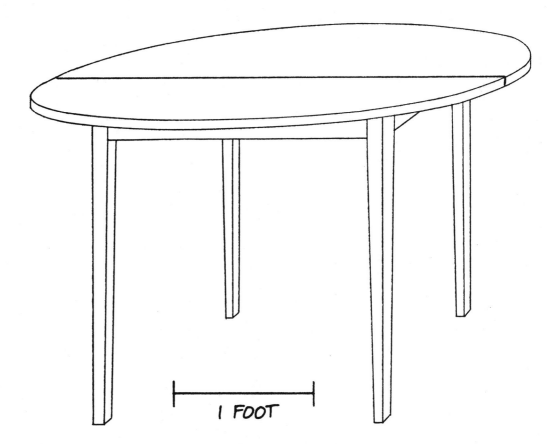

Perspective of the round extension table.

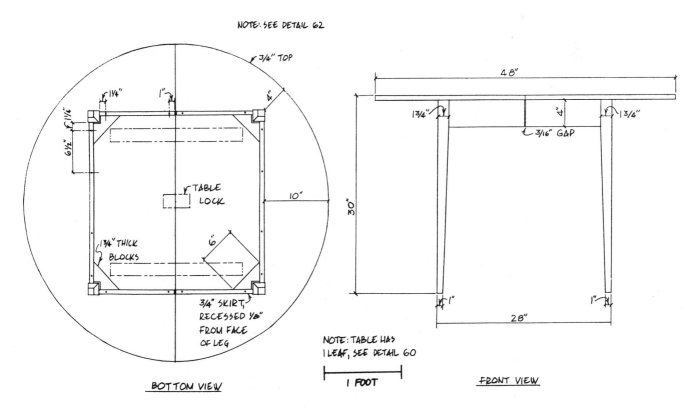

NOTE: SEE DETAIL 62

3/4" TOP

1¼"

1"

4"

1¼"

6½"

TABLE
LOCK

10"

1¾" THICK
BLOCKS

6"

3/4" SKIRT,
RECESSED ¼"
FROM FACE
OF LEG

BOTTOM VIEW

48"

1¾"

4"

3/16" GAP

1¾"

30"

1"

1"

28"

NOTE: TABLE HAS
1 LEAF, SEE DETAIL 60

1 FOOT

FRONT VIEW

Front and bottom views of the round extension table.

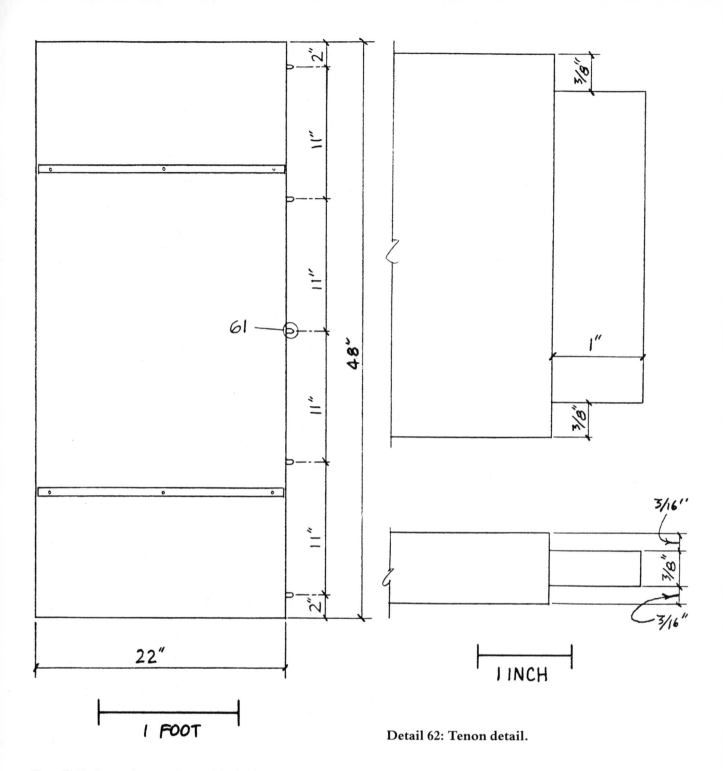

2"

11"

11"

61

48"

11"

11"

2"

22"

1 FOOT

Detail 60: Round extension table leaf.

3/8"

1"

3/8"

3/16"

3/8"

3/16"

1 INCH

Detail 62: Tenon detail.

Half-Round Table

As an occasional table, the half-round table can be stored against a wall
when not in use. It can also be used as a table for magazines, gloves,
telephones, etc. With a simple swing of the leg, it converts to a fully round
table that can seat four.

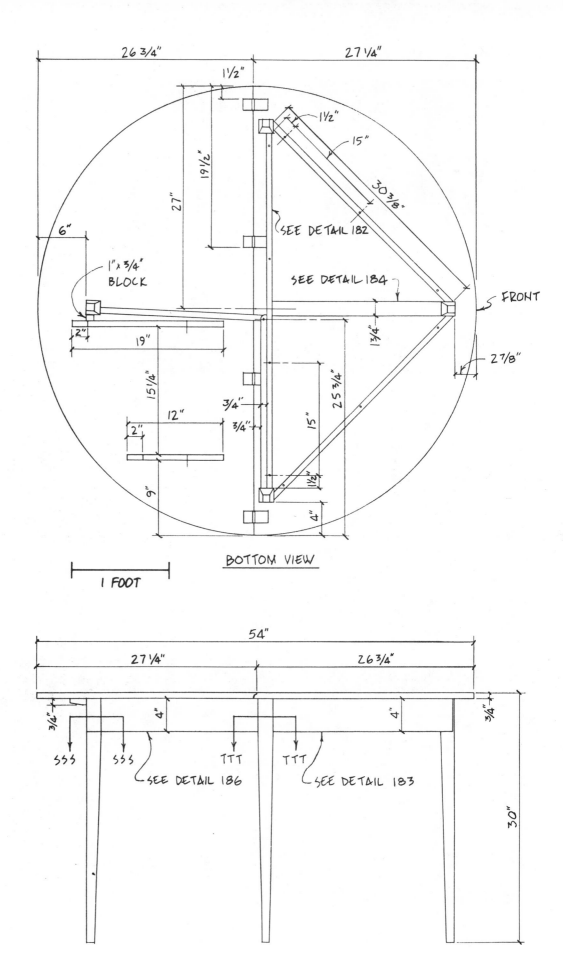

Bottom and right-side views of the half-round table.

Thos. Moser relaxes on an
inverted arm bench.

New Gloucester rocker.

Bowback stool and custom cupboard.

Table maximus (closed).

Table maximus (extended).

B

Twenty-four inch coffee table.

Six-foot trestle desk variation and bowback chair.

Bowfront glove table.

C

Panel desk.

Clockwise from far left: Continuous arm chair; Gates cabinet (custom lateral-file interior); custom bookcase; and bowfront desk.

D

High desk (left-hand).

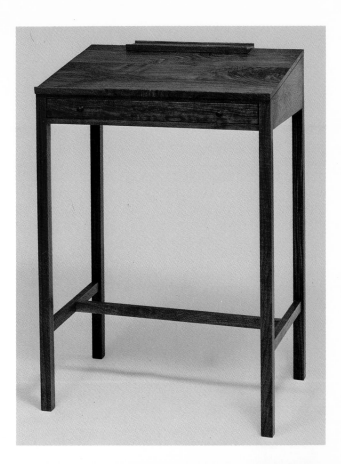

Lectern desk.

At left, tall desk with pigeonholes and bowback stool. At right, high desk (right-hand) and studio stool.

At left, Dr. White's chest. At right, seven-drawer dresser.

Three-door sideboard.

F

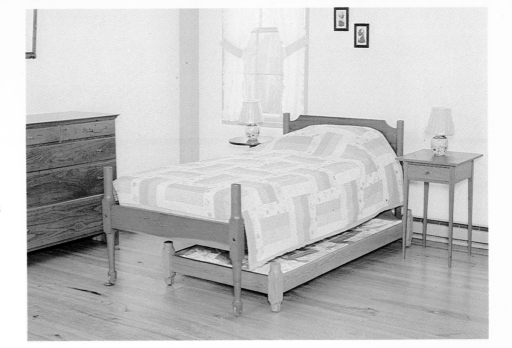

From left to right: five-drawer chest; low-post bed; custom trundle bed; and sidestand.

Clockwise from rear left: endchest with drawers; bed with panel headboard and custom blanket chest in front of it; wall clock; endchest with doors; two-stepper; fanback chair and game table; triangular étagère; 24-inch coffee table and bowback bench.

Wall clock and continuous arm display.

(Left) tall clock and 16-inch roundstand #2.

From left: bowback chair; slant-top desk; corner cupboard; two-door endchest; custom daybed; and three-drawer endchest.

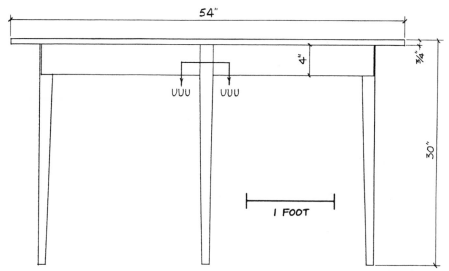

Front view of the half-round table.

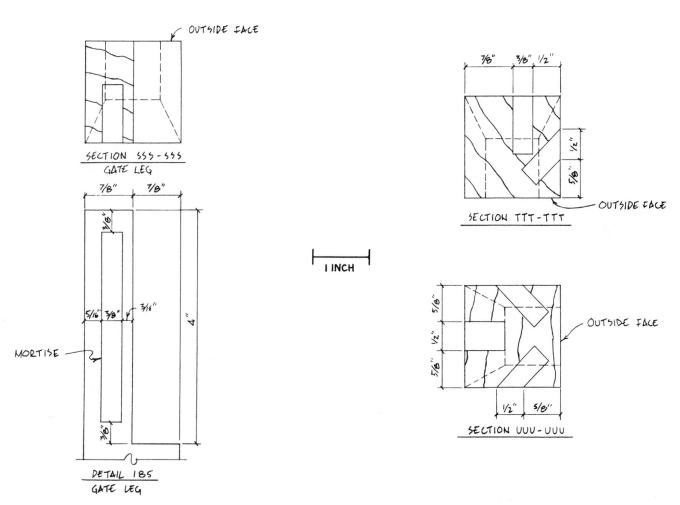

Detail 185 and sections TTT-TTT and UUU-UUU.

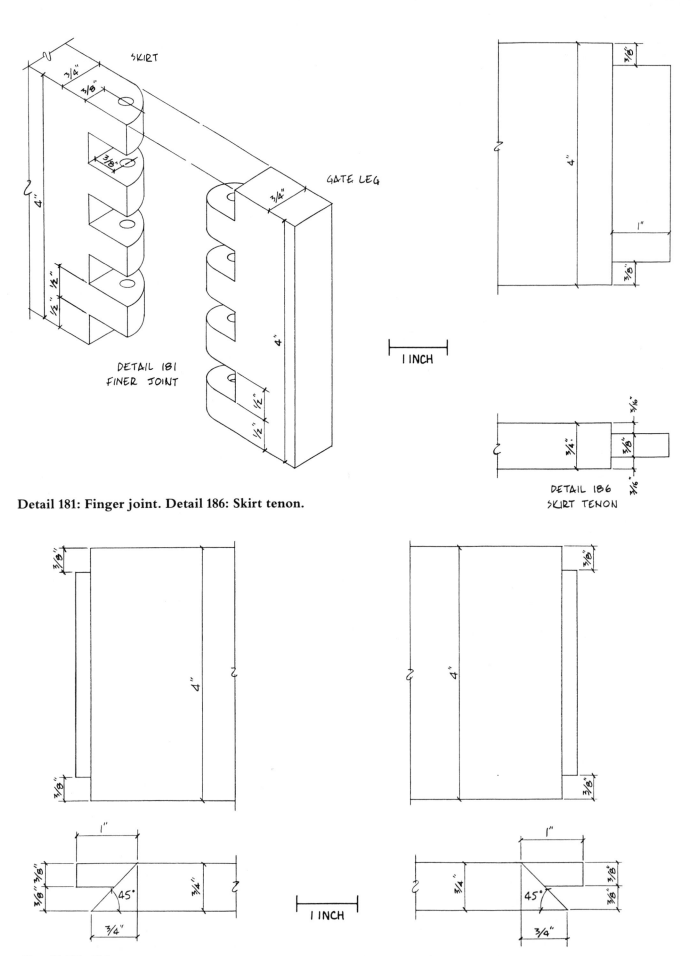

SKIRT

3/4"
3/8"
3/8"
4"
1/2" 1/2"
1/2"

DETAIL 181
FINER JOINT

GATE LEG

3/4"
4"
1/2"
1/2"

Detail 181: Finger joint. Detail 186: Skirt tenon.

3/8"
4"
1"
3/8"

1 INCH

3/16"
3/4"
3/8"
3/16"

DETAIL 186
SKIRT TENON

3/8"
4"
3/8"

3/8"
4"
3/8"

1"
3/8" 3/8"
45°
3/4"
3/4"

1 INCH

1"
3/4
45°
3/4"
3/8" 3/8"

Detail 183: Skirt tenons.

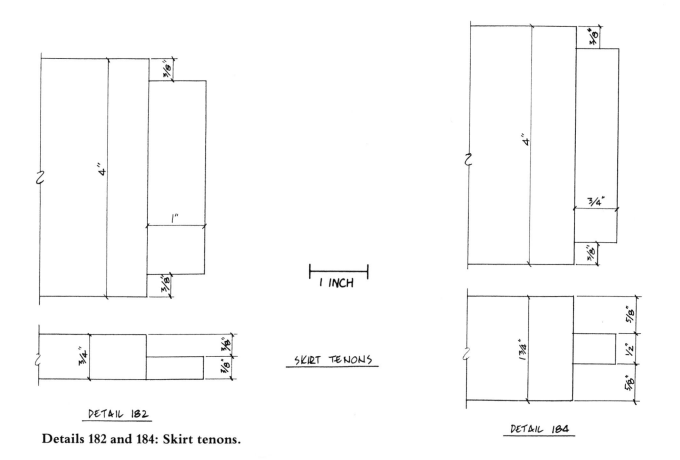

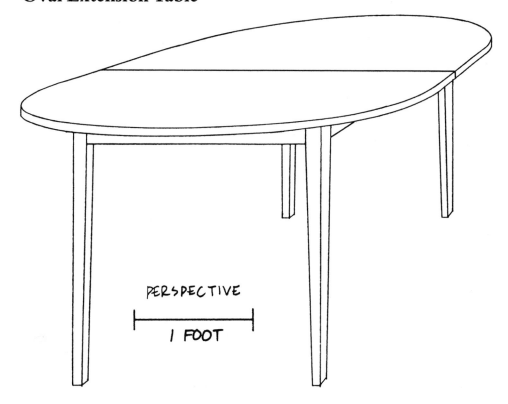

Details 182 and 184: Skirt tenons.

SKIRT TENONS

1 INCH

DETAIL 182

DETAIL 184

Oval Extension Table

PERSPECTIVE

1 FOOT

The oval extension table is more ambitious than a simple round extension table, but it is not as complex as the maximus form. It can seat six without the extension, and eight with the extension.

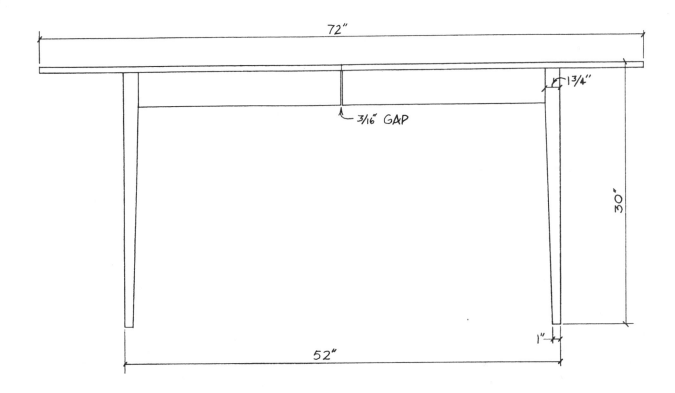

72"

1 3/4"

3/16" GAP

30"

52"

1"

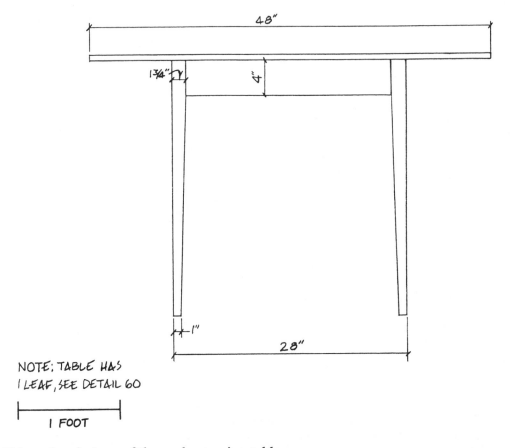

48"

1 3/4"

4"

1"

28"

NOTE: TABLE HAS
1 LEAF, SEE DETAIL 60

1 FOOT

Side and end views of the oval extension table.

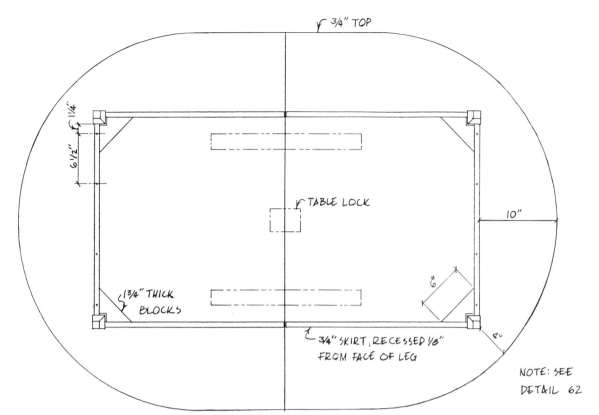

3/4" TOP

1 1/4"

6 1/2"

TABLE LOCK

10"

6"

1 3/4" THICK BLOCKS

3/4" SKIRT, RECESSED 1/8" FROM FACE OF LEG

8"

NOTE: SEE DETAIL 62

Bottom view of the oval extension table. For details 60 and 62, see the round extension table, page 62.

Round-Ring Extension Table

The use of the constantly curving perimeter skirt or apron brings a note of elegance to the round-ring extension table. The placement of the leg allows one to see the leg face and not just the sharp edge. The design has an advantage over the others in that the apron is near the perimeter, which allows room for leg crossing without striking your knee on the underside of the table.

Closeup of the legs on the round-ring extension table.

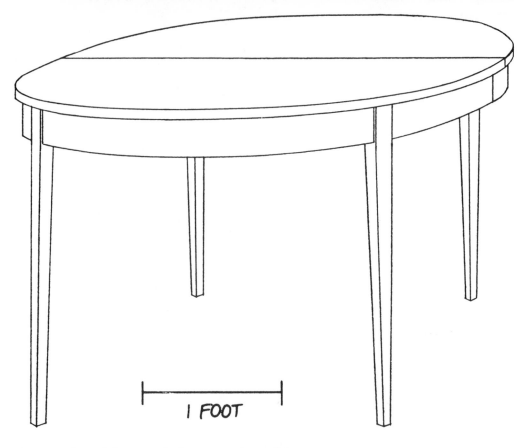

1 FOOT

Perspective of the round-ring extension table.

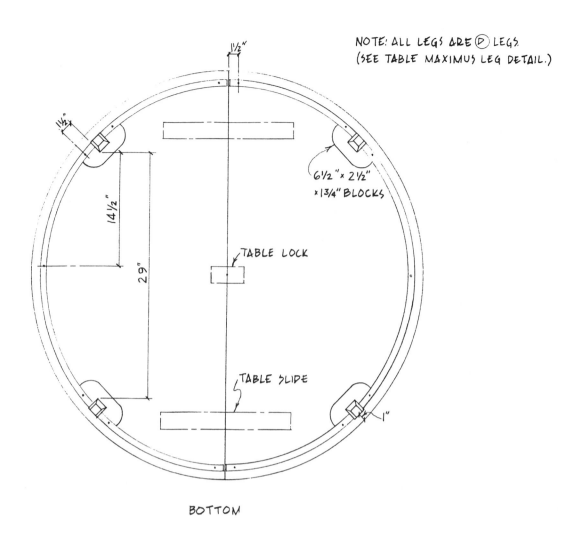

NOTE: ALL LEGS ARE (P) LEGS.
(SEE TABLE MAXIMUS LEG DETAIL.)

1½"

1½"

14½"

29"

6½" x 2½" x 1¾" BLOCKS

TABLE LOCK

TABLE SLIDE

1"

BOTTOM

NOTE: SEE DETAIL B3

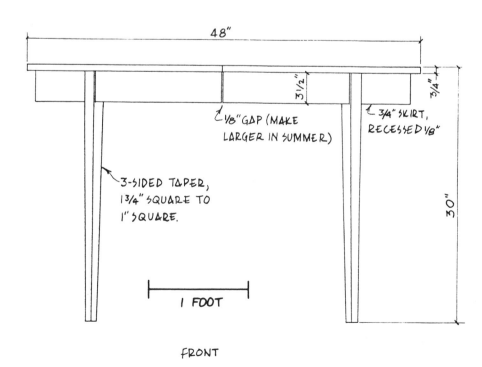

48"

3½"

¾"

⅛" GAP (MAKE LARGER IN SUMMER)

¾" SKIRT, RECESSED ⅛"

3-SIDED TAPER, 1¾" SQUARE TO 1" SQUARE.

30"

1 FOOT

FRONT

Bottom and side views of the round-ring extension table.

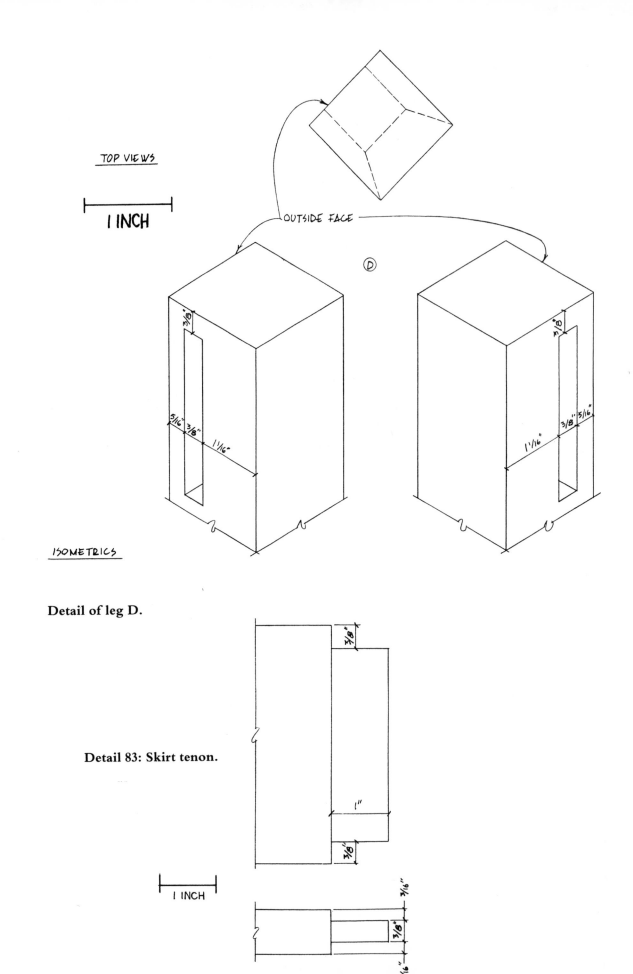

1 INCH

OUTSIDE FACE

Ⓓ

3/8"

5/16" 3/8" 1 1/16"

3/8"

1 1/16" 3/8" 5/16"

ISOMETRICS

Detail of leg D.

Detail 83: Skirt tenon.

3/8"

1"

3/8"

1 INCH

5/16"

3/8"

3/16"

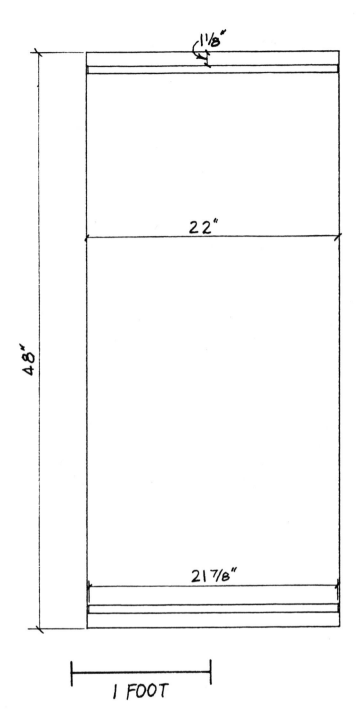

Round-ring leaf detail.

Oval-Ring Extension Table

This variation of the ring table can seat an additional two people in comfort. The additional legs give added support without interfering with chair placement.

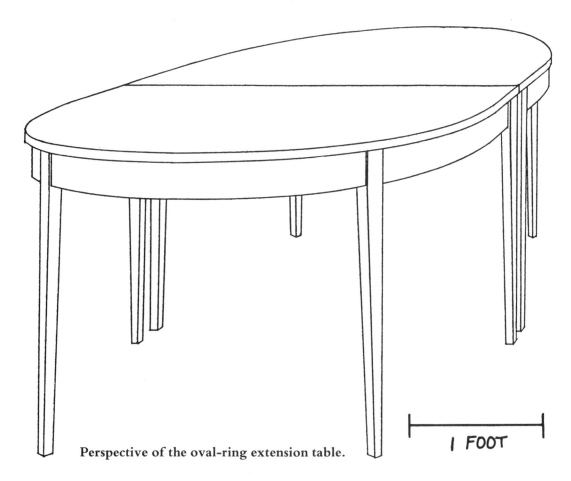

1 FOOT

Perspective of the oval-ring extension table.

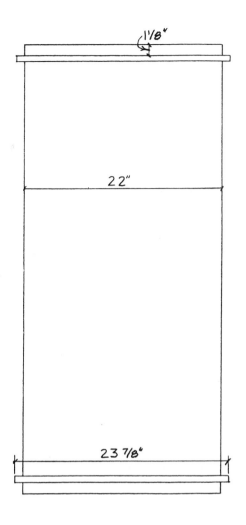

OVAL RING LEAVES

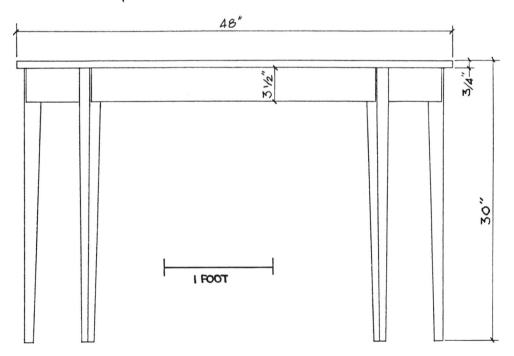

OVAL RING — END VIEW

End view and leaf details for the oval-ring extension table.

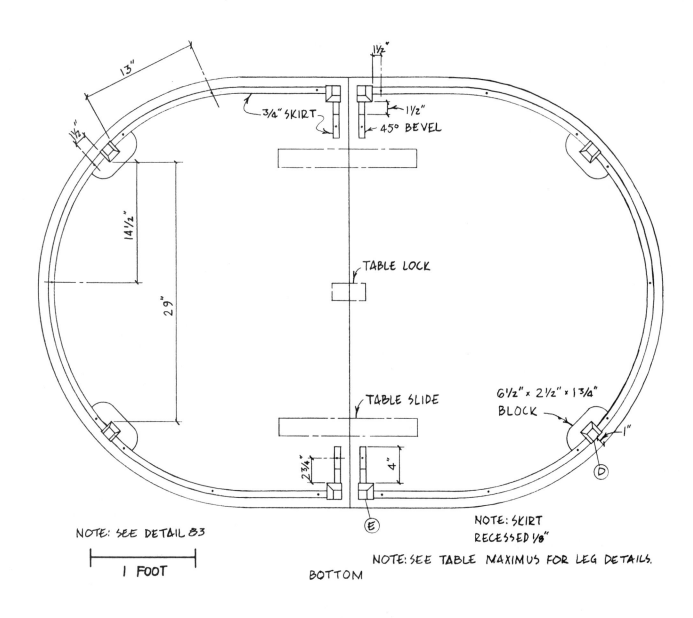

13"

1½"

3/4" SKIRT

1½"

1½"

45° BEVEL

14½"

29"

TABLE LOCK

TABLE SLIDE

6½" × 2½" × 1¾"
BLOCK

1"

Ⓓ

2¾"

4"

Ⓔ

NOTE: SEE DETAIL 83

| 1 FOOT |

NOTE: SKIRT
RECESSED ⅛"

NOTE: SEE TABLE MAXIMUS FOR LEG DETAILS.

BOTTOM

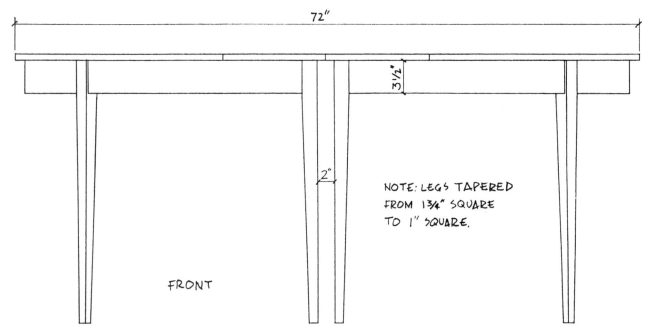

72"

3½"

2"

NOTE: LEGS TAPERED
FROM 1¾" SQUARE
TO 1" SQUARE.

FRONT

Bottom and front views of the oval-ring extension table.

Coffee Table (24-inch)

Our forefathers used a serving table about 27 inches (68.5 cm) high that had a surface from which tea could be served, but it was not used in front of a sofa or couch as is the contemporary coffee table. The 24-inch coffee table can go in front of a sofa seating three, and can be used in the center of a living-room area without taking up too much room. The drawers are useful for holding magazines, etc.

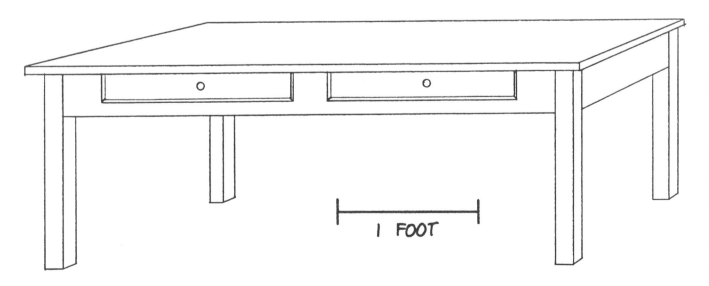

Perspective of 24-inch coffee table.

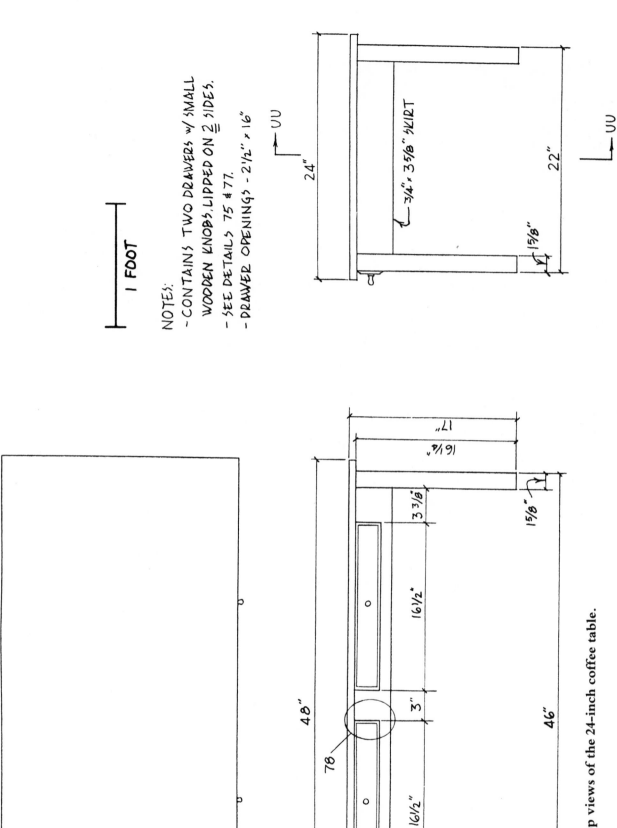

I FOOT

NOTES:
- CONTAINS TWO DRAWERS w/ SMALL WOODEN KNOBS. LIPPED ON 2 SIDES.
- SEE DETAILS 75 #77.
- DRAWER OPENINGS - 2½" x 16"

24"

← UU

3/4" x 3 5/8" SKIRT

22"

1 5/8"

← UU

17"

19 5/8"

3 3/8"

16½"

3"

78

16½"

2½"

3 3/8"

48"

46"

1 5/8"

End, front and top views of the 24-inch coffee table.

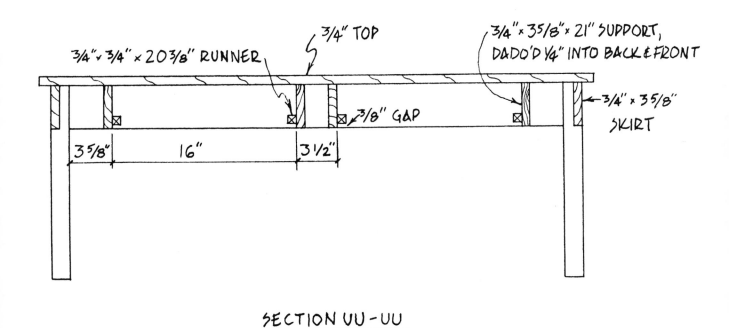

3/4" × 3/4" × 20 3/8" RUNNER

3/4" TOP

3/4" × 35/8" × 21" SUPPORT, DADO'D 1/4" INTO BACK & FRONT

3/8" GAP

3/4" × 35/8" SKIRT

3 5/8"

16"

3 1/2"

SECTION UU-UU

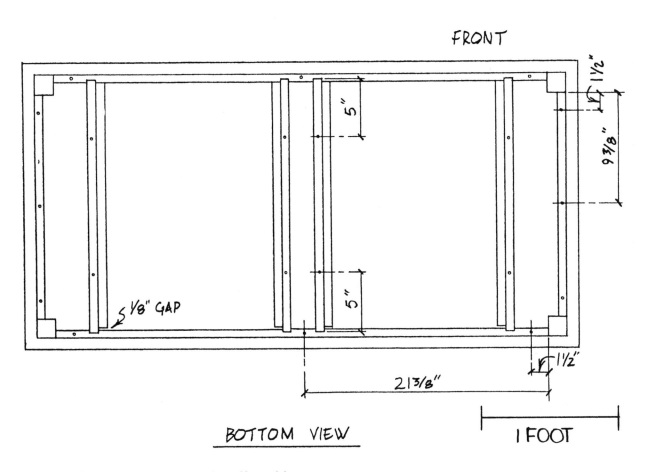

FRONT

1 1/2"

5"

9 3/8"

1/8" GAP

5"

1 1/2"

21 3/8"

BOTTOM VIEW

1 FOOT

Bottom and side views of the 24-inch coffee table.

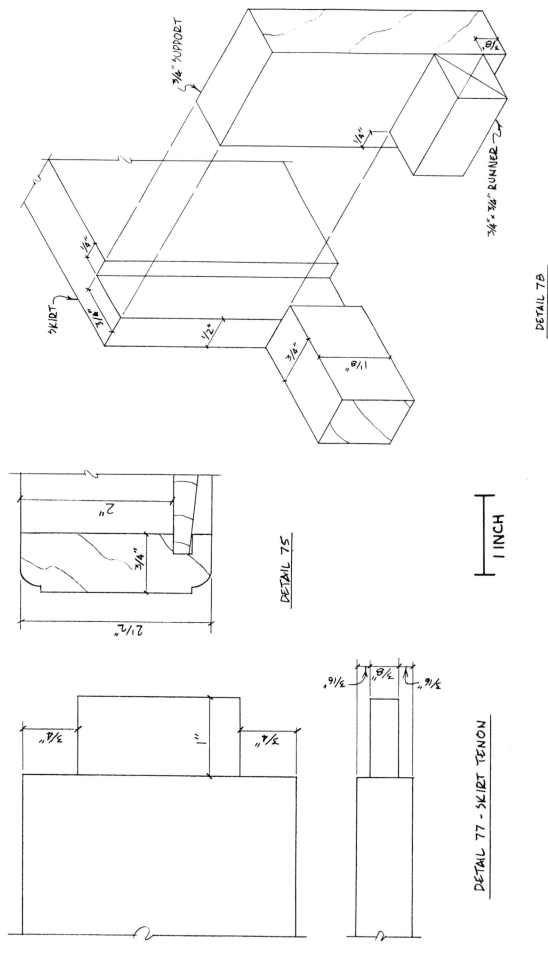

3/4" SUPPORT

1/8"

1/4"

3/4" × 3/4" RUNNER

DETAIL 78

1/4"

SKIRT

3/4"

1/2"

3/4"

1 1/8"

2"

3/4"

2 1/2"

DETAIL 75

1 INCH

3/4"

1"

3/4"

3/16"

3/8"

3/16"

DETAIL 77 - SKIRT TENON

Detail 77: Skirt tenon. Detail 75: Drawer front. Detail 78: Interior construction. For drawer and knob details, see the Appendix on case details (page 315).

Knee Table

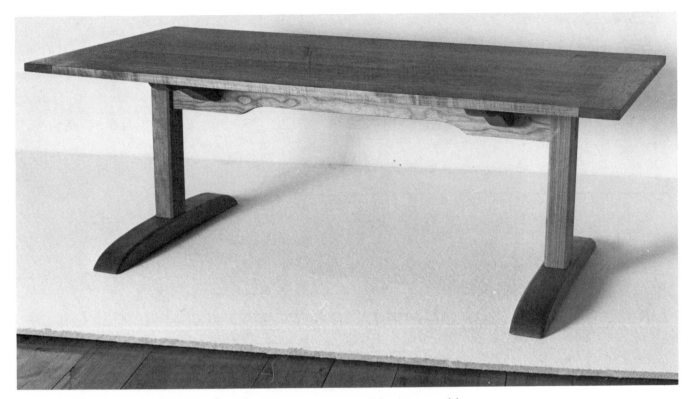

This miniature trestle table has all of the characteristics of the larger table, but is considerably scaled down. Its 17-inch (43.2-cm) height is standard and works well with the average-size couch or lounge chair. If the table is designed to go with a more contemporary couch, which might be lower, then a few inches can be taken from its height.

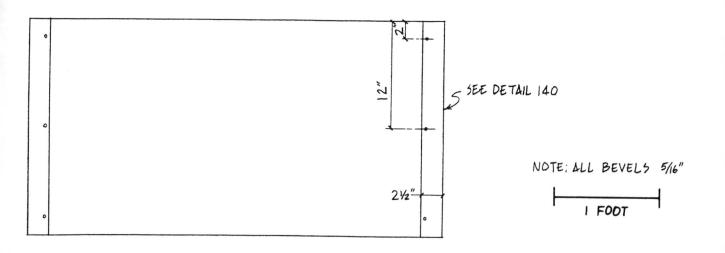

SEE DETAIL 140

NOTE: ALL BEVELS 5/16"

1 FOOT

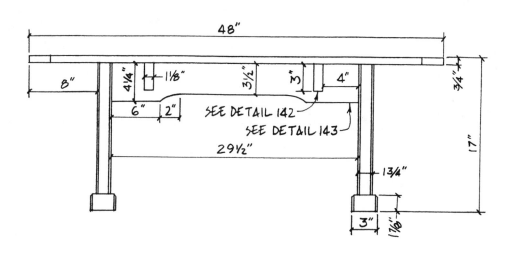

SEE DETAIL 142

SEE DETAIL 143

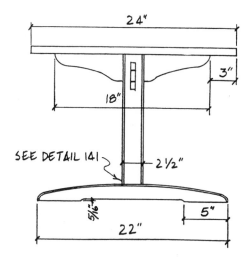

SEE DETAIL 141

Front, side and top views of the knee table.

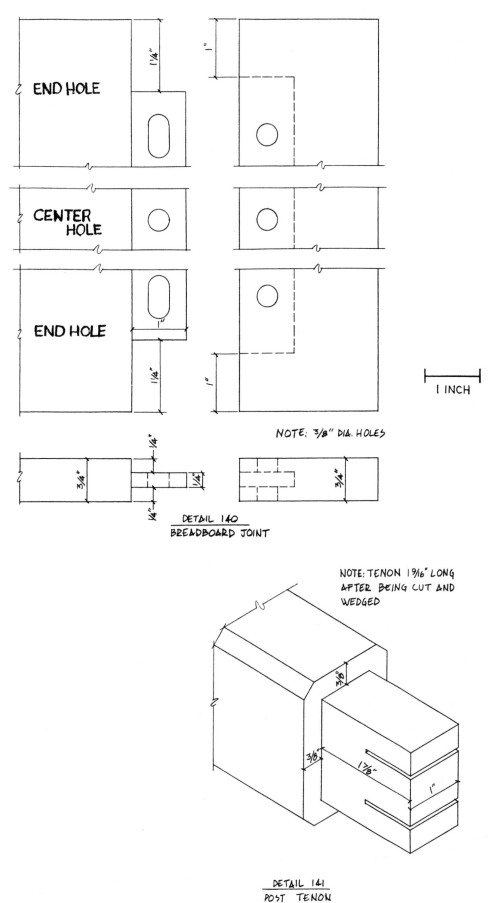

END HOLE

1¼"

CENTER HOLE

END HOLE

1¼"

1"

1"

1 INCH

NOTE: ⅜" DIA. HOLES

¼"

3/4"

¼"

¼"

3/4"

DETAIL 140
BREADBOARD JOINT

NOTE: TENON 1 9/16" LONG
AFTER BEING CUT AND
WEDGED

⅜"

⅜"

1 7/8"

1"

DETAIL 141
POST TENON

Detail 140: Breadboard joint. Detail 141: Post tenon.

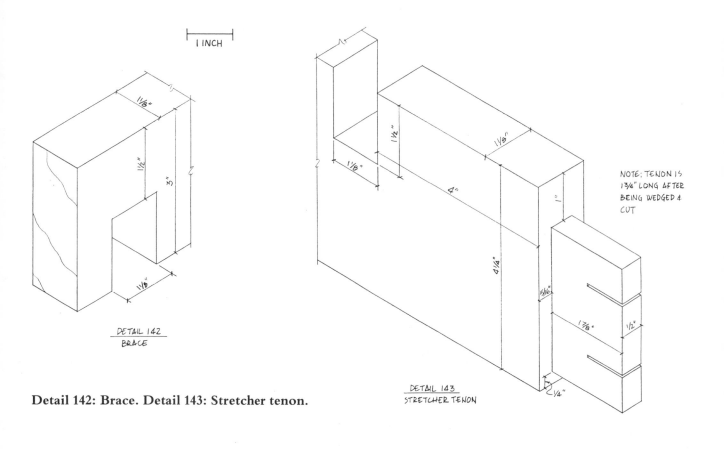

1 INCH

1 1/8"

1 1/2"

3"

1 1/8"

DETAIL 142
BRACE

1 1/8"

1 1/2"

1 1/8"

4"

1"

4 1/4"

5/16"

1 7/8"

1/2"

1/4"

NOTE: TENON IS
1 3/4" LONG AFTER
BEING WEDGED &
CUT

DETAIL 143
STRETCHER TENON

Detail 142: Brace. Detail 143: Stretcher tenon.

Coffee Table (30-inch)

Unlike the knee table and the 24-inch coffee table, this form has a strict contemporary feeling. The fact that the drawer is concealed in the apron offers a cleanliness of line not found in traditional lipped or flush drawers. The 30-inch (76.2-cm) width of this table makes it ideal for an L-shaped couch or square seating arrangement.

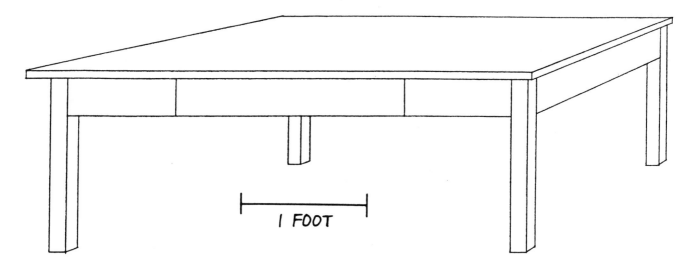

Perspective of 30-inch coffee table.

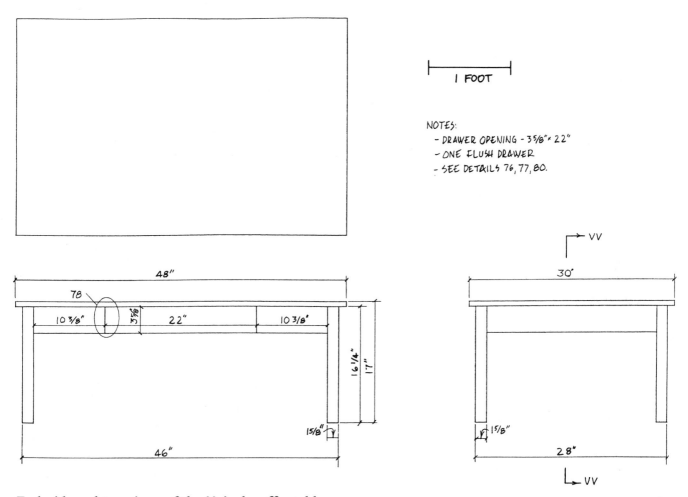

NOTES:
- DRAWER OPENING - 3⅝" × 22"
- ONE FLUSH DRAWER
- SEE DETAILS 76, 77, 80.

1 FOOT

48"

78

10 3/8"   3⅝   22"   10 3/8"

16 1/4"   17"

15/8"

46"

30'

15/8"   28"

VV

End, side and top views of the 30-inch coffee table.

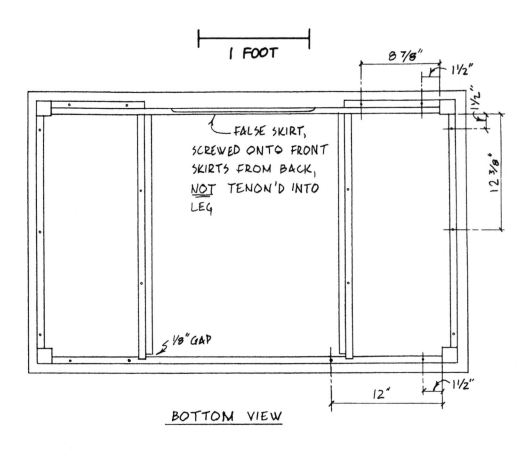

├─ 1 FOOT ─┤

8 7/8"

1 1/2"

1 1/2"

12 3/8"

FALSE SKIRT,
SCREWED ONTO FRONT
SKIRTS FROM BACK,
NOT TENON'D INTO
LEG

1/8" GAP

12"

1 1/2"

BOTTOM VIEW

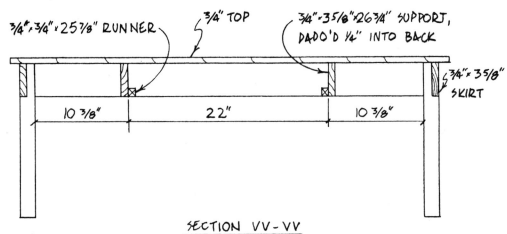

3/4"×3/4"×25 7/8" RUNNER

3/4" TOP

3/4"×3 5/8"×26 3/4" SUPPORT,
DADO'D 1/4" INTO BACK

3/4"×3 5/8"
SKIRT

10 3/8"   22"   10 3/8"

SECTION VV-VV

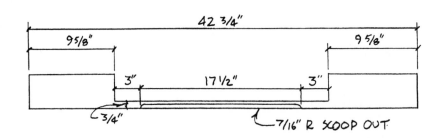

42 3/4"

9 5/8"   9 5/8"

3"   17 1/2"   3"

3/4"

7/16" R SCOOP OUT

DETAIL 80 - REFER ALSO TO 79
FRONT VIEW OF FALSE SKIRT

Bottom view, section VV-VV and detail 80 (front skirt).

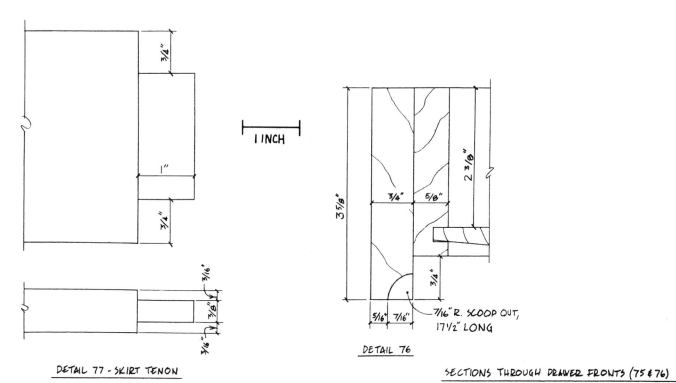

3/4"
1"
3/4"

1 INCH

3/16"
3/8"
3/16"

DETAIL 77 - SKIRT TENON

3/4" 5/8"
2 3/8"
3 5/8"
3/4"
5/16" 7/16"
7/16" R. SCOOP OUT,
17 1/2" LONG

DETAIL 76

SECTIONS THROUGH DRAWER FRONTS (75 & 76)

Detail 77: Skirt tenon. Detail 76: Drawer front. For drawer details, see the Appendix on case details (page 315).

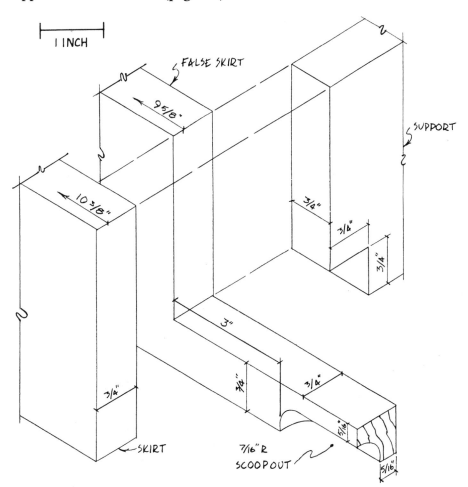

1 INCH

FALSE SKIRT

9 5/8"

SUPPORT

10 3/8"

3/4"
3/4"
3/4"

Detail 79: Interior construction.

3/4"

3"

3/4"
3/4"

SKIRT

7/16" R
SCOOP OUT

5/16"
5/16"

DETAIL 79 - REFER TO DETAIL 80 ALSO

Glove Table

NOTES:
- TWO DRAWERS
- 3/4" TOP
- 1" OVERHANG ALL AROUND
- SEE DETAILS 83 & 84

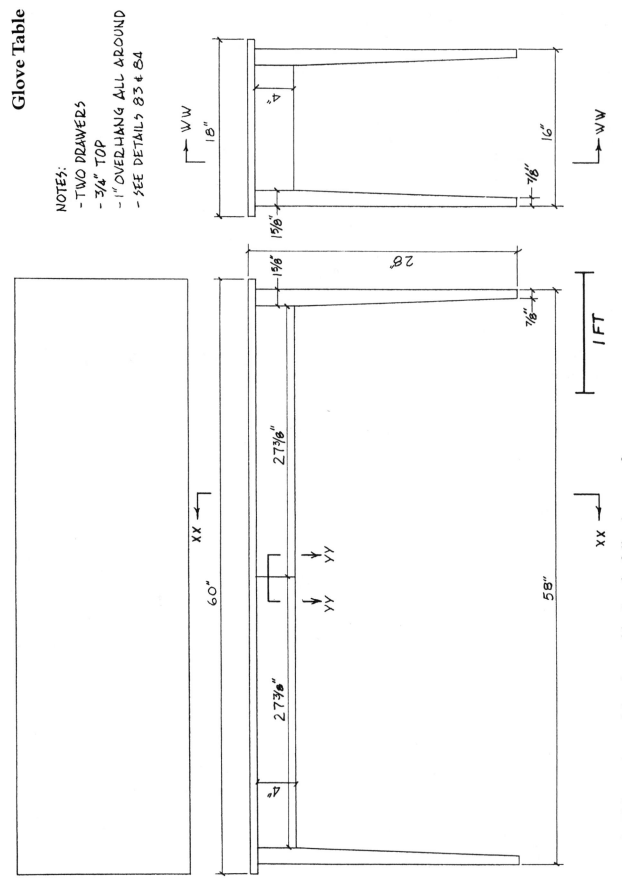

End and front views of the glove table. See the following page for a photograph and perspective.

The glove table was designed to be placed in the entrance hall of a home, where it was used to hold the mail, the keys to the house, gloves and mittens, hats, etc. It works well in this way, but it also works well behind a couch, where it is sometimes referred to as a parsons table. Again, the height can be slightly varied, 2 or 3 inches (5.1 or 7.6 cm) in either direction, without taking away from the overall delicate feeling that this table displays. The drawers concealed in the apron give the table a purity of line uninterrupted with hardware of handles of any sort.

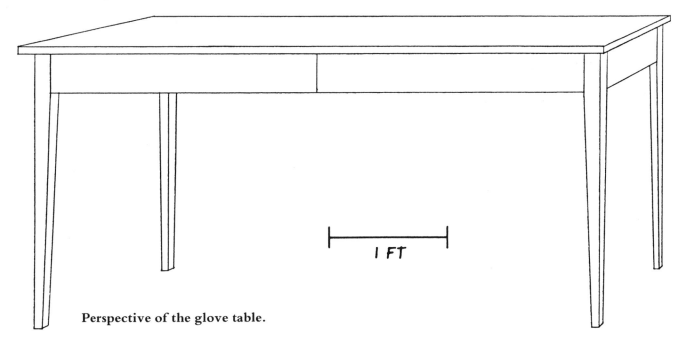

I FT

Perspective of the glove table.

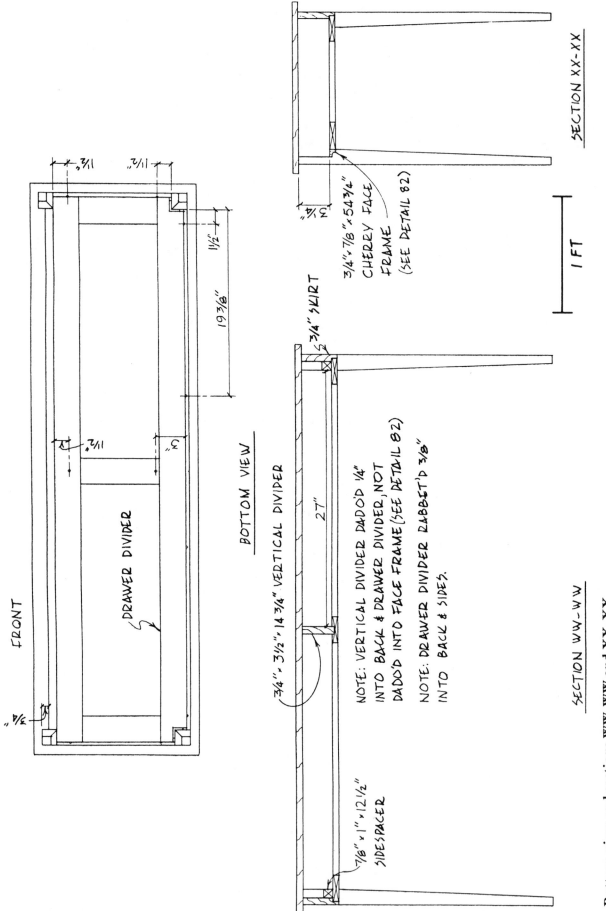

FRONT

DRAWER DIVIDER

3/4"

1 1/2" 1 1/2"

1 1/2"

19 3/8"

1 1/2"

3"

BOTTOM VIEW

3/4" · 7/8 " x 54 3/4"
CHERRY FACE
FRAME
(SEE DETAIL 82)

3/8"
3

1 FT

SECTION XX-XX

3/4" SKIRT

3/4" · 3 1/2" · 14 3/4" VERTICAL DIVIDER

27"

7/8" · 1" · 12 1/2"
SIDE SPACER

NOTE: VERTICAL DIVIDER DADO'D 1/4"
INTO BACK & DRAWER DIVIDER, NOT
DADO'D INTO FACE FRAME (SEE DETAIL 82)

NOTE: DRAWER DIVIDER RABBIT'D 3/8"
INTO BACK & SIDES.

SECTION WW-WW

Bottom view and sections WW-WW and XX-XX.

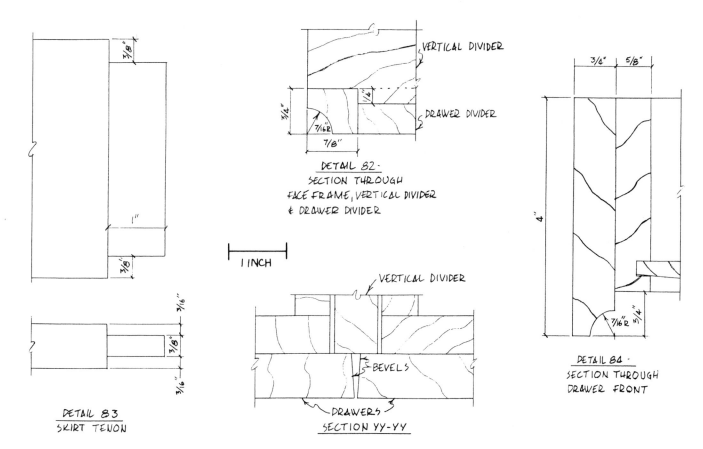

VERTICAL DIVIDER

DRAWER DIVIDER

DETAIL 82·
SECTION THROUGH
FACE FRAME, VERTICAL DIVIDER
& DRAWER DIVIDER

1 INCH

VERTICAL DIVIDER

BEVELS

DRAWERS
SECTION YY-YY

DETAIL 83
SKIRT TENON

DETAIL 84 ·
SECTION THROUGH
DRAWER FRONT

Detail 83 (skirt tenon), Detail 82 (face frame), Detail 84 (drawer front) and section YY-YY.

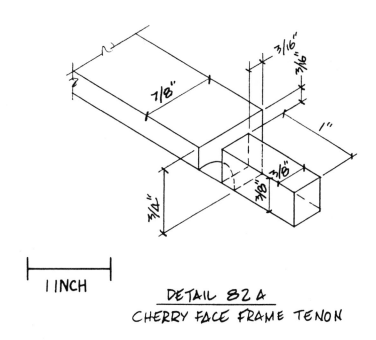

1 INCH

DETAIL 82 A
CHERRY FACE FRAME TENON

Detail 82A: Frame tenon.

Bowfront Glove Table

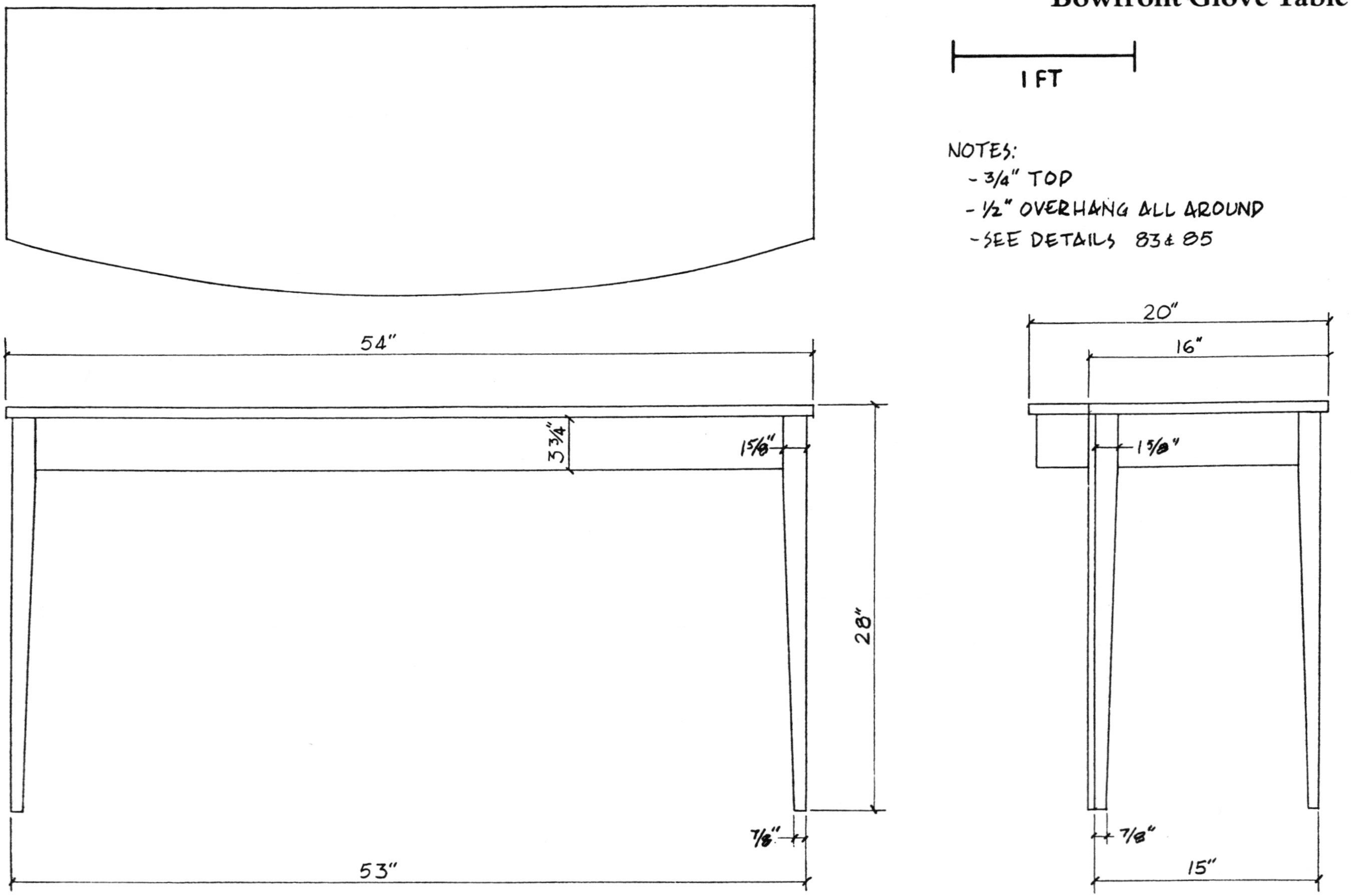

1 FT

NOTES:
- 3/4" TOP
- 1/2" OVERHANG ALL AROUND
- SEE DETAILS, 83 & 85

20"

16"

1 5/8"

15"

7/8"

28"

1 5/8"

3 3/4"

7/8"

54"

53"

End, top and side views of the bowfront glove table. See the following page for a photograph and perspective.

Serving the same function as the straight-front glove table, the bowfront glove table adds another dimension with its convex frontal curve. This table was not designed to house a drawer, although I suppose one could be adapted to it.

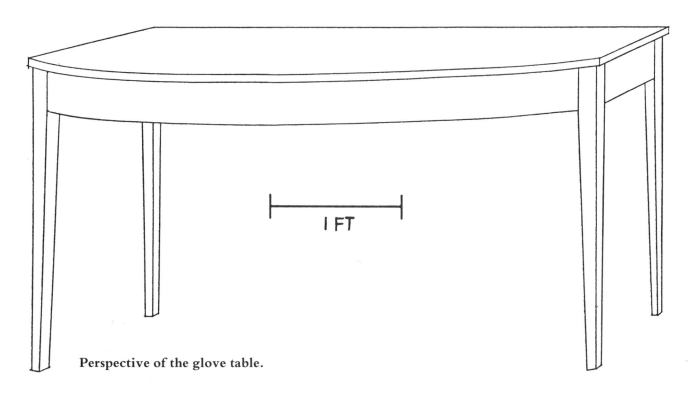

Perspective of the glove table.

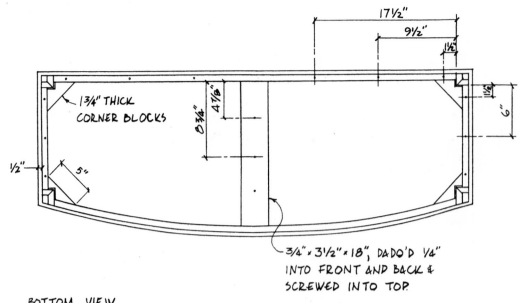

17½"

9½"

1½"

1¾" THICK
CORNER BLOCKS

4⅛"

ø¾"

6"

1½"

½"

5"

3/4" × 3½" × 18", DADO'D ¼"
INTO FRONT AND BACK &
SCREWED INTO TOP.

BOTTOM VIEW

1 FT

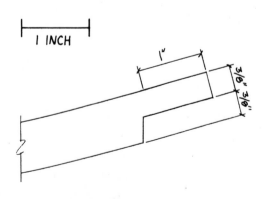

3/8"

3/8"

Bottom view of the bowfront glove table and Detail 85 (skirt tenon).

1 INCH

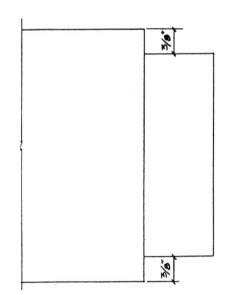

1"

3/8"

3/8"

DETAIL 85
FRONT SKIRT TENON

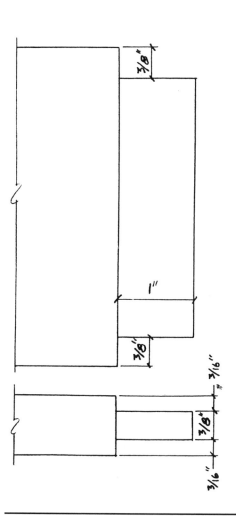

1 INCH

Detail 83: Skirt tenon.

Vault Table

The early cabinetmaker could not have created the vault table because the technology for doing so simply wasn't available. This contemporary table requires a precision in bending that can only be achieved through a multi-ply laminate or through highly controlled steam bending. The table works well in any area where one wants to avoid a ponderous form. The edge of the tabletop has a deep bevel that allows the top to float free of the base.

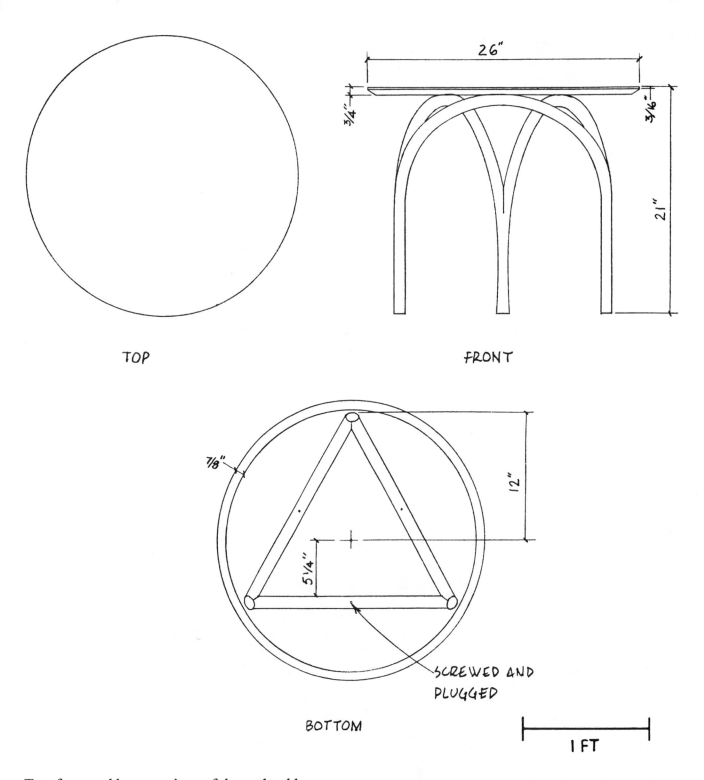

TOP

FRONT

26"

3/4"

3/16"

21"

7/8"

12"

5¼"

SCREWED AND
PLUGGED

BOTTOM

1 FT

Top, front and bottom views of the vault table.

DESKS

If a dining table averages 30 inches (76.2 cm) in height, so then does a desk. Most American manufacturers of desks make them between 29 and 29½ inches (73.6 and 74.9 cm) high, while in Europe they are made at about 28½ inches (72.4 cm) in height. What accounts for this difference I have not been able to determine, but I do know from empirical testing that a desk measuring 29½ to 30 inches is in most cases at a perfect height. One advantage to going a little higher is that there exists more space between the bottom of the desk top—be it a drawer or an apron—and the floor, which gives more leg room. Any work surface that is more than 36 inches (.91 m) deep becomes increasingly less useful as its depth increases, for it is impossible for a seated person on one side of a desk to reach across 40 inches (1.0 m). In order to grasp an object on the other side of the desk, one would have to stand up.

An office desk can be a formidable barrier to human communication. The stereotype of the banker seated on one side of a monster desk and the intimidated customer on the other does not enhance human interaction. It is for this reason that I am partial to a combination desk and writing table where the user of the desk is not so far, psychologically, from others seated across from him.

Panel Desk (see following page)

The panel desk is the most ambitious piece of furniture depicted—ambitious both in the variety of joint work necessary to build it and in sheer volume. When completed, this desk weighs close to 300 pounds and is made of 350 board feet of wood. Throughout the desk all the surfaces, both concealed and visible, are made up of floating panels. The panels, in addition to providing interesting visual patterns, also allow the wood an opportunity to expand and contract with heat and humidity changes. The writing trays that appear on each side of the desk are a combination pen drawer and a platform on which to spill out additional work.

Panel desk.

Back of the panel desk.

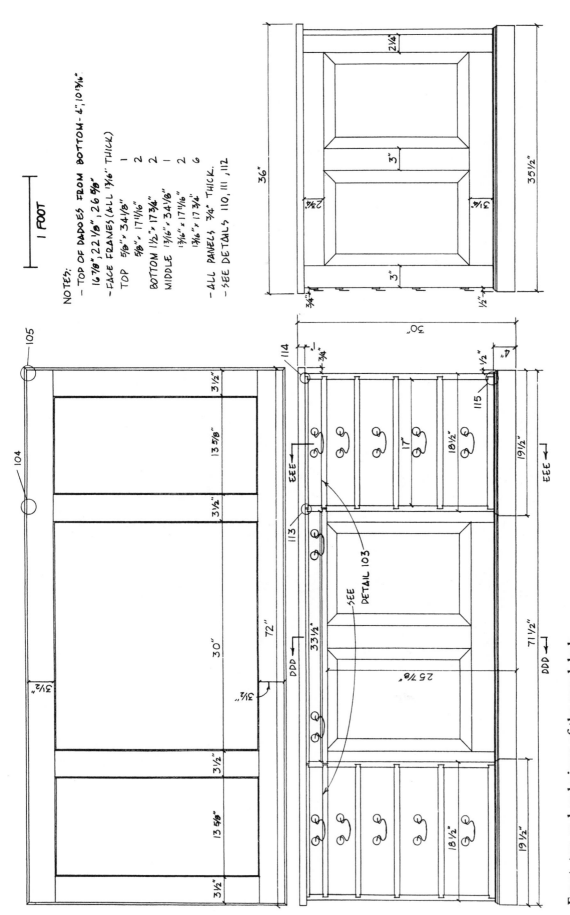

Front, top and end views of the panel desk.

NOTES:
— TOP OF DADOES FROM BOTTOM — 4", 10 13/16"
  16 7/8", 22 1/8", 26 5/8"
— FACE FRAMES (ALL 13/16" THICK)
  TOP   5/8" × 34 1/8"   1
         5/8" × 17 11/16"   2
                               2
  BOTTOM 1 1/2" × 17 3/4"   1
  MIDDLE 13/16" × 34 1/8"   2
         13/16" × 17 11/16"
         13/16" × 17 3/4"   6
— ALL PANELS 3/4" THICK.
— SEE DETAILS 110, 111, 112

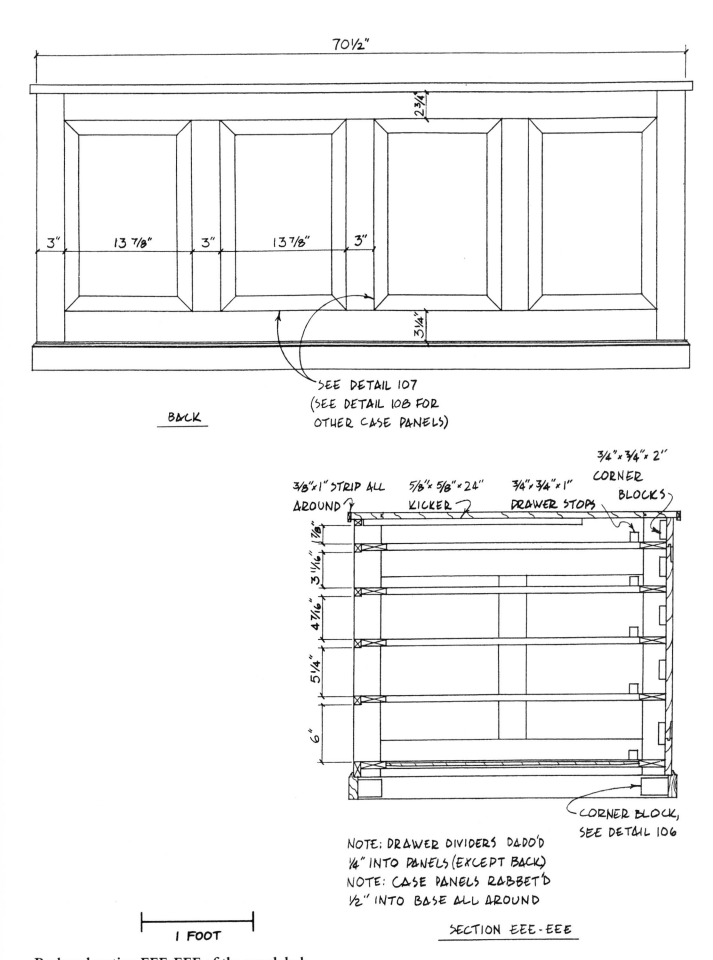

70½"

2¾"

3" 13⅞" 3" 13⅞" 3"

3¼"

SEE DETAIL 107
(SEE DETAIL 108 FOR
OTHER CASE PANELS)

BACK

3/8"×1" STRIP ALL
AROUND

5/8"×5/8"×24"
KICKER

3/4"×3/4"×1"
DRAWER STOPS

3/4"×3/4"×2"
CORNER
BLOCKS

1⅛"

3 11/16"

4 7/16"

5¼"

6"

CORNER BLOCK,
SEE DETAIL 106

NOTE: DRAWER DIVIDERS DADO'D
¼" INTO PANELS (EXCEPT BACK)
NOTE: CASE PANELS RABBET'D
½" INTO BASE ALL AROUND

SECTION EEE-EEE

1 FOOT

Back and section EEE-EEE of the panel desk.

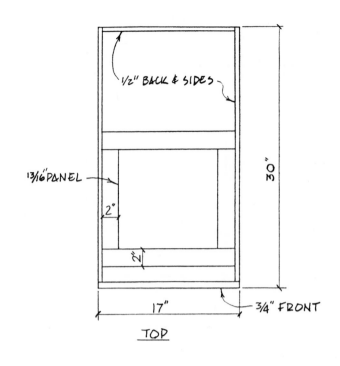

½" BACK & SIDES

13/16" PANEL

30"

2"

2"

17"

¾" FRONT

TOP

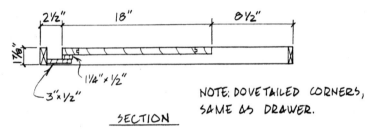

2½"

18"

8½"

17/8"

1¼" × ½"

3" × ½"

SECTION

NOTE: DOVETAILED CORNERS, SAME AS DRAWER.

DETAIL 103
PULL OUT SHELF

Detail 103 (shelf) and section DDD-DDD.

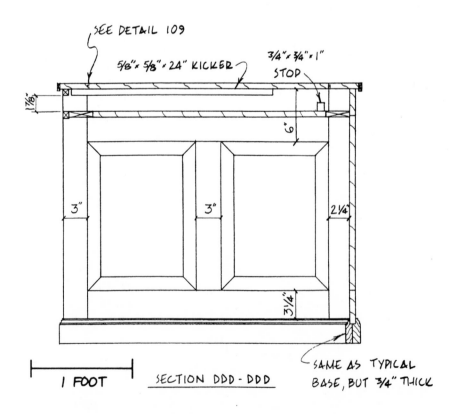

SEE DETAIL 109

5/8" × 5/8" × 24" KICKER

¾" × ¾" × 1"
STOP

17/8"

6"

3"

3"

2¼"

3¼"

1 FOOT

SECTION DDD-DDD

SAME AS TYPICAL BASE, BUT ¾" THICK

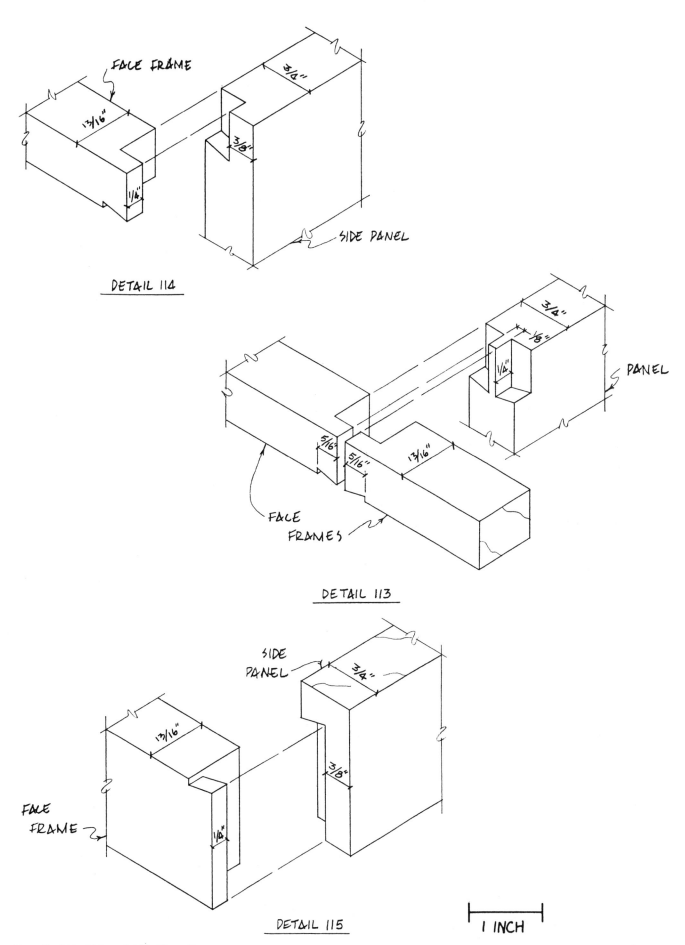

FACE FRAME

3/4"

13/16"

3/8"

1/4"

SIDE PANEL

DETAIL 114

3/4"

1/8"

1/4"

PANEL

5/16"

5/16"

13/16"

FACE FRAMES

DETAIL 113

SIDE PANEL

3/4"

13/16"

3/8"

FACE FRAME

1/4"

DETAIL 115

1 INCH

Details 113, 114 and 115: Face frames.

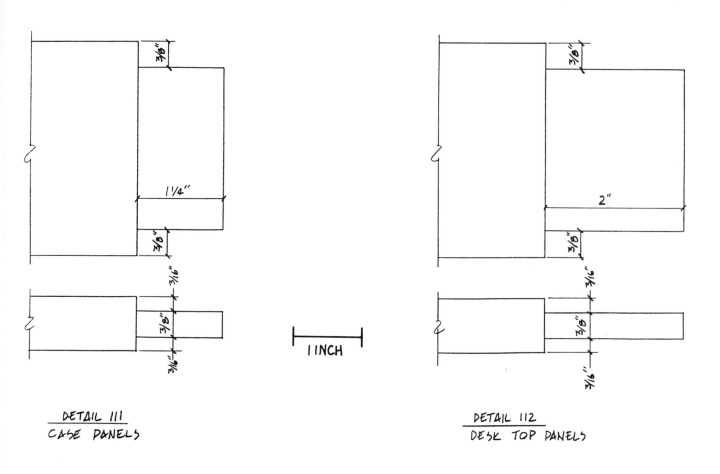

DETAIL 111
CASE PANELS

DETAIL 112
DESK TOP PANELS

1 INCH

RAIL TENONS

Details 111 and 112: Tenon details.

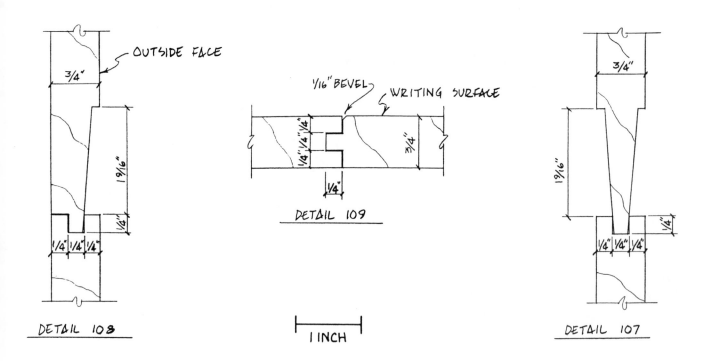

DETAIL 108

DETAIL 109

DETAIL 107

1 INCH

SECTIONS THROUGH RAILS & PANELS

Details 107, 108, and 109: Frame and panel.

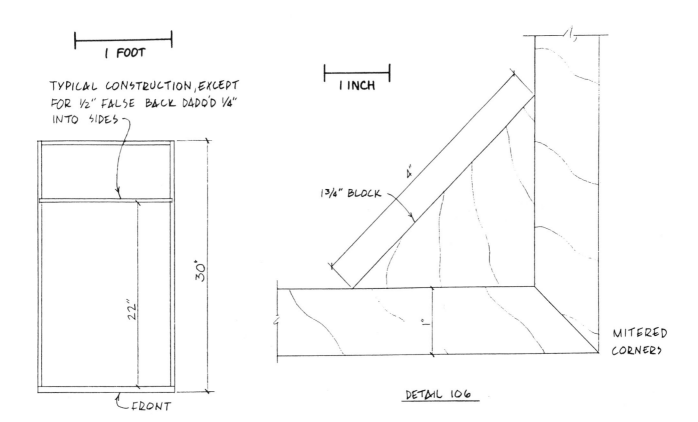

1 FOOT

TYPICAL CONSTRUCTION, EXCEPT
FOR ½" FALSE BACK DADO'D ¼"
INTO SIDES

30"

22"

FRONT

DETAIL 110
DRAWERS

1 INCH

1¾" BLOCK

4"

1"

MITERED
CORNERS

DETAIL 106

Detail 106: Corner. Detail 110: Drawers. For drawer details, see the Appendix on case details.

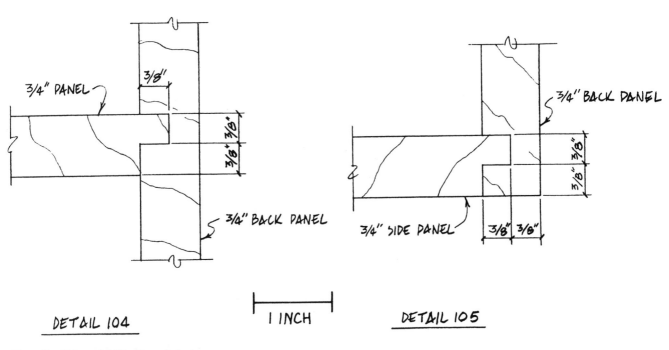

3/4" PANEL

3/8"

3/8" 3/8"

3/4" BACK PANEL

DETAIL 104

1 INCH

3/4" BACK PANEL

3/4" SIDE PANEL

3/8" 3/8"

3/8"

3/8"

DETAIL 105

Details 104 and 105: Case joints.

Bowfront Table
Credenza

The bowfront table credenza incorporates the bow so that it houses three shallow drawers and can be used against a wall. This piece also serves as a writing table and as a conference table. The bowfront desk also achieves a much more personal atmosphere than a massive desk.

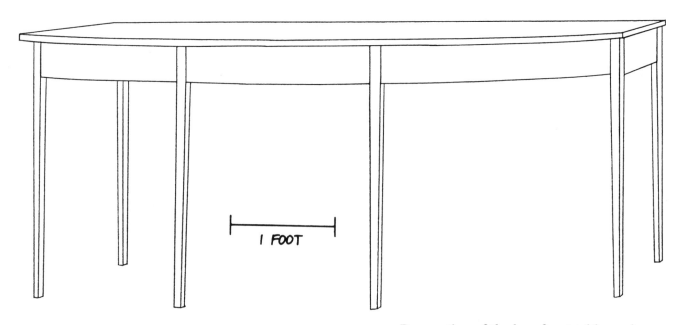

1 FOOT

Perspective of the bowfront table credenza.

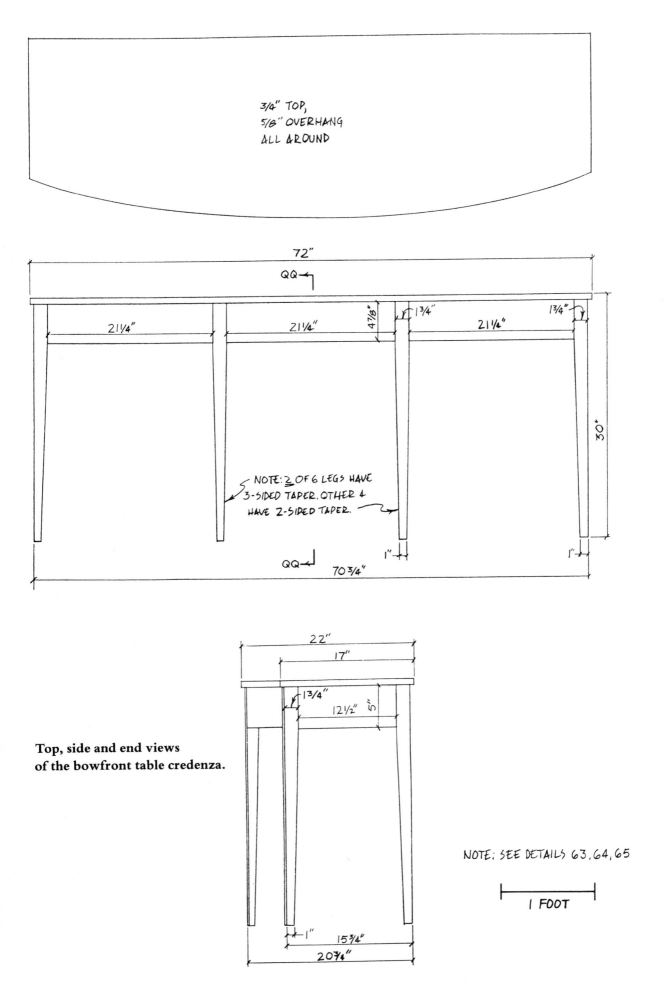

3/4" TOP,
5/8" OVERHANG
ALL AROUND

72"

QQ ←

21¼"   21¼"   4⅞"   1¾"   21¼"   1¾"

30'

NOTE: 2 OF 6 LEGS HAVE
3-SIDED TAPER. OTHER 4
HAVE 2-SIDED TAPER.

1"   1"

QQ ←
70¾"

22"

17"

1¾"
12½"   5"

**Top, side and end views
of the bowfront table credenza.**

1"   15¾"

20¾"

NOTE: SEE DETAILS 63, 64, 65

1 FOOT

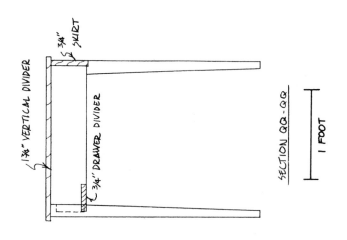

34" SKIRT

1¾" VERTICAL DIVIDER

34" DRAWER DIVIDER

SECTION QQ-QQ

1 FOOT

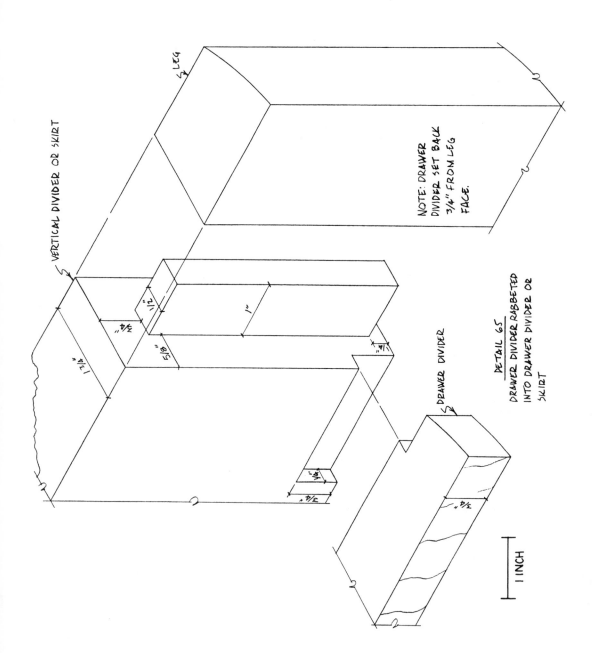

LEG

VERTICAL DIVIDER OR SKIRT

NOTE: DRAWER DIVIDER SET BACK 3/4" FROM LEG FACE.

VERTICAL DIVIDER

1½"

3/4"

1"

5/8"

1"

1 3/4"

3/4"

⅛"

DRAWER DIVIDER

3/4"

DETAIL 65
DRAWER DIVIDER RABBETED INTO DRAWER DIVIDER OR SKIRT

1 INCH

Detail 65 (drawer divider) and section QQ-QQ.

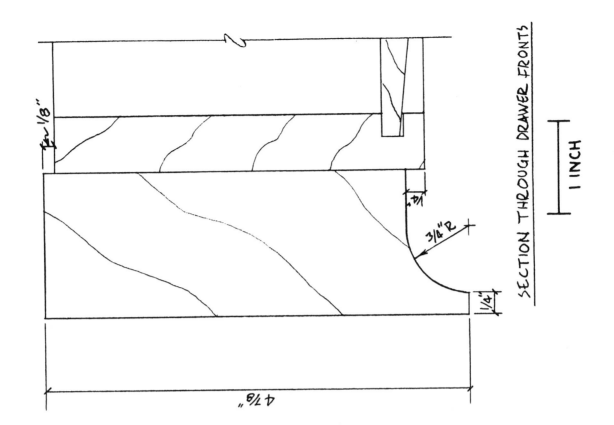

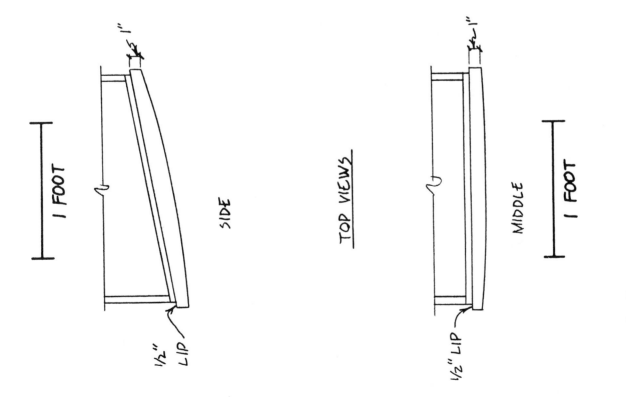

SECTION THROUGH DRAWER FRONTS

1 INCH

4 7/8"

1/8"

3/4" R

1/4"

1/4"

TOP VIEWS

1 FOOT

1/2" LIP

SIDE

1"

1 FOOT

1/2" LIP

MIDDLE

1"

Drawer details.

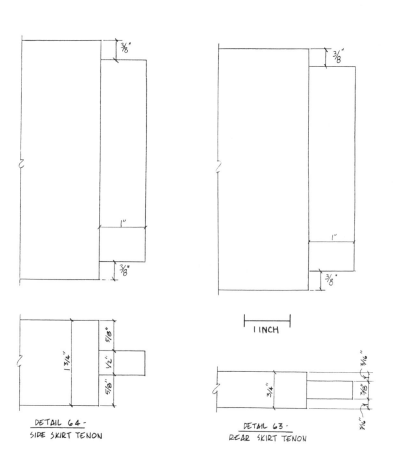

Details 63 and 64: Skirt tenons.

|← 1 INCH →|

DETAIL 64 -
SIDE SKIRT TENON

DETAIL 63 -
REAR SKIRT TENON

Trestle Table Desk

This combination of a trestle table and a writing table with drawers is unique in my experience. As a trestle table, it has the advantage of free space beneath the table, can be quickly disassembled, and also provides an attractive conference table and writing table. The nature of the structure prohibits more than 36 inches (91.4 cm) in width, but that should be adequate for any desk in any case.

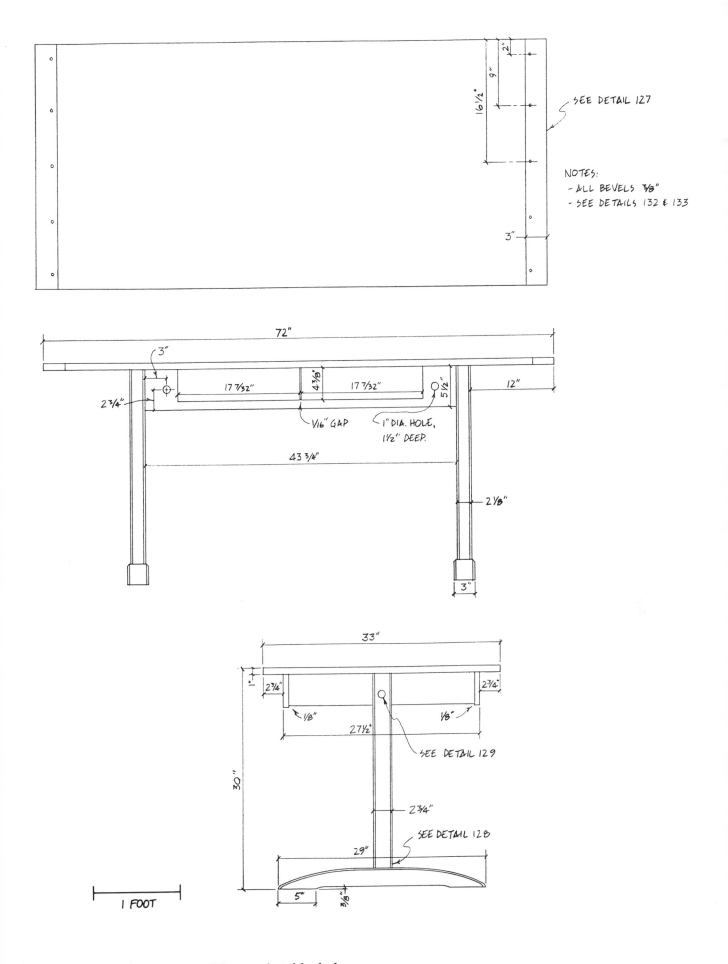

Front, top and end views of the trestle table desk.

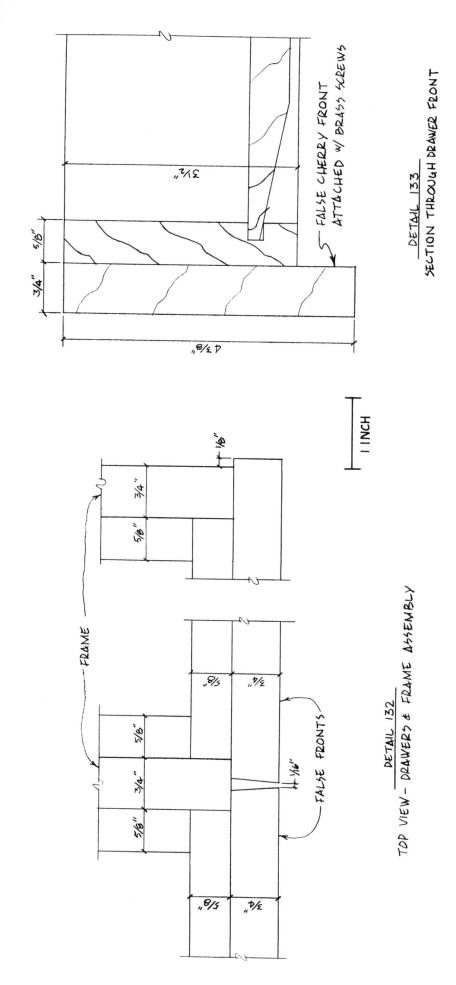

3½"

5/8"

3/4"

4 3/8"

FALSE CHERRY FRONT
ATTACHED W/ BRASS SCREWS

DETAIL 133
SECTION THROUGH DRAWER FRONT

1 INCH

3/4"

5/8"

1/8"

FRAME

5/8"

3/4"

5/8"

3/4"

1/16"

FALSE FRONTS

5/8"

3/4"

DETAIL 132
TOP VIEW – DRAWERS & FRAME ASSEMBLY

Details 132 and 133: Drawer details.

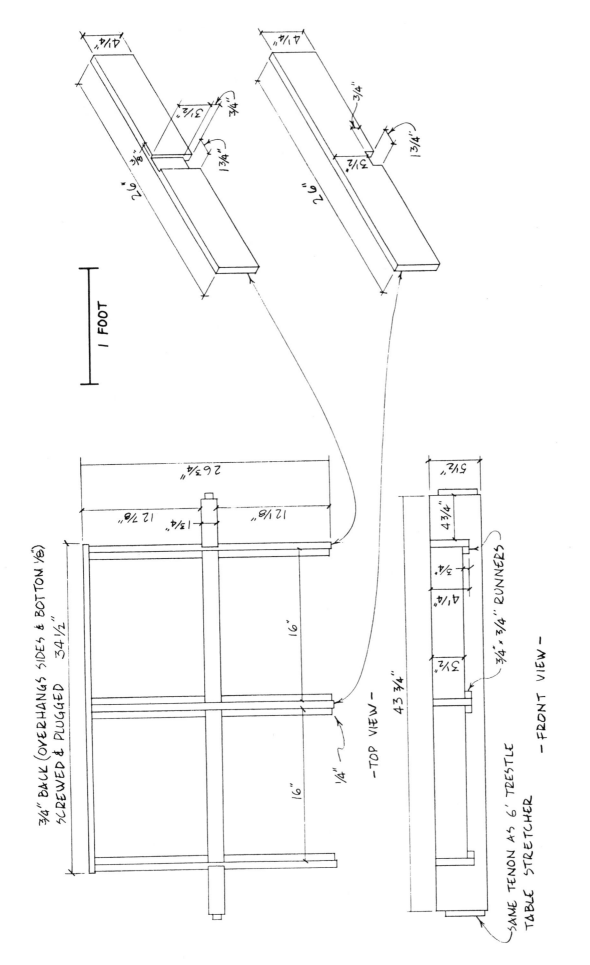

4 1/4"

3 1/2"   3/4"

13/4"

2'6"

3/8"

4 1/4"

3/4"

3 1/2"   13/4"

2'6"

1 FOOT

3/4" BACK (OVERHANGS SIDES & BOTTOM 1/8")
SCREWED & PLUGGED   34 1/2"

26 3/4"

12 7/8"   13/4"   12 7/8"

16"

16"

1/4"

—TOP VIEW—

5 1/2"

4 3/4"

3/4"

4 1/4"

3 1/2"

43 3/4"

SAME TENON AS 6' TRESTLE
TABLE STRETCHER

3/4" x 3/4" RUNNERS

—FRONT VIEW—

Stretcher and drawer frame assembly. For further details, see the trestle table (pages 44 to 46).

Lectern Desk

Many people who work at a desk for more or less a 40 hour week experience lower back pain. Some of the back pain can be relieved by occasionally standing while working. The lectern desk is good for this purpose. It is sufficiently small to be used in almost any office in conjunction with the traditional 30-inch (76.2-cm)-high desk without cluttering up the room and can also be used as a lectern or speaker's rostrum.

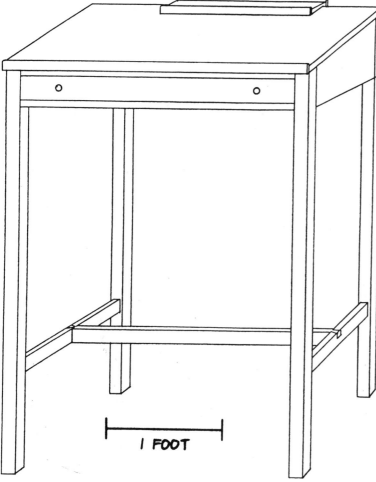

1 FOOT

Perpective of the lectern desk.

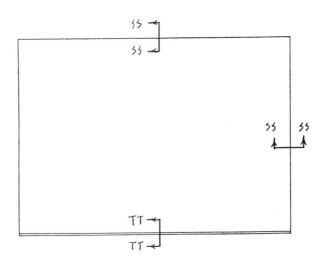

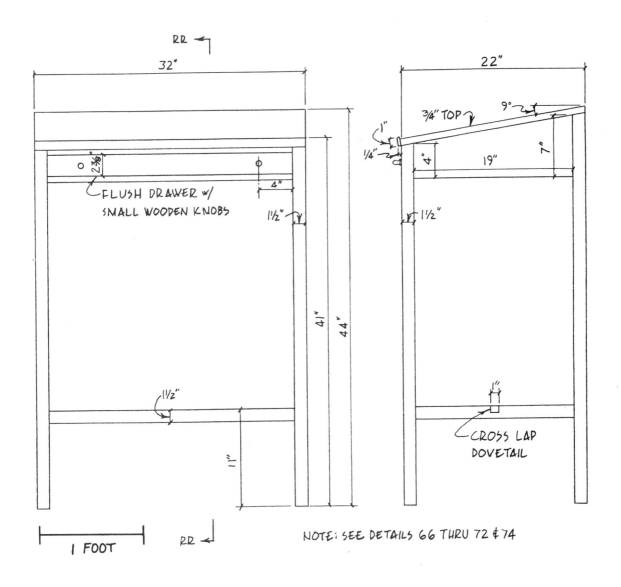

Front, side and top views of the lectern desk.

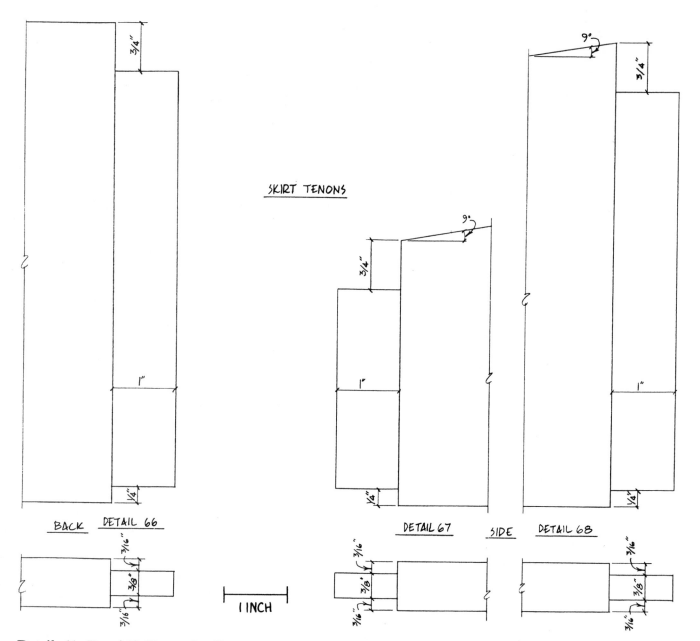

SKIRT TENONS

3/4"

1"

1/4"

BACK   DETAIL 66

9°

3/4"

1"

1/4"

DETAIL 67   SIDE   DETAIL 68

9°

3/4"

1"

1/4"

3/16"

3/8"

3/16"

⊢ 1 INCH ⊣

3/16"

3/8"

3/16"

3/16"

3/8"

3/16"

Details 66, 67 and 68: Tenon details.

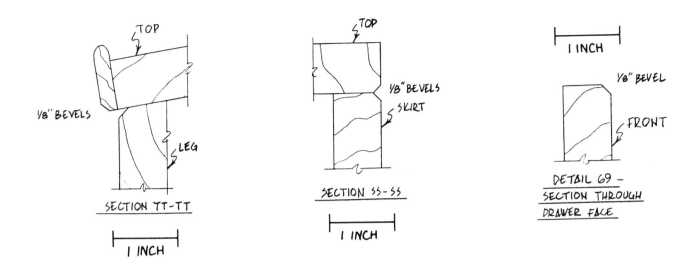

⅛" BEVELS

LEG

SECTION TT-TT

1 INCH

TOP

⅛" BEVELS

SKIRT

SECTION SS-SS

1 INCH

1 INCH

⅛" BEVEL

FRONT

DETAIL 69 –
SECTION THROUGH
DRAWER FACE

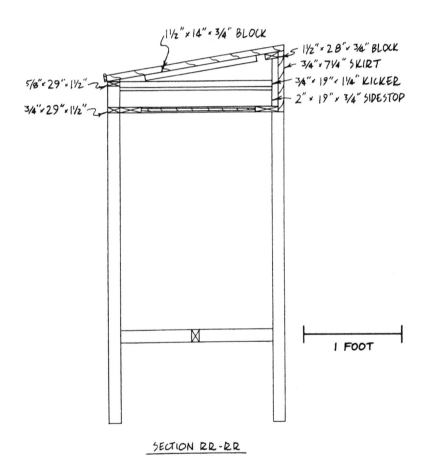

1½" × 14" × ¾" BLOCK

1½" × 28" × ¾" BLOCK

¾" × 7¼" SKIRT

¾" × 19" × 1¼" KICKER

2" × 19" × ¾" SIDESTOP

5/8" × 29" × 1½"

¾" × 29" × 1½"

SECTION RR-RR

1 FOOT

Detail 69 (drawer front) and sections TT-TT, SS-SS and RR-RR.

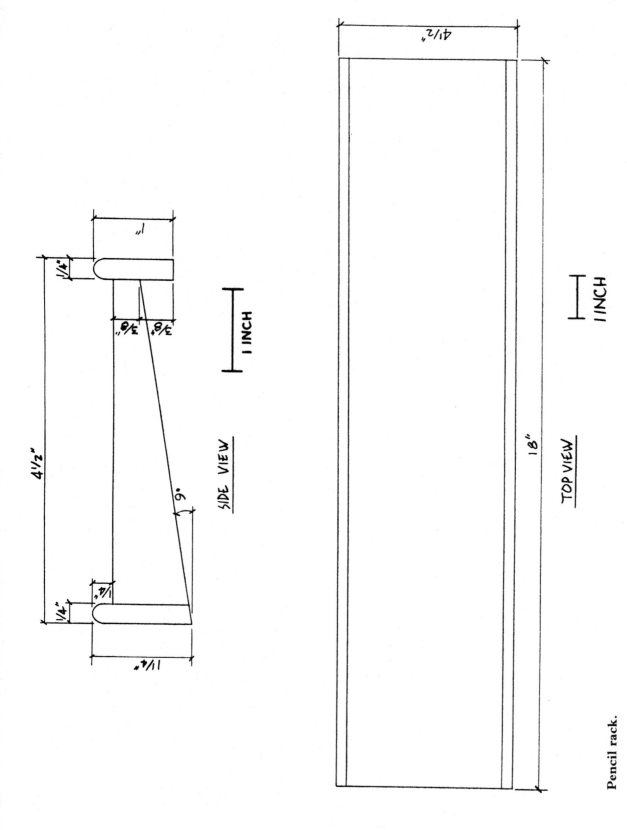

SIDE VIEW

1"

1/4"

3/8" 3/16"

4 1/2"

9°

1 INCH

1/4"

1/4"

1 1/4"

TOP VIEW

4 1/2"

18"

1 INCH

Pencil rack.

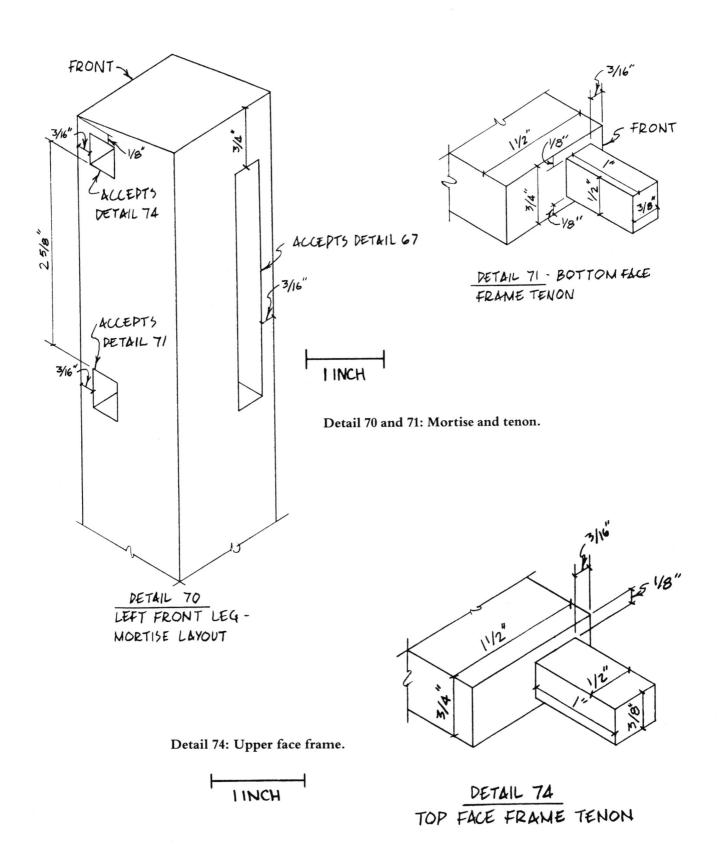

FRONT

3/16"
1/8"
ACCEPTS DETAIL 74

3/4"

2 5/8"

ACCEPTS DETAIL 67

3/16"

ACCEPTS DETAIL 71

3/16"

DETAIL 70
LEFT FRONT LEG -
MORTISE LAYOUT

1 INCH

Detail 70 and 71: Mortise and tenon.

3/16"

1 1/2"   1/8"   FRONT

3/4"   1/2"   1"   3/8"

1/8"

DETAIL 71 - BOTTOM FACE
FRAME TENON

Detail 74: Upper face frame.

1 INCH

3/16"

1 1/2"   1/8"

3/4"   1/2"   1"   3/8"

DETAIL 74
TOP FACE FRAME TENON

High Desk

The high desk offers a 43-inch (1.0-m)-high writing surface that is ideal for standing while working. The lower cross rail is brought somewhat forward to provide a place to rest one's foot while working. The flat surface, or return, can be either at the right or left side, and offers a place to put a telephone, cup of coffee, or any other object that would otherwise slide down the slanted desk surface. This is an ideal solution for a person who wants to think on his feet or work while standing.

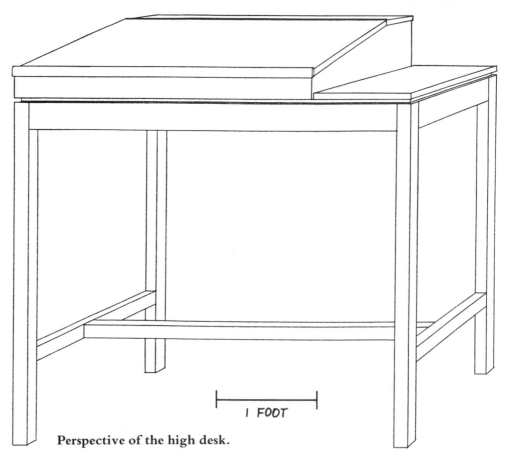

1 FOOT

Perspective of the high desk.

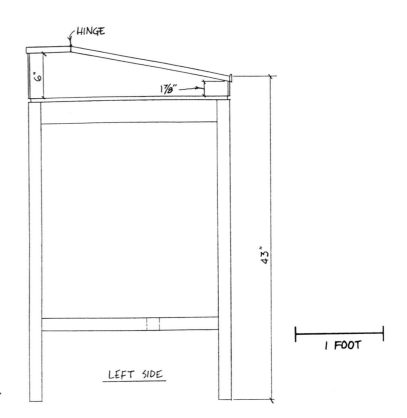

HINGE

6"

1⅞"

43"

LEFT SIDE

1 FOOT

Top, bottom and side views of the high desk.

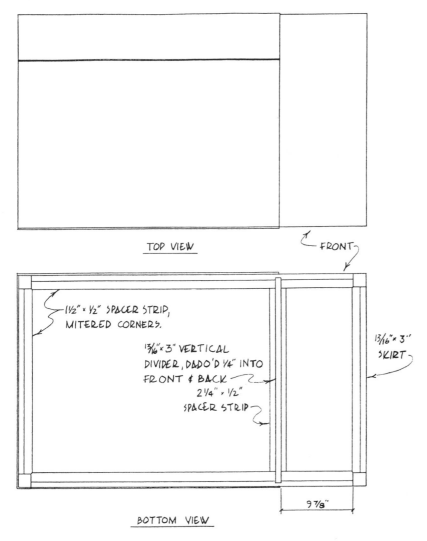

TOP VIEW

FRONT

1½" × ½" SPACER STRIP,
MITERED CORNERS.

13/16" × 3" VERTICAL
DIVIDER, DADO'D ¼" INTO
FRONT & BACK

2¼" × ½"
SPACER STRIP

13/16" × 3"
SKIRT

9⅞"

BOTTOM VIEW

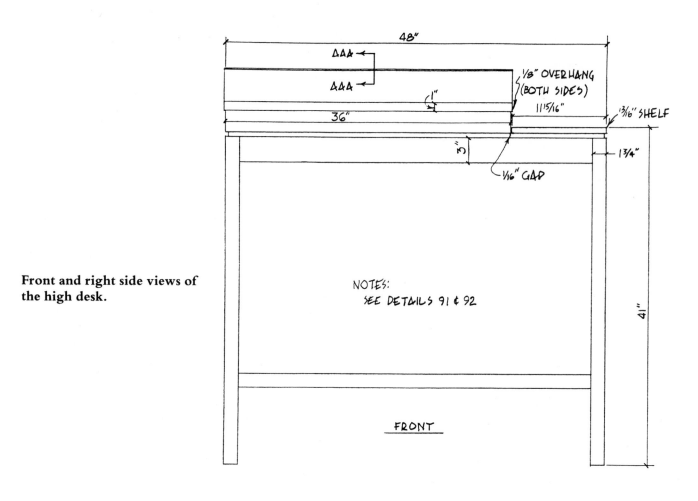

Front and right side views of the high desk.

NOTES:
SEE DETAILS 91 & 92

48"

⊿⊿⊿

⊿⊿⊿

⅛" OVERHANG
(BOTH SIDES)

1"

11¹⁵/₁₆"

1³/₁₆" SHELF

36"

3"

1³/₄"

¹/₁₆" GAP

41"

FRONT

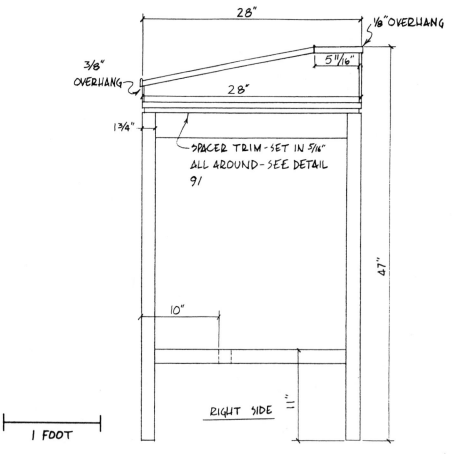

28"

⅛" OVERHANG

3/8"
OVERHANG

5 ¹¹/₁₆"

28"

1³/₄"

SPACER TRIM – SET IN 5/16"
ALL AROUND – SEE DETAIL
91

47"

10"

1"

RIGHT SIDE

1 FOOT

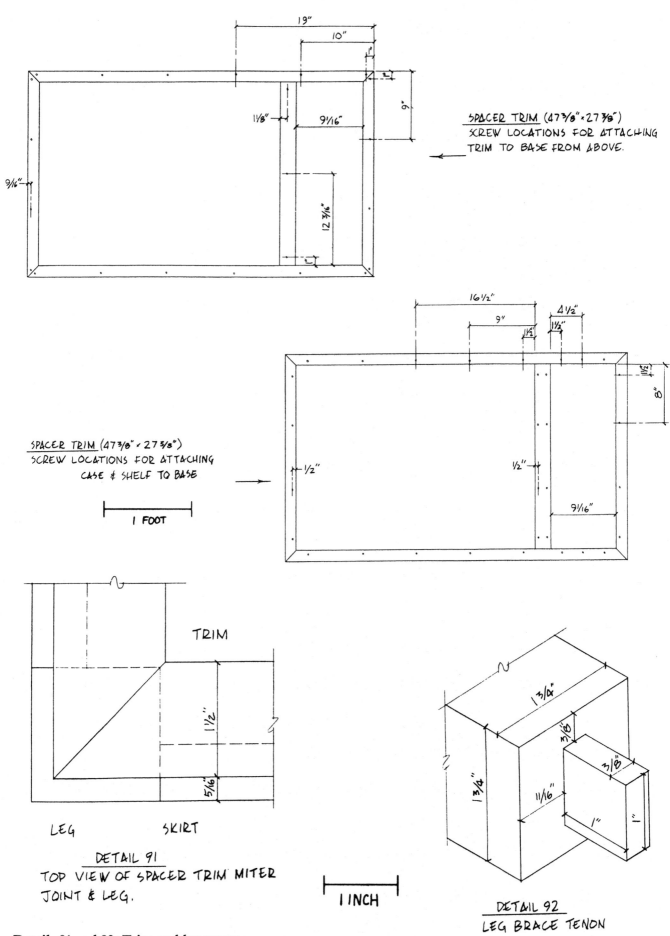

19"

10"

1"

9"

1⅛" 9¹/₁₆"

12 ³/₁₆"

1"

9/16"

SPACER TRIM (47⅜" × 27⅜")
SCREW LOCATIONS FOR ATTACHING
TRIM TO BASE FROM ABOVE.

16½"

9"

4½"

1½" 1½"

1½"

8"

½"

½"

9¹/₁₆"

SPACER TRIM (47⅜" × 27⅜")
SCREW LOCATIONS FOR ATTACHING
CASE & SHELF TO BASE

1 FOOT

TRIM

1½"

5/16"

LEG   SKIRT

DETAIL 91
TOP VIEW OF SPACER TRIM MITER
JOINT & LEG.

1 INCH

1 3/4"

3/8"

3/8"

1 3/4"

11/16"

1"

1"

DETAIL 92
LEG BRACE TENON

Details 91 and 92: Trim and leg tenon.

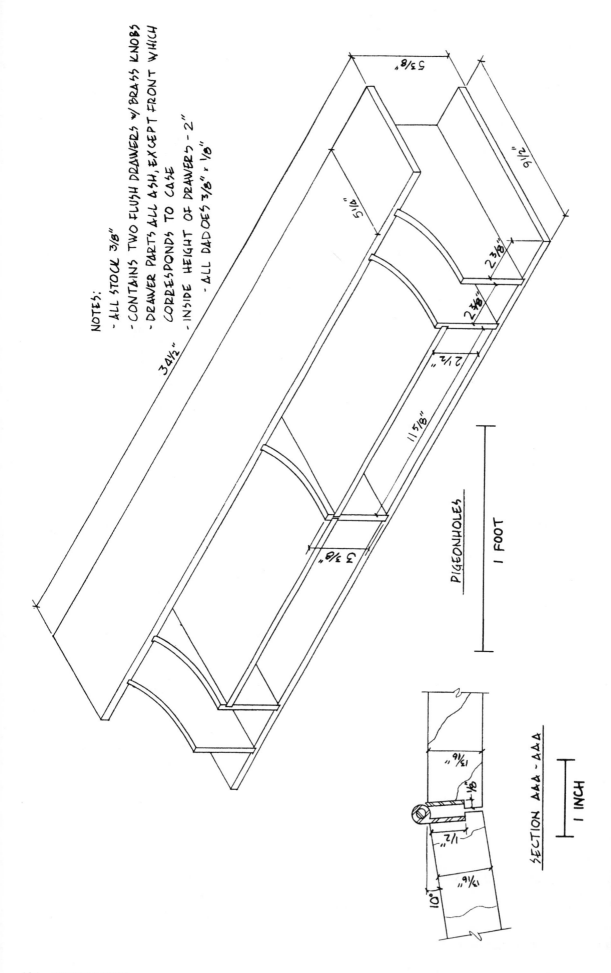

NOTES:
- ALL STOCK 3/8"
- CONTAINS TWO FLUSH DRAWERS W/ BRASS KNOBS
- DRAWER PARTS ALL ASH, EXCEPT FRONT WHICH CORRESPONDS TO CASE
- INSIDE HEIGHT OF DRAWERS - 2"
- ALL DADOES 3/8" x 1/8"

5 3/8"

9 1/2"

2 3/8"

2 3/8"

2 1/2"

5 1/4"

11 5/8"

3 3/8"

30 1/2"

PIGEONHOLES

1 FOOT

SECTION AAA - AAA

1 INCH

13 1/16"

1/8"

1/2"

13 1/16"

10°

Pigeonholes interior of high desk.

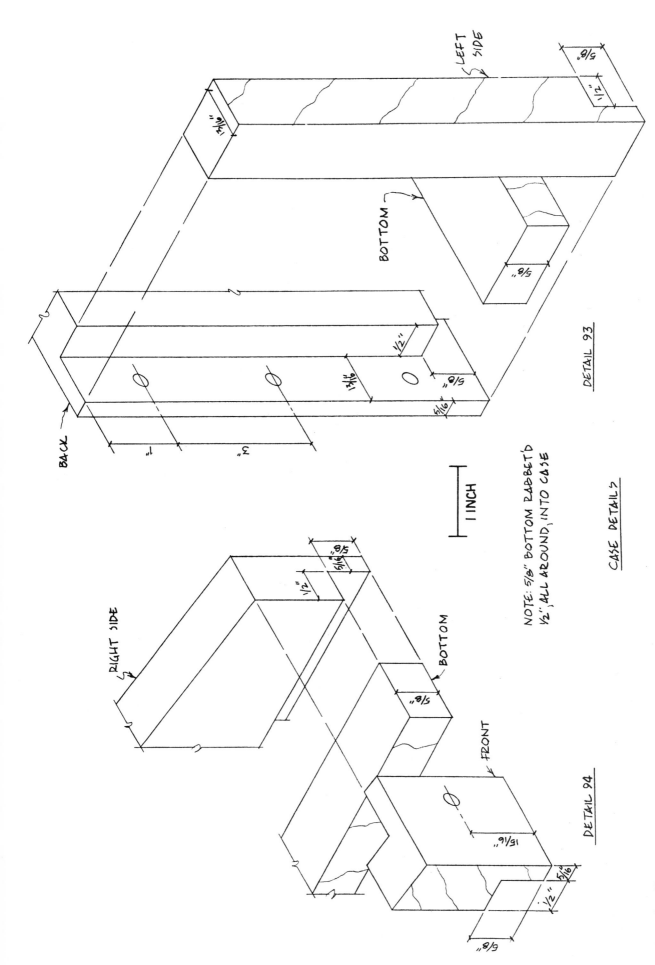

NOTE: 5/8" BOTTOM RABBET'D 1/2", ALL AROUND, INTO CASE

CASE DETAILS

DETAIL 93

DETAIL 94

| 1 INCH

Case details.

Standing Desk

The standing desk incorporates the same features as the high desk in terms of utility, but it also has several additional storage spaces. The upper pigeonholes are ideal for storing stationery, pamphlets and writing material of all types. The eight-inch (20.3-cm) surface is sufficiently deep to allow a telephone to be placed on it. Beneath the lid, of course, are the small drawers that can be used for odds and ends, and beneath the whole is a good-size drawer for writing materials.

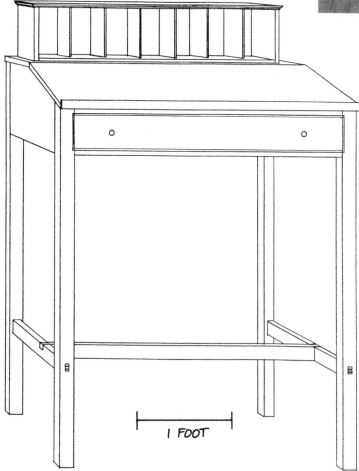

1 FOOT

Perspective of the standing desk.

NOTE: 1/8" OVERHANG BACK
AND SIDES, 3/8" IN FRONT.

1 FOOT

10"

18 5/8"

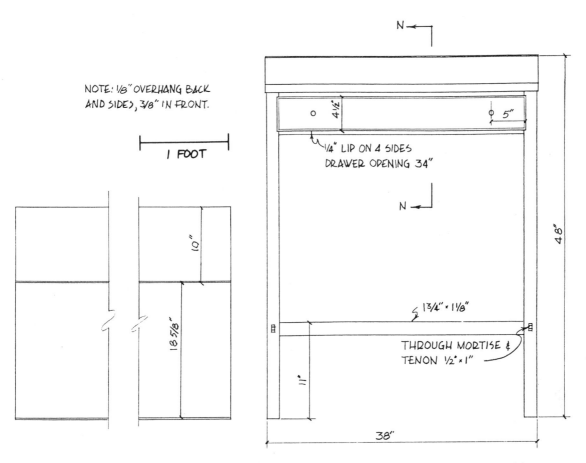

N ←

4 1/2"

5"

1/4" LIP ON 4 SIDES
DRAWER OPENING 34"

N ←

48"

13/4" × 11/8"

THROUGH MORTISE &
TENON 1/2" × 1"

11"

38"

NOTE: ALSO SEE DETAILS 12 THRU 18

1/4" THICK, EXTENDS
1/4" ABOVE DESK SURFACE

Side, front, and top views of the standing desk.

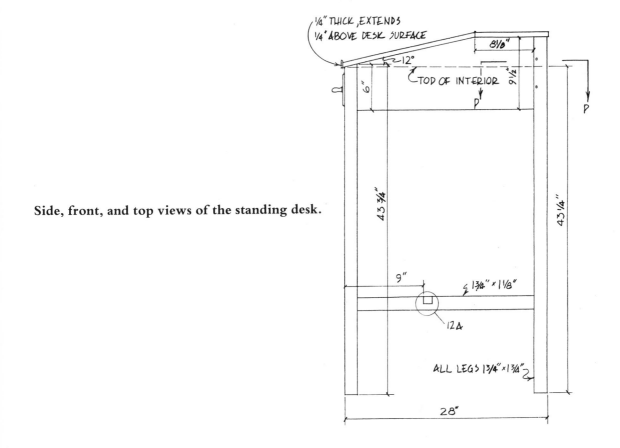

8 1/8"

12°

TOP OF INTERIOR

9 1/2"

6"

P

P

43 3/4"

43 1/4"

9"

13/4" × 11/8"

12A

ALL LEGS 13/4" × 13/4"

28"

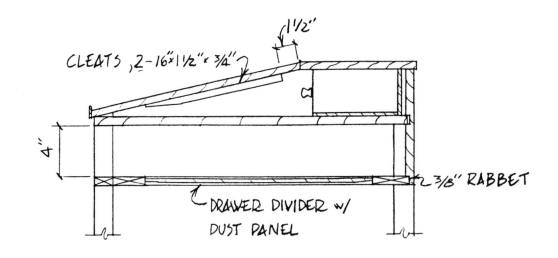

CLEATS, 2-16"×1½"×¾"

1½"

4"

3/8" RABBET

DRAWER DIVIDER w/ DUST PANEL

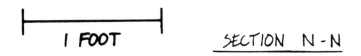

1 FOOT

SECTION N-N

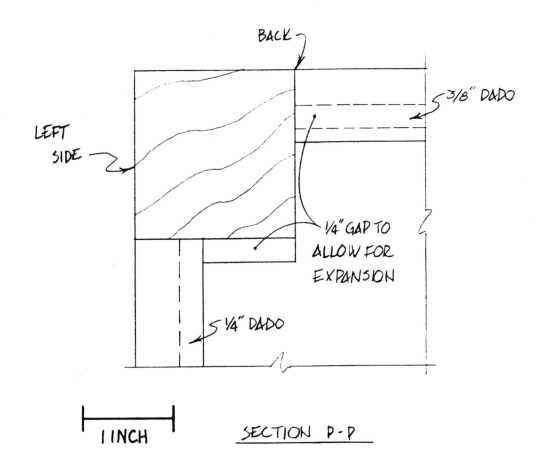

BACK

3/8" DADO

LEFT SIDE

¼" GAP TO ALLOW FOR EXPANSION

¼" DADO

1 INCH

SECTION P-P

Sections NN and PP: Case and leg cross sections.

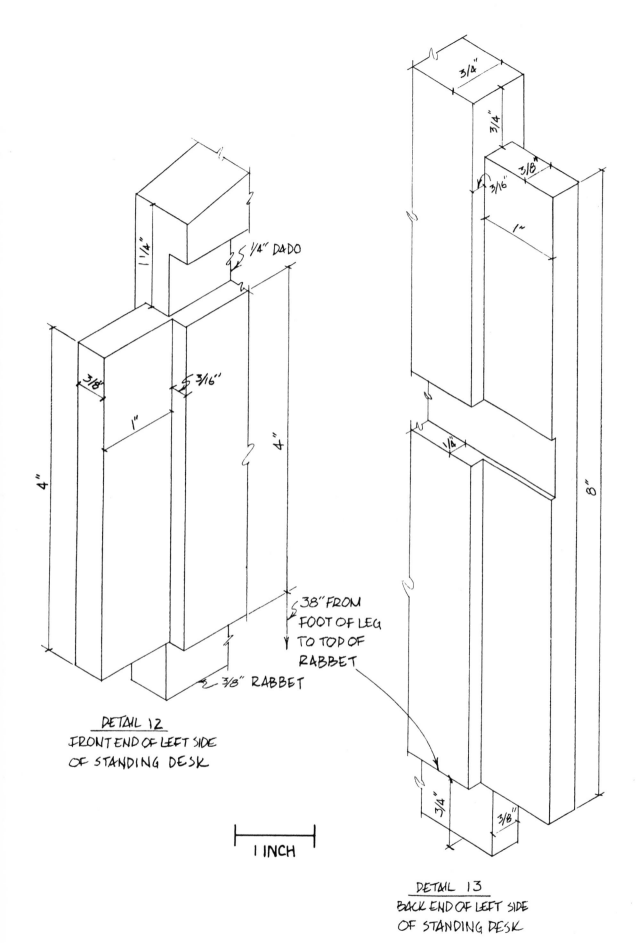

1¼"

¼" DADO

3/8"

3/16"

1"

4"

4"

38" FROM
FOOT OF LEG
TO TOP OF
RABBET

3/8" RABBET

DETAIL 12
FRONT END OF LEFT SIDE
OF STANDING DESK

1 INCH

3/4"

3/4"

3/8"

3/16"

1"

1/8"

8"

3/4"

3/8"

DETAIL 13
BACK END OF LEFT SIDE
OF STANDING DESK

Details 12 and 13: Tenon details.

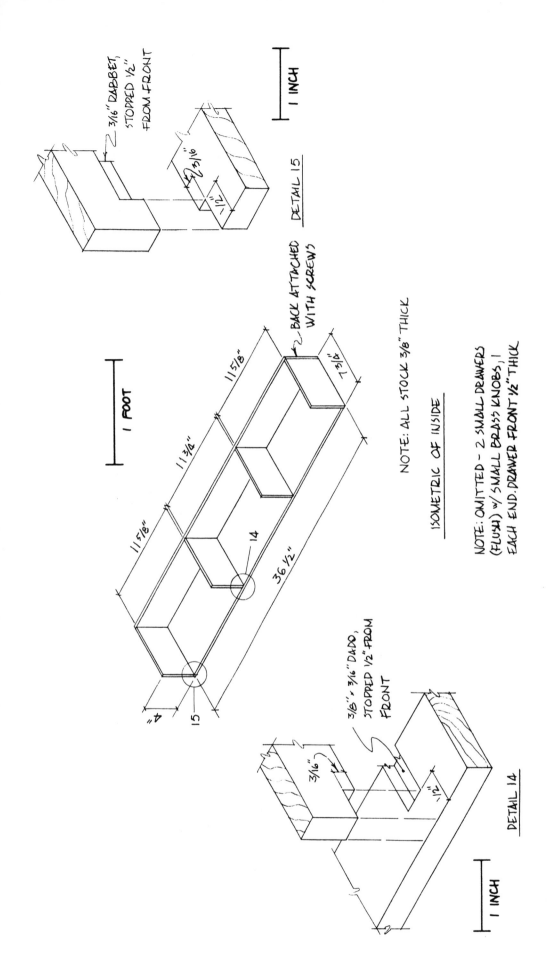

3/16" RABBET, STOPPED 1/2" FROM FRONT

3/16"

1/2"

DETAIL 15

1 INCH

BACK ATTACHED WITH SCREWS

11 5/8"

11 3/2"

11 5/8"

36 1/2"

4"

7 3/4"

14

15

1 FOOT

NOTE: ALL STOCK 3/8" THICK

ISOMETRIC OF INSIDE

NOTE: OMITTED - 2 SMALL DRAWERS (FLUSH) W/ SMALL BRASS KNOBS, 1 EACH END. DRAWER FRONT 1/2" THICK

3/8" x 3/16" DADO, STOPPED 1/2" FROM FRONT

3/16"

1/2"

DETAIL 14

1 INCH

Details 14 and 15: Interior details.

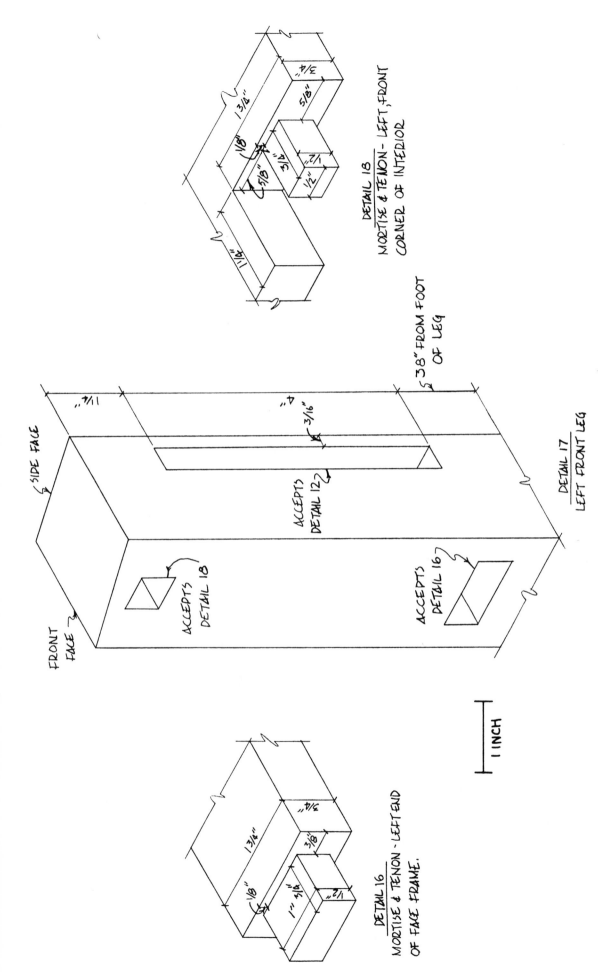

DETAIL 18
MORTISE & TENON - LEFT, FRONT CORNER OF INTERIOR

DETAIL 17
LEFT FRONT LEG

DETAIL 16
MORTISE & TENON - LEFT END OF FACE FRAME.

Details 16, 17 and 18: Mortise and tenon.

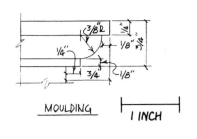

MOULDING

|← 1 INCH →|

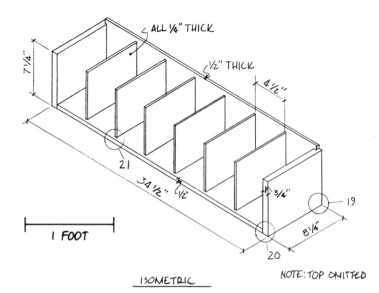

ISOMETRIC

NOTE: TOP OMITTED

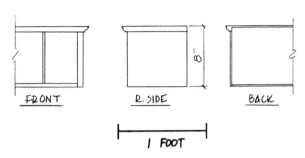

FRONT   R. SIDE   BACK

|← 1 FOOT →|

Pigeonhole assembly.

Detail 12A: Dovetail.

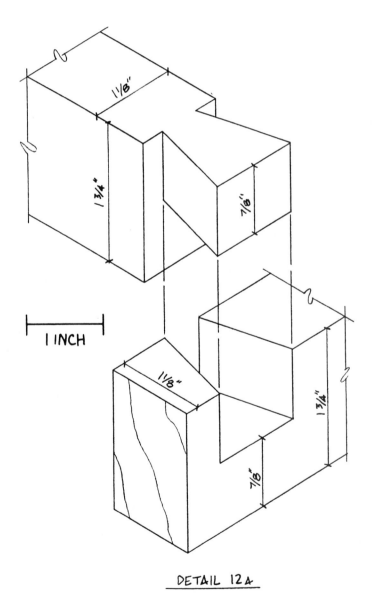

|← 1 INCH →|

DETAIL 12A

Cupboard Desk

The cupboard desk was inspired by a Shaker design of the early 19th century. As we have built this desk over the years, a number of changes have taken place, particularly in the depth of the desk. It started out around 11 inches (27.9 cm) deep, and has been growing to the point where it is now 15 inches (38.1 cm) deep. The purpose of this added depth is to give the desk greater stability. When the desk lid is dropped forward and is in use, it is cantilevered fairly far forward from the center of gravity. Since anyone sitting on the lid could topple the desk forward, place toggle bolts near the top to anchor it to the wall. On the left is an exterior view of the cupboard desk. Below is an interior view of the cupboard desk.

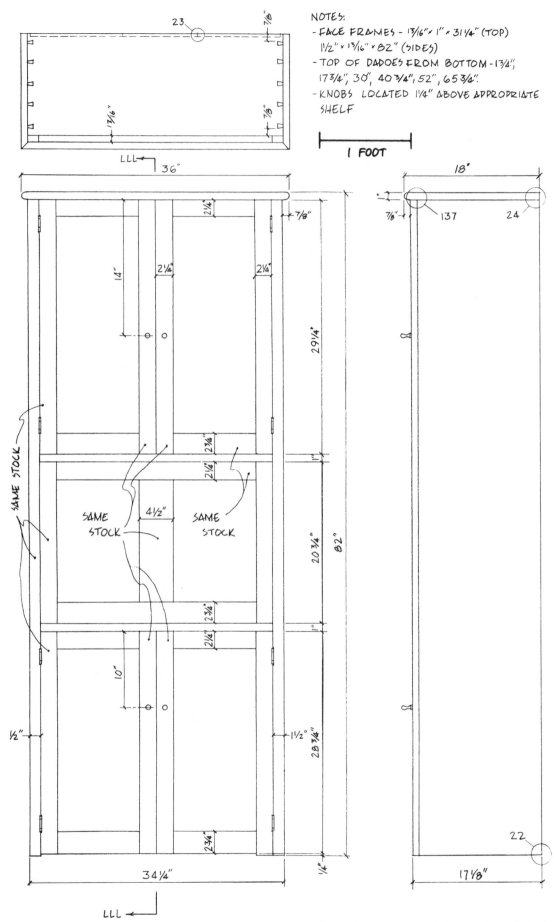

NOTES:
- FACE FRAMES - 13/16" × 1" × 31 1/4" (TOP)
  1 1/2" × 13/16" × 82" (SIDES)
- TOP OF DADOES FROM BOTTOM - 1 3/4",
  17 3/4", 30", 40 3/4", 52", 65 3/4".
- KNOBS LOCATED 1 1/4" ABOVE APPROPRIATE
  SHELF

1 FOOT

Front, side and top views of the cupboard desk.

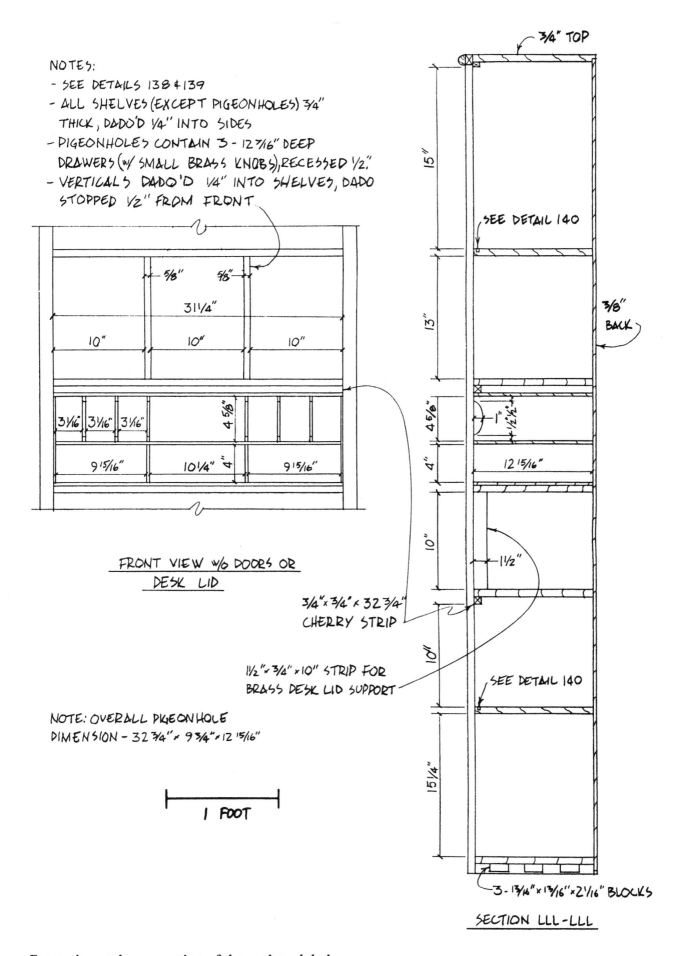

NOTES:
- SEE DETAILS 138 & 139
- ALL SHELVES (EXCEPT PIGEONHOLES) ¾"
  THICK, DADO'D ¼" INTO SIDES
- PIGEONHOLES CONTAIN 3 - 12⅞" DEEP
  DRAWERS (w/ SMALL BRASS KNOBS), RECESSED ½"
- VERTICALS DADO'D ¼" INTO SHELVES, DADO
  STOPPED ½" FROM FRONT

⅝" ⅝"
31¼"
10" 10" 10"

3 1/16" 3 1/16" 3 1/16" 4 ⅝"

9 15/16" 10¼" 4" 9 15/16"

FRONT VIEW w/o DOORS OR
DESK LID

¾" × ¾" × 32¾"
CHERRY STRIP

1½" × ¾" × 10" STRIP FOR
BRASS DESK LID SUPPORT

NOTE: OVERALL PIGEONHOLE
DIMENSION - 32¾" × 9¾" × 12 15/16"

|← 1 FOOT →|

¾" TOP

15"

SEE DETAIL 140

13"

3/8"
BACK

4 ⅝" 1" 1½" 2½"

4" 12 15/16"

10" 1½"

10"

SEE DETAIL 140

15¼"

3 - 1¾" × 1¾6" × 2 1/16" BLOCKS

SECTION LLL-LLL

Front view and cross section of the cupboard desk.

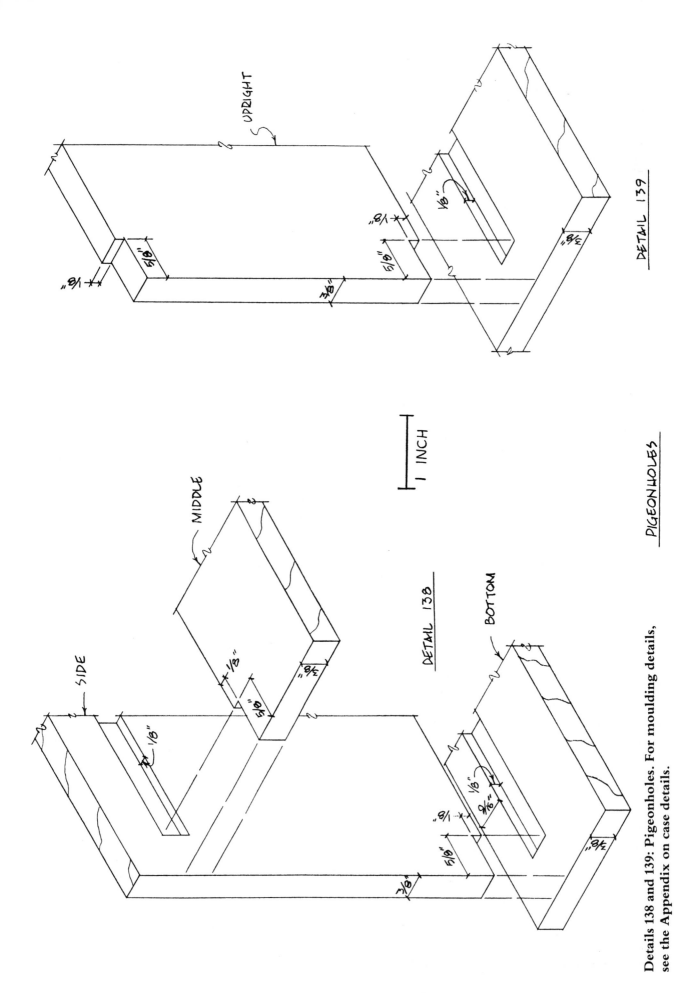

UPRIGHT

DETAIL 139

1 INCH

MIDDLE

SIDE

DETAIL 138

BOTTOM

PIGEONHOLES

Details 138 and 139: Pigeonholes. For moulding details,
see the Appendix on case details.

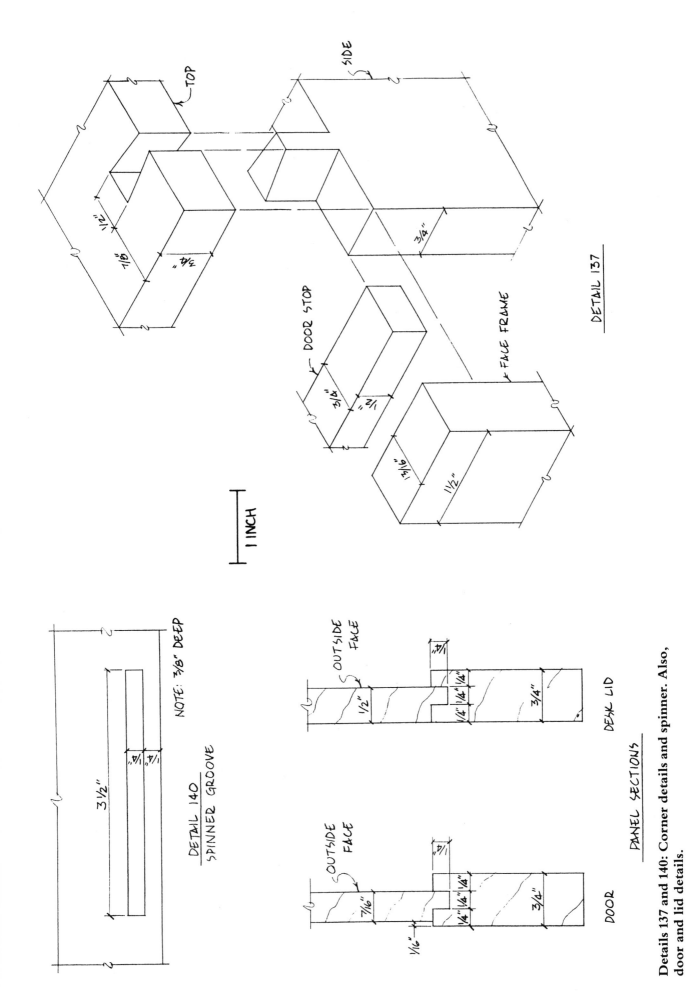

TOP

SIDE

1 1/2"

7/8"

3/4"

3/4"

DETAIL 137

DOOR STOP

3/4"

1/2"

FACE FRAME

1 3/4"

1 1/2"

1 INCH

3 1/2"

1/4"

NOTE: 3/8" DEEP

DETAIL 140
SPINNER GROOVE

OUTSIDE FACE

1/4"

1/2"

1/4" 1/4"

3/4"

DESK LID

OUTSIDE FACE

1/4"

7/8"

1/16"

1/4" 1/4"

3/4"

DOOR

PANEL SECTIONS

Details 137 and 140: Corner details and spinner. Also, door and lid details.

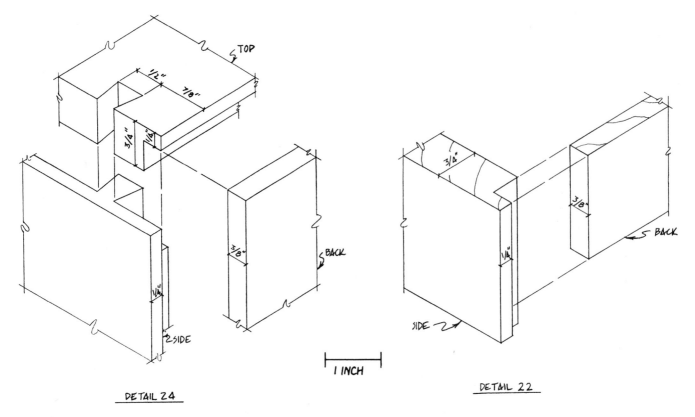

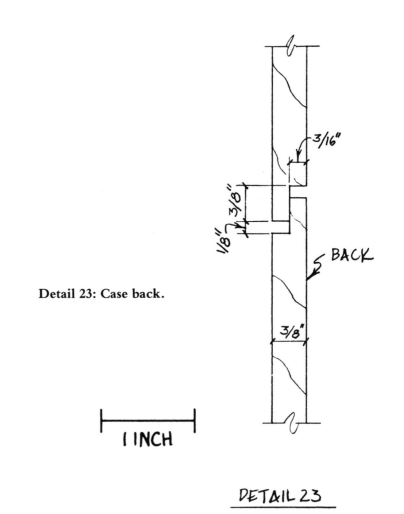

Desk-On-Frame

The desk-on-frame was originally called the ladies desk, and for the first several years of its history we didn't encounter any reactions to this name. But with the increasing sensitivity of both men and women toward sexual egalitarianism, this name began to carry a negative connotation. No man would buy the desk for fear of being stigmatized, and most women avoided buying it because they didn't like the condescension. So we changed the name to desk-on-frame, which, incidentally, is a much more appropriate description of what it is. On the right is an exterior view of the desk-on-frame. Below is an interior view.

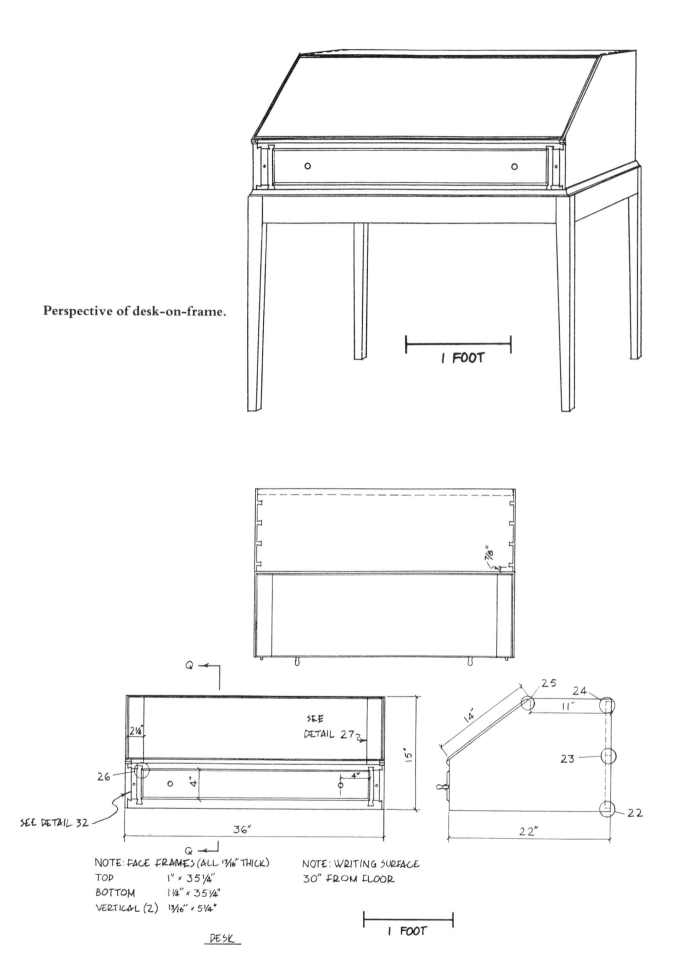

Perspective of desk-on-frame.

SEE DETAIL 27

15"

2¼"

26

4"

4"

SEE DETAIL 32

36"

Q

Q

7/8"

25   24

14"   11"

23

22"   22

NOTE: FACE FRAMES (ALL ¹³/₁₆" THICK)
TOP   1" × 35¼"
BOTTOM   1¼" × 35¼"
VERTICAL (2) ¹³/₁₆" × 5¼"

NOTE: WRITING SURFACE
30" FROM FLOOR

DESK

1 FOOT

1 FOOT

End, front and top views of the case.

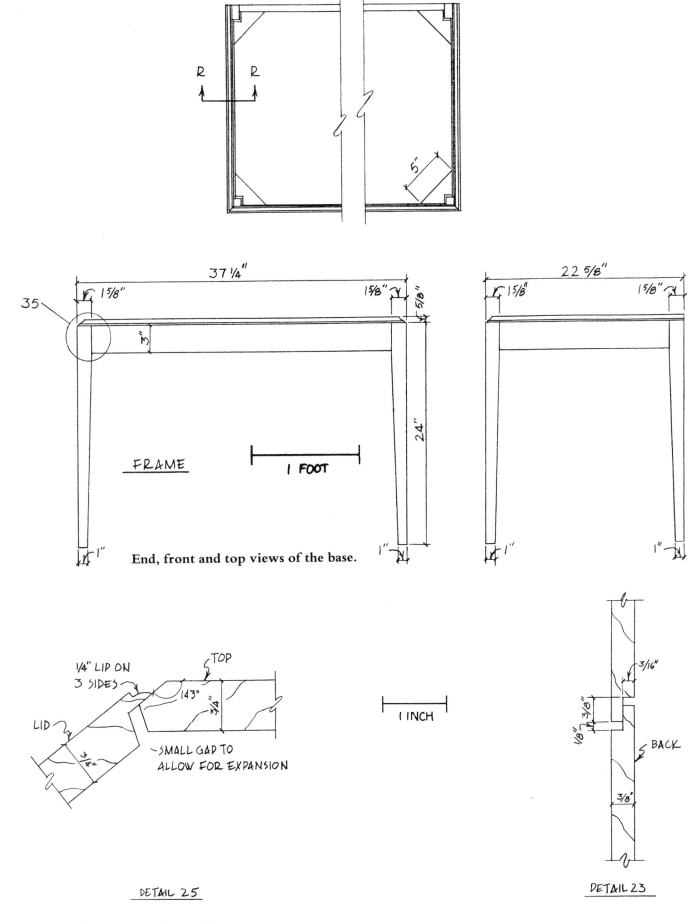

End, front and top views of the base.

FRAME

R   R

37 1/4"

1 5/8"

1 5/8"

5/8"

35

3"

24"

1"

1 FOOT

22 5/8"

1 5/8"

1 5/8"

1"

1"

1/4" LIP ON
3 SIDES

TOP

143°

3/4"

LID

3/4"

SMALL GAP TO
ALLOW FOR EXPANSION

1 INCH

3/16"

1/8" 3/8"

BACK

3/8"

DETAIL 25

DETAIL 23

Details 23 and 25: Back and lid.

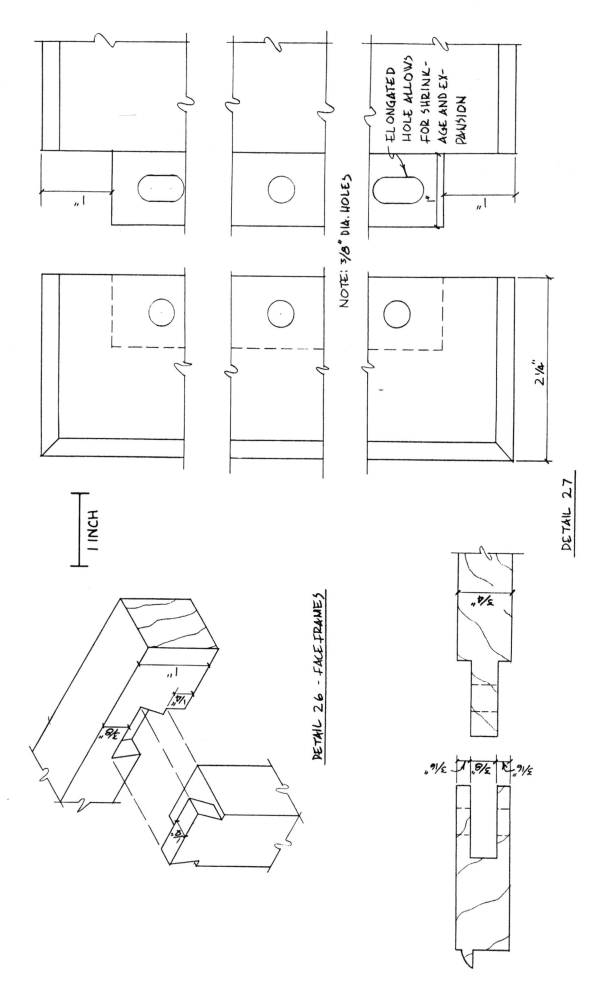

NOTE: 3/8" DIA. HOLES

ELONGATED HOLE ALLOWS FOR SHRINK- AGE AND EX- PANSION

1"

1"

2 1/4"

DETAIL 27

1 INCH

DETAIL 26 - FACE FRAME

1"

1/4"

3/8"

1/8"

3/4"

3/16"   3/8"   3/16"

Details 26 and 27: Face frame and lid tenon details.

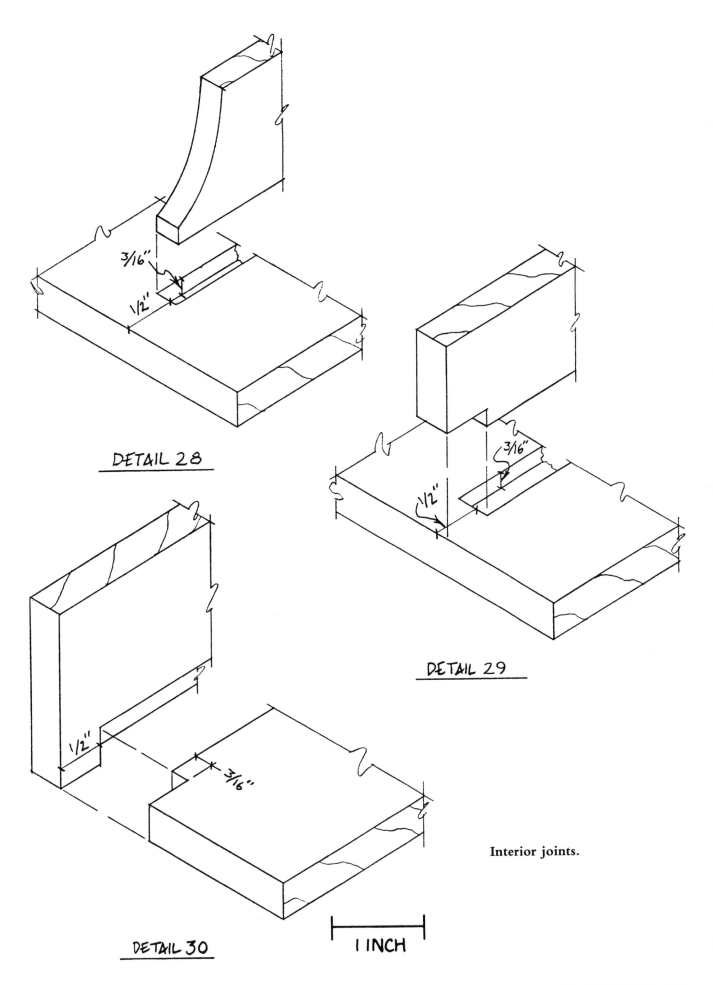

DETAIL 28

DETAIL 29

DETAIL 30

3/16"

1/2"

1/2"

3/16"

1/2"

3/16"

Interior joints.

1 INCH

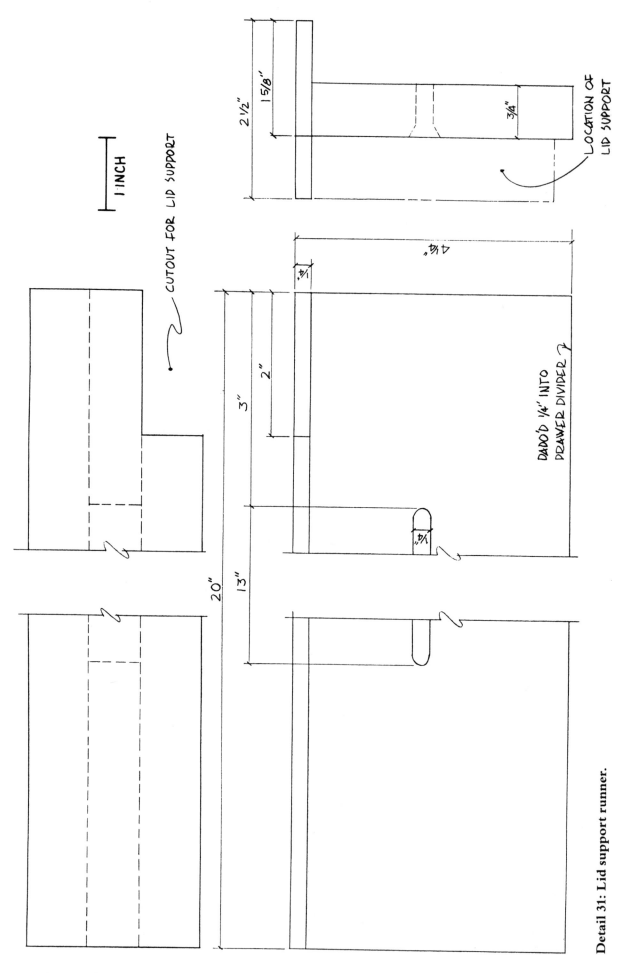

1 INCH

CUTOUT FOR LID SUPPORT

2 1/2"

1 5/8"

3/4"

LOCATION OF LID SUPPORT

4 1/2"

1/4"

3"

2"

20"

13"

1/4"

DADO'D 1/4" INTO DRAWER DIVIDER

1/4"

Detail 31: Lid support runner.

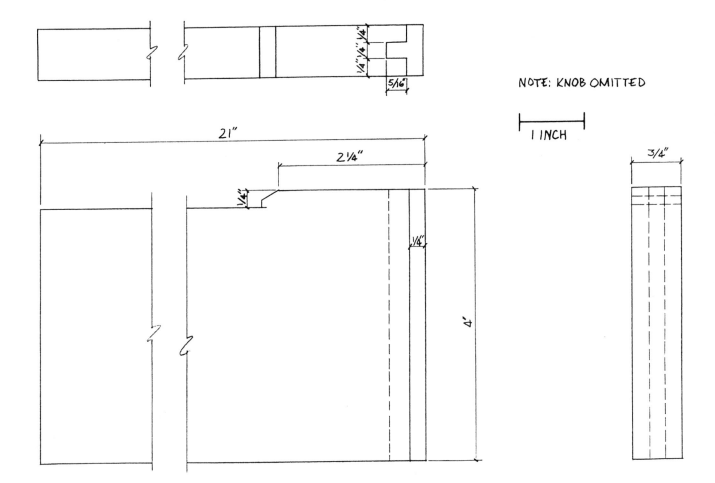

NOTE: KNOB OMITTED

1 INCH

Detail 32: Lid support.

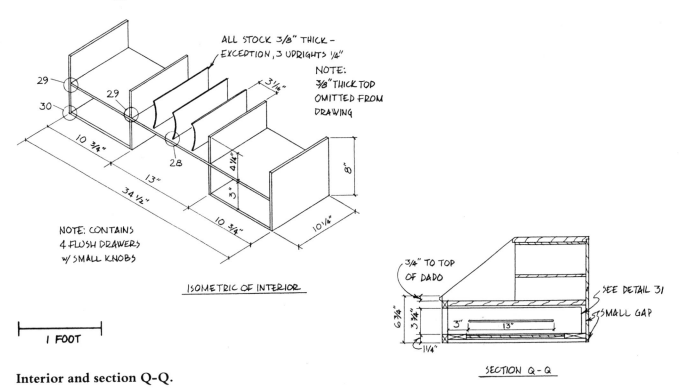

ALL STOCK 3/8" THICK –
EXCEPTION, 3 UPRIGHTS 1/4"

NOTE:
3/8" THICK TOP
OMITTED FROM
DRAWING

NOTE: CONTAINS
4 FLUSH DRAWERS
w/ SMALL KNOBS

ISOMETRIC OF INTERIOR

1 FOOT

3/4" TO TOP
OF DADO

SEE DETAIL 31

SMALL GAP

SECTION Q - Q

Interior and section Q-Q.

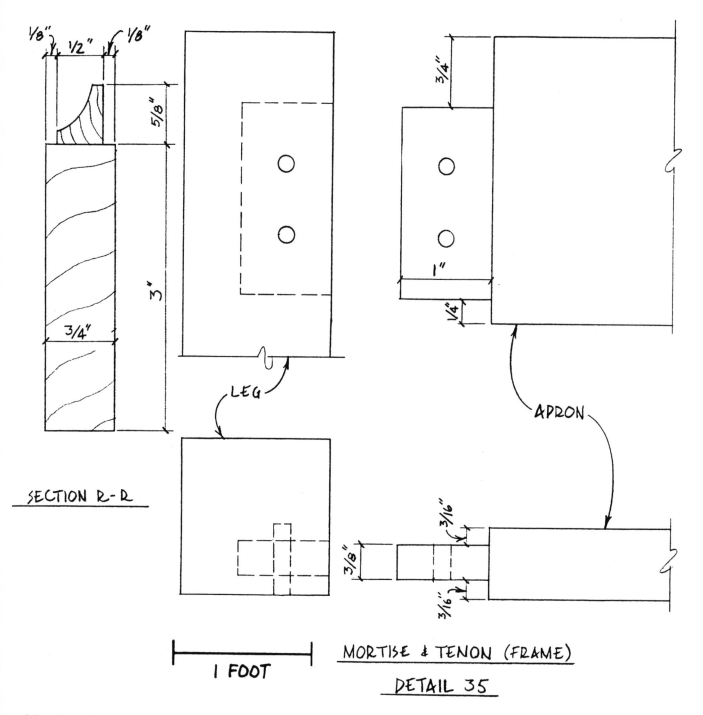

1/8" 1/2" 1/8"

5/8"

3"

3/4"

SECTION R-R

LEG

1 FOOT

3/4"

1"

1/4"

APRON

3/16"

3/8"

3/16"

MORTISE & TENON (FRAME)

DETAIL 35

Mortise and tenon on base and section R-R.

Slant-Top Desk

The slant-top desk has its origin in the mid-18th century and served as the basis for what historians call the Governor Winthrop desk or the secretary desk. It began as a very simple arrangement of three or four drawers with a folding slant top, and evolved over the years to a more ornate structure with acanthus leaves, ball-and-claw feet, quartered pilasters, and other ornamentation. This version is much more simplified and most of its parts are purely functional, the exception being the ogee feet. With a flip of a hand, its lid can be shut and the support slides pushed in.

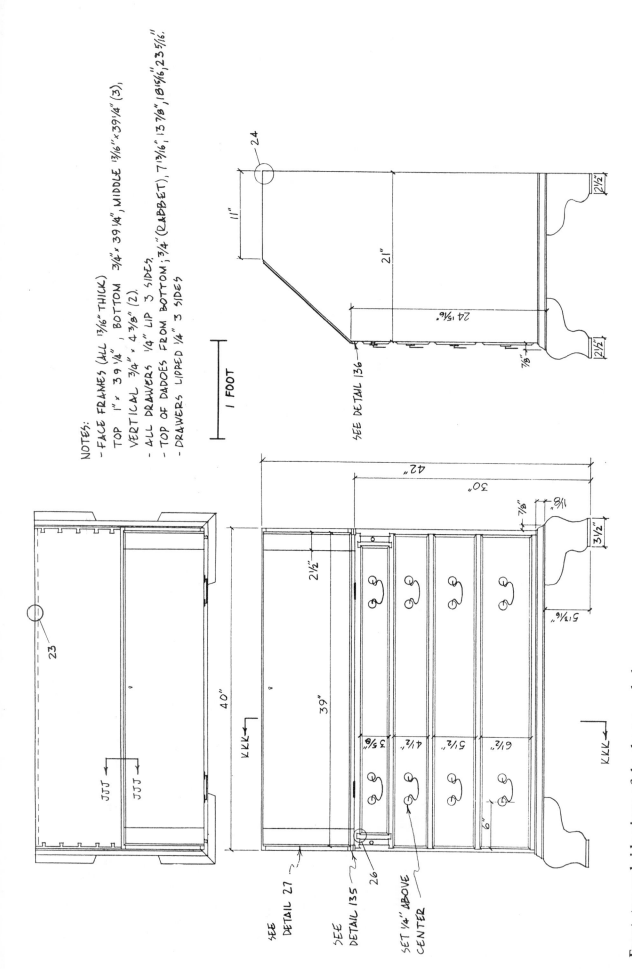

NOTES:
- FACE FRAMES (ALL ¹³/₁₆" THICK)
  TOP 1" × 39¼", BOTTOM ¾" × 39¼", MIDDLE ¹³/₁₆" × 39¼" (3),
  VERTICAL ¾" × 4⅜" (2).
- ALL DRAWERS ¼" LIP 3 SIDES.
- TOP OF DADOES FROM BOTTOM; ¾" (RABBET), 7¹³/₁₆", 13⅞", 18¹⁵/₁₆", 23⁵/₁₆".
- DRAWERS LIPPED ¼" 3 SIDES

1 FOOT

24

11"

21"

24¹⁵/₁₆"

7/8"

2½"

2½"

SEE DETAIL 136

42"

30"

7/8"

11/8"

3½"

5¹³/₁₆"

2½"

39"

40"

23

JJJ

JJJ

3⅝"

4½"

5½"

6½"

6"

26

KKK

KKK

SEE DETAIL 27

SEE DETAIL 135

SET ¼" ABOVE CENTER

Front, top and side views of the slant-top desk.

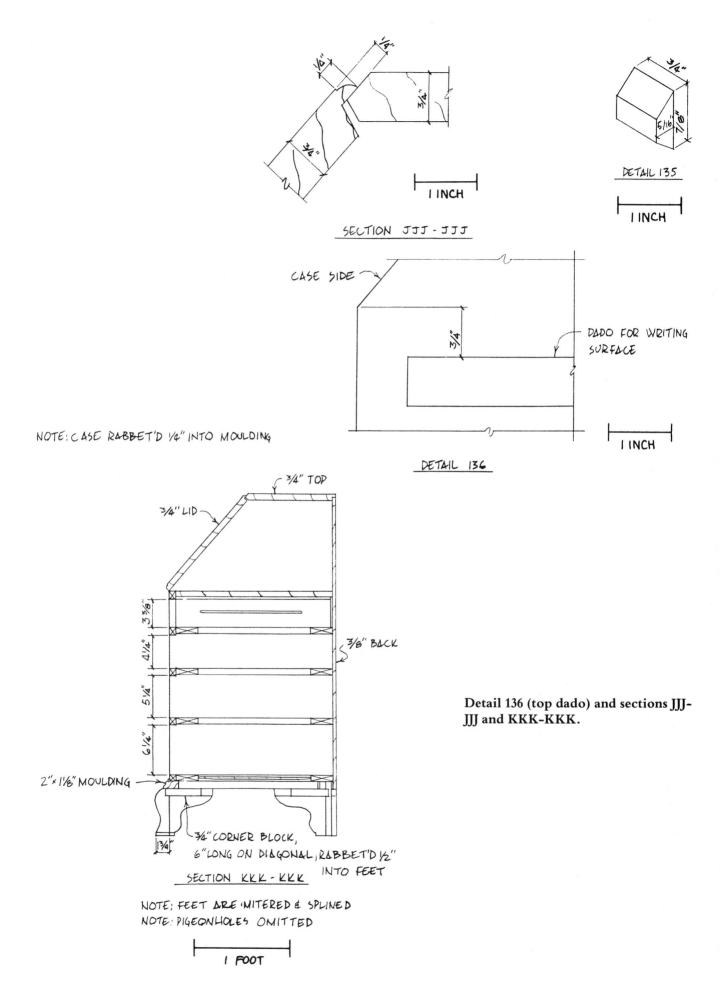

SECTION JJJ-JJJ

DETAIL 135

1 INCH

CASE SIDE

3/4"

DADO FOR WRITING SURFACE

NOTE: CASE RABBET'D 1/4" INTO MOULDING

DETAIL 136

1 INCH

Detail 136 (top dado) and sections JJJ-JJJ and KKK-KKK.

3/4" TOP

3/4" LID

3 5/8"

4 1/4"

3/8" BACK

5 1/4"

6 1/4"

2" x 1 1/8" MOULDING

1 3/4"

3/4" CORNER BLOCK, 6" LONG ON DIAGONAL, RABBET'D 1/2" INTO FEET

SECTION KKK-KKK

NOTE: FEET ARE MITERED & SPLINED
NOTE: PIGEONHOLES OMITTED

1 FOOT

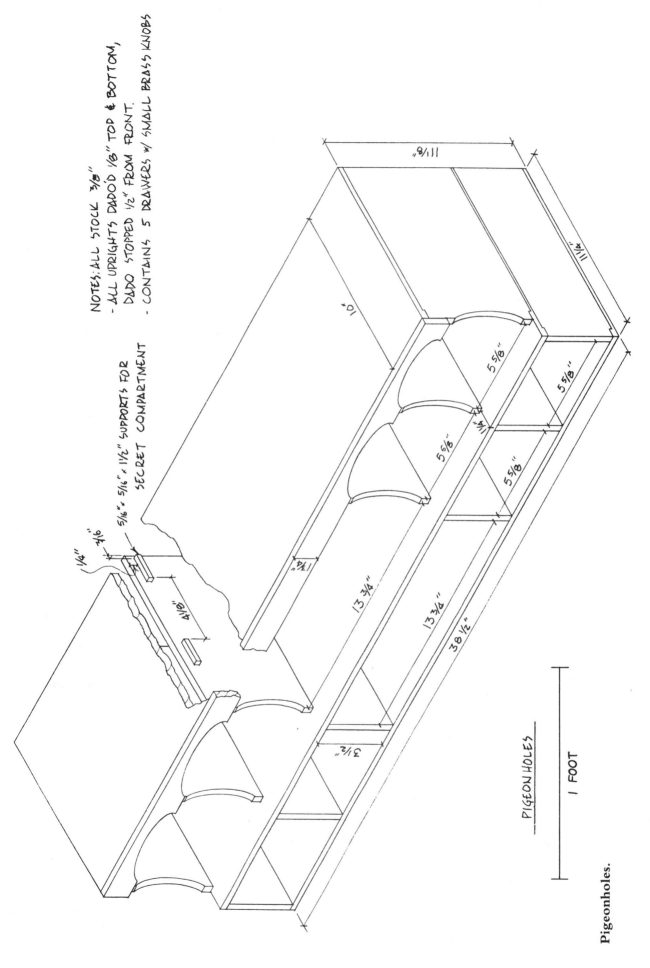

NOTES: ALL STOCK 3/8"
- ALL UPRIGHTS DADO'D 1/8" TOP & BOTTOM,
  DADO STOPPED 1/2" FROM FRONT.
- CONTAINS 5 DRAWERS w/ SMALL BRASS KNOBS

5/16" 5/16" x 1 1/2" SUPPORTS FOR
SECRET COMPARTMENT

1/4"
3/16"

4 1/8"

11/8"

10"

11/8"

5 5/8"

5 5/8"

5 5/8"

5 5/8"

1 3/4"

13 3/4"

13 3/4"

38 1/2"

3 1/2"

PIGEON HOLES

1 FOOT

Pigeonholes.

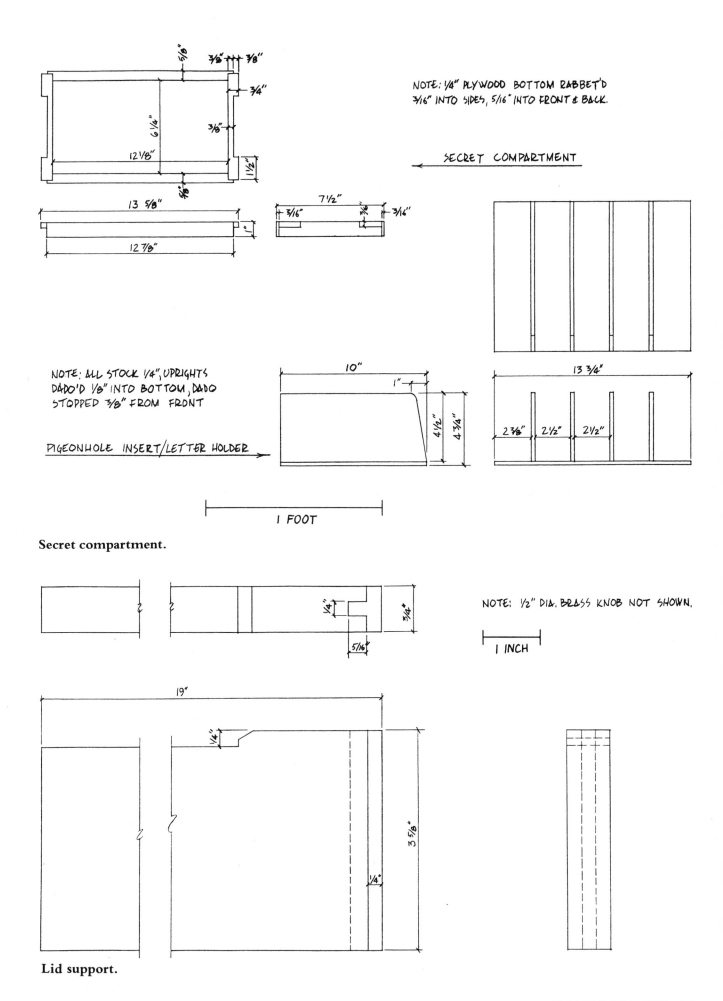

NOTE: ¼" PLYWOOD BOTTOM RABBET'D 3/16" INTO SIDES, 5/16" INTO FRONT & BACK.

SECRET COMPARTMENT

NOTE: ALL STOCK ¼", UPRIGHTS DADO'D ⅛" INTO BOTTOM, DADO STOPPED ⅜" FROM FRONT

PIGEONHOLE INSERT/LETTER HOLDER

1 FOOT

Secret compartment.

NOTE: ½" DIA. BRASS KNOB NOT SHOWN.

1 INCH

Lid support.

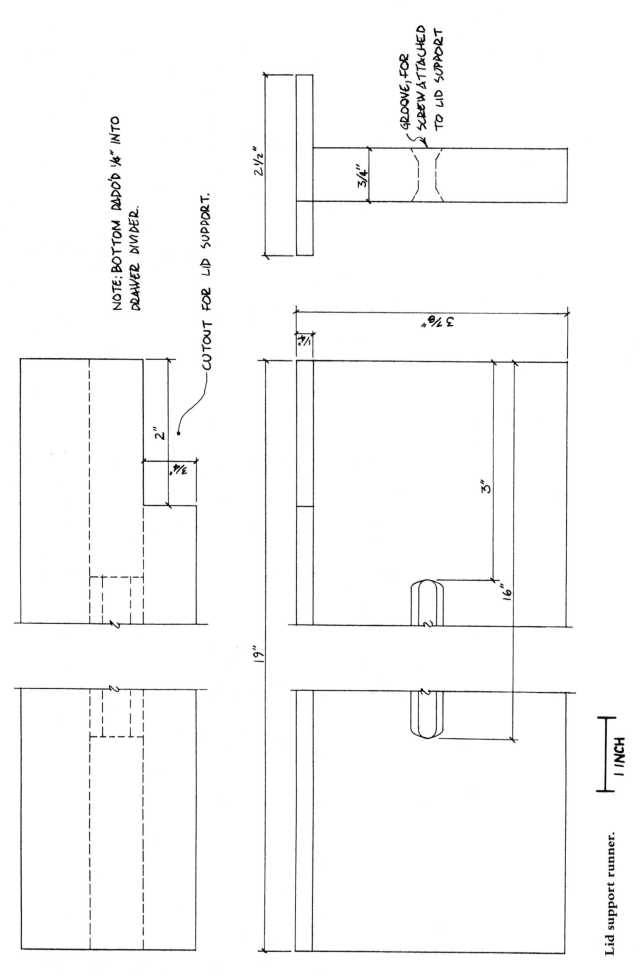

NOTE: BOTTOM DADO'D 1/4" INTO DRAWER DIVIDER.

CUTOUT FOR LID SUPPORT.

2"

3/4"

2 1/2"

3/4"

GROOVE, FOR SCREW ATTACHED TO LID SUPPORT

3 7/8"

1/4"

3"

16"

19"

1 INCH

Lid support runner.

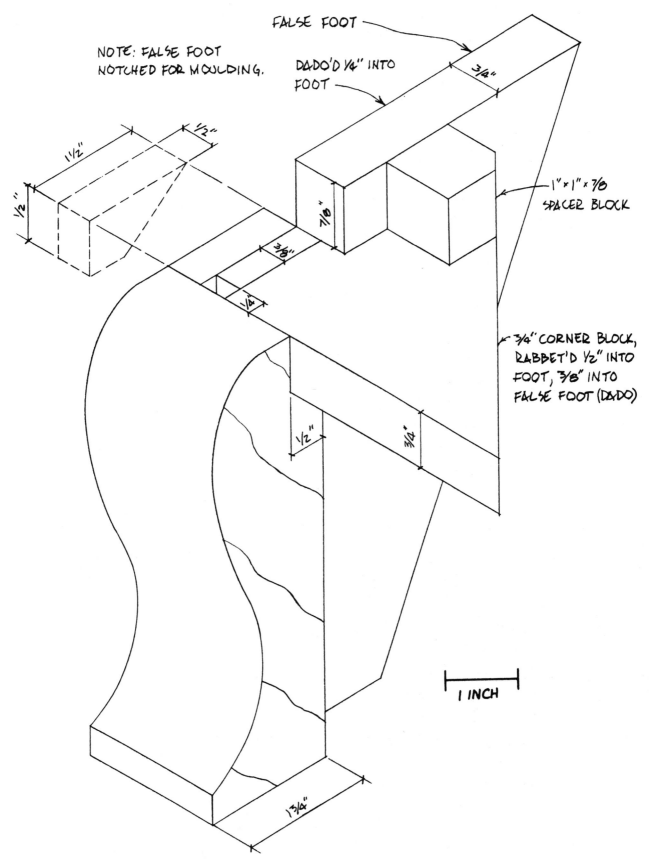

NOTE: FALSE FOOT NOTCHED FOR MOULDING.

FALSE FOOT

DADO'D ¼" INTO FOOT

¾"

1½"

½"

½"

⅞"

⅜"

¼"

1" × 1" × ⅞
SPACER BLOCK

¾" CORNER BLOCK,
RABBET'D ½" INTO
FOOT, ⅜" INTO
FALSE FOOT (DADO)

½"

¾"

1 INCH

1¾"

Back and left foot details.

CASES AND CHESTS

Very few generalizations can be made about cases and chests since they exist in such variety. The depth of a usable chest of drawers can be between 16 and 20 inches (40.6 and 50.8 cm), and heights vary considerably. The working height of the average table is 30 inches (76.2 cm), and a sideboard or serving table can be between 32 and 36 inches (.81 and .91 m). Most sideboards beyond 32 inches in height tend to be unusable under window openings. The standard height of kitchen counters is 36 inches, so casework designed to work as a counter should be 36 inches.

Work surfaces to be used while standing are usually about 42 inches (1.06 m) high. The universal height for American tavern bars is 42 inches. When a cupboard or chest is higher than five feet (1.5 m), its top surface becomes almost unusable since it is impossible to see what's on it. The width of cases varies considerably, and the designer should keep an eye on proportion. As the case gets higher, it has to be widened to maintain proportion. Most casework is built to contain objects, and so in designing we usually start with the object to be contained and move outward. Visually, however, we work from the outside in—proportion is vital!

Wardrobe

The wardrobe has its best use as a storage space for clothing. In houses or apartments that lack closet space, the wardrobe is an ideal solution. It is sufficiently deep inside to take a coat hanger carrying almost any size garment. The interior of the wardrobe can be arranged to fit a number of purposes. We have built them to house everything from sheet music to architectural drawings, and all types of clothing.

Wardrobe.

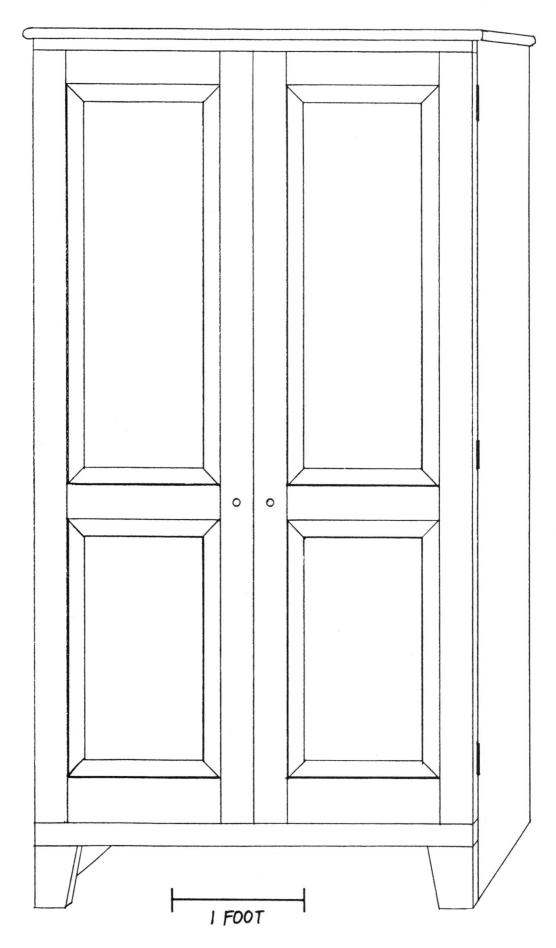

I FOOT

Perspective of wardrobe.

Wardrobe (Interior #1)

Wardrobe (interior #1).

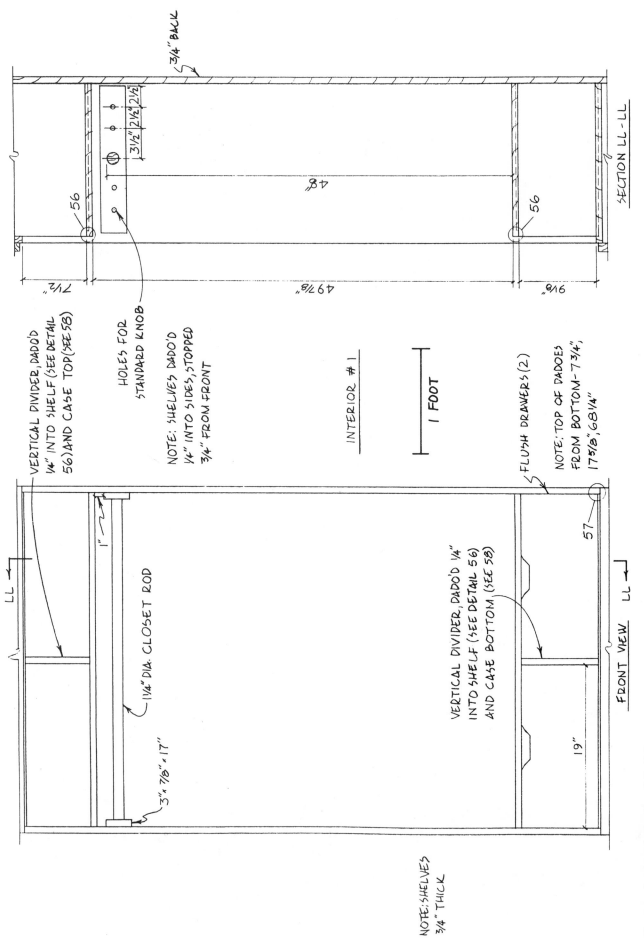

3/4" BACK

SECTION LL-LL

3½" 2½" 2½"

48"

56

56

7½"

49⅞"

9⅞"

VERTICAL DIVIDER, DADO'D ¼" INTO SHELF (SEE DETAIL 56) AND CASE TOP (SEE 58)

HOLES FOR STANDARD KNOB

NOTE: SHELVES DADO'D ¼" INTO SIDES, STOPPED ¾" FROM FRONT

INTERIOR #1

1 FOOT

FLUSH DRAWERS (2)

NOTE: TOP OF DADOES FROM BOTTOM-7¾", 17⅝", 68¼"

LL

1"

1¼" DIA. CLOSET ROD

3" 7/8" 17"

VERTICAL DIVIDER, DADO'D ¼" INTO SHELF (SEE DETAIL 56) AND CASE BOTTOM (SEE 58)

57

19"

FRONT VIEW   LL

NOTE: SHELVES ¾" THICK

Front view and section LL-LL.

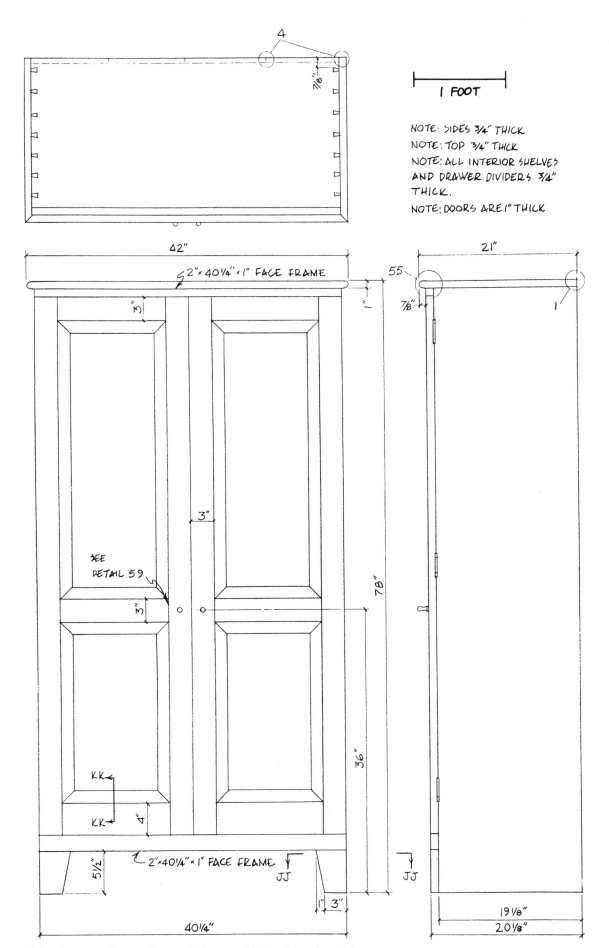

Side, front and top views of the wardrobe (interior #1).

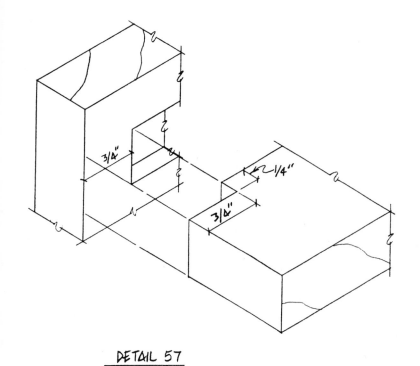

DETAIL 57

NOTE: ALL DADOES SHOWN
ARE 3/4" x 1/4".

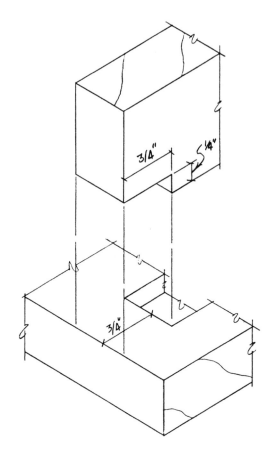

DETAIL 56

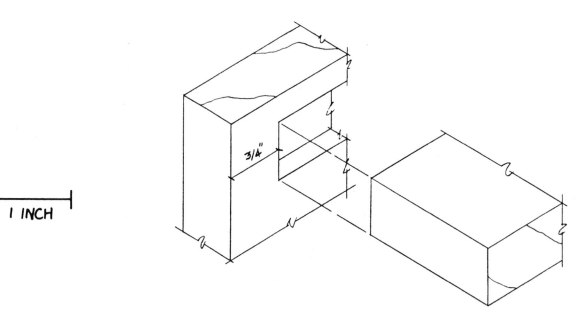

1 INCH

DETAIL 58

Details 56, 57 and 58: Dadoes.

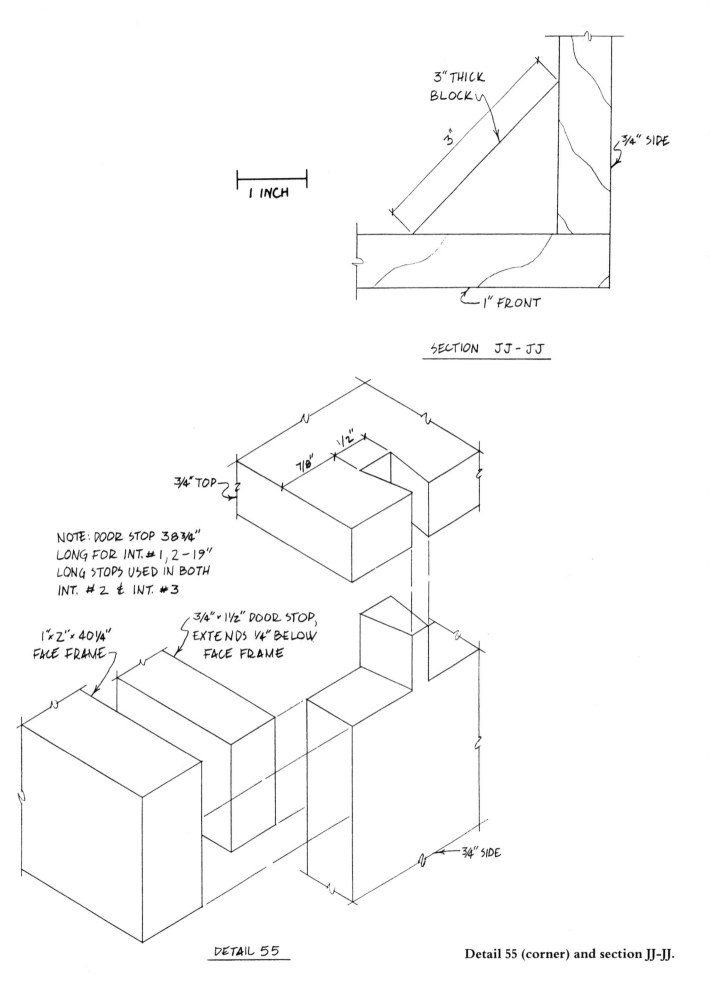

3" THICK
BLOCK

3"

3/4" SIDE

1 INCH

1" FRONT

SECTION JJ-JJ

3/4" TOP

7/8"   1/2"

NOTE: DOOR STOP 38 3/4"
LONG FOR INT.#1, 2-19"
LONG STOPS USED IN BOTH
INT.#2 & INT.#3

3/4" × 1 1/2" DOOR STOP,
EXTENDS 1/4" BELOW
FACE FRAME

1"× 2"× 40 1/4"
FACE FRAME

3/4" SIDE

DETAIL 55

Detail 55 (corner) and section JJ-JJ.

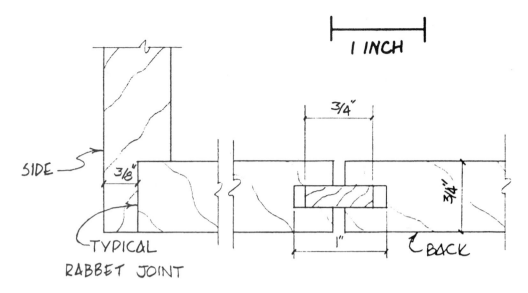

1 INCH

SIDE

3/8"

TYPICAL
RABBET JOINT

3/4"

3/4"

1"

BACK

Detail 4: Back cross section.

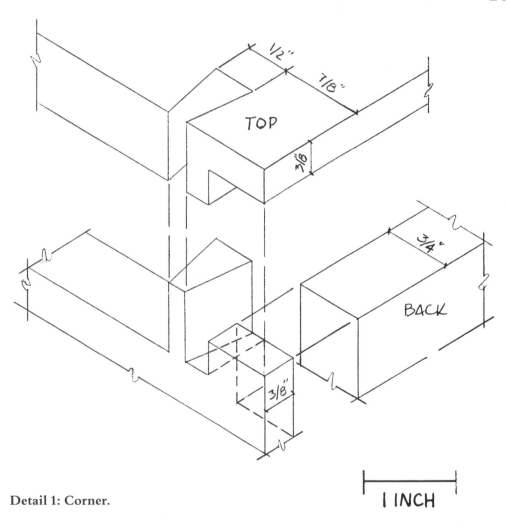

1/2"

7/8"

TOP

3/8"

3/4"

BACK

3/8"

1 INCH

Detail 1: Corner.

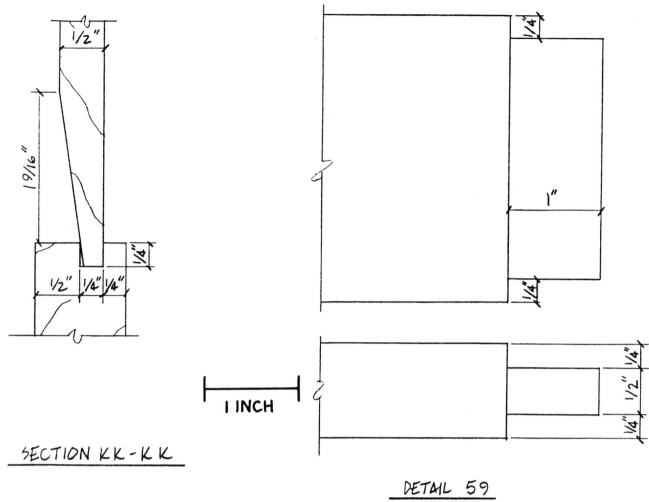

SECTION KK-KK

|← 1 INCH →|

DETAIL 59
MORTISE & TENON, MIDDLE STILE

Detail 59 (mortise and tenon) and section KK-KK.

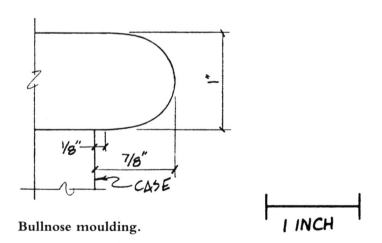

Bullnose moulding.

|← 1 INCH →|

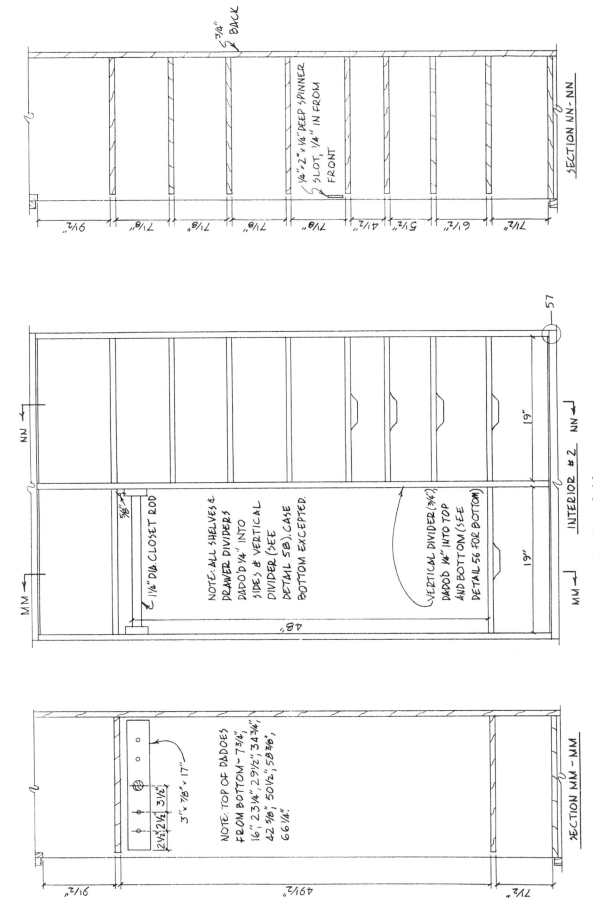

SECTION NN-NN

3/4" BACK

1/4" x 2" x 1/4" DEEP SPINNER SLOT, 1/4" IN FROM FRONT

9 1/16", 7 1/8", 7 1/8", 7 1/8", 7 1/8", 4 1/2", 5 1/2", 6 1/8", 7 1/2"

1 FOOT

57

19"

INTERIOR #2

NN

MM

19"

NN

MM

5/8"

1 1/4" DIA. CLOSET ROD

NOTE: ALL SHELVES & DRAWER DIVIDERS DADO'D 1/4" INTO SIDES & VERTICAL DIVIDER (SEE DETAIL 58). CASE BOTTOM EXCEPTED.

VERTICAL DIVIDER (3/4") DADO'D 1/4" INTO TOP AND BOTTOM (SEE DETAIL 56 FOR BOTTOM)

48"

SECTION MM-MM

NOTE: TOP OF DADOES FROM BOTTOM~ 7 3/4", 16", 23 1/4", 29 1/2", 34 3/4", 42 5/8", 50 1/2", 58 3/8", 66 1/4".

3" x 7/8" x 17"

2 1/2", 2 1/2", 3 1/2"

9 1/16", 49 1/2", 7 1/2"

Sections MM and NN of wardrobe (interior #2). For details and side, top, and front views, see pages 158 to 163. See the following page for a photograph of the wardrobe (interior #2).

This wardrobe (interior #2) offers a compromise between a closet and a chest of drawers.

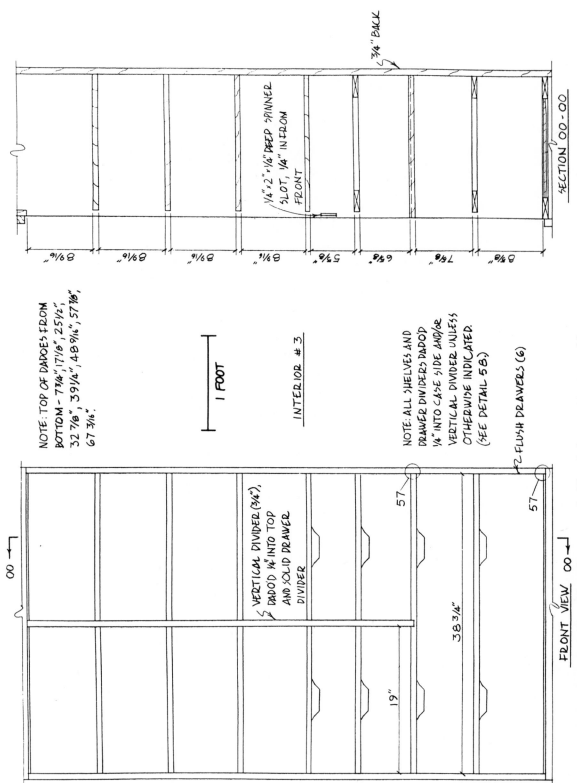

SECTION OO - OO

8 9/16" 8 9/16" 8 9/16" 8 9/16" 5 5/8" 6 5/8" 7 5/8" 8 3/8"

¾" BACK

¼" x 2 - ¼" DEEP SPINNER
SLOT, ¼" IN FROM
FRONT

NOTE: TOP OF DADOES FROM
BOTTOM - 7¾", 17⅛", 25½",
32⅞", 39¼", 48 9/16", 57⅛",
67 3/16".

1 FOOT

INTERIOR #3

VERTICAL DIVIDER (¾"),
DADO'D ¼" INTO TOP
AND SOLID DRAWER
DIVIDER

NOTE: ALL SHELVES AND
DRAWER DIVIDERS DADO'D
¼" INTO CASE SIDE AND/OR
VERTICAL DIVIDER UNLESS
OTHERWISE INDICATED.
(SEE DETAIL 5B.)

2 FLUSH DRAWERS (6)

57

57

38¾"

19"

OO

FRONT VIEW OO

This wardrobe (interior #3) offers far more shelf and drawer space and is used where clothes-hanging capacity is not necessary. For details and side, top and front views, see pages 158 to 163.

Ten-Drawer
Dresser

The ten-drawer dresser takes up minimum floor space, yet provides maximum storage capacity. The drawers of all of these dressers are graduated, which allows a variety of drawer depths to accommodate a variety of contents. A very bulky sweater or ski outfit will take eight or nine inches (20.3 or 22.8 cm) of drawer depth, whereas smaller items such as socks or handkerchiefs don't require this much depth and would be lost in the bottom of a eight-inch drawer.

CROSS LAP JOINT
NOTE: VERT. DIVIDERS
DADO'D ¼" INTO DRAWER DIV.

1⅛" × 2½" KICKER,
16 5/16" LONG

3"

1" THICK VERT. DIVIDERS

3"

6"

6⅜"

6¾"

7⅛"

7⅝"

8"

8⅜"

8¾"

3"

3 - 1 3/16" × 1 3/16" × 2 1/16" BLKS.

SECTION E-E

1 FOOT

Perspective of the ten-drawer dresser. For drawer details, see the Appendix for case details.

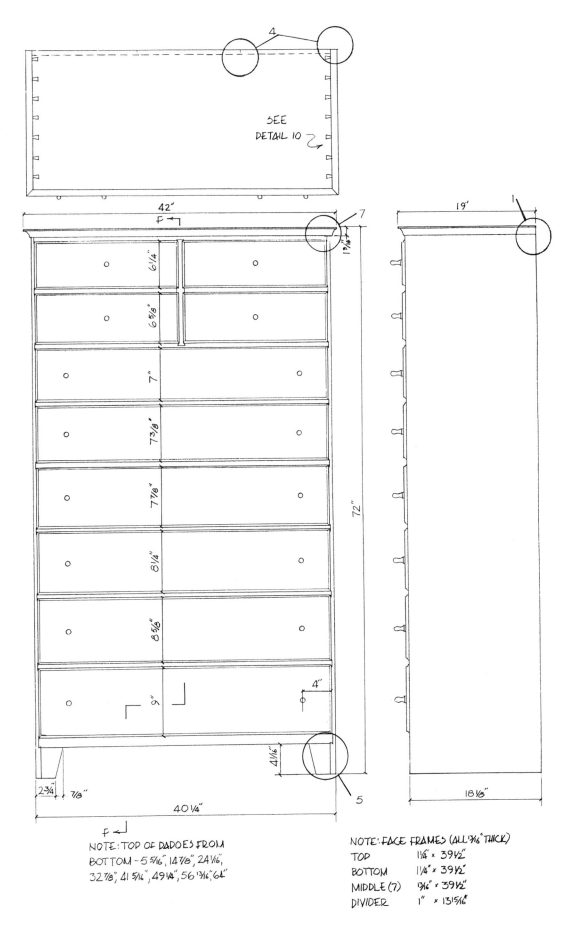

4

SEE
DETAIL 10

7

42"

6 1/4"

6 5/8"

7"

7 3/8"

7 7/8"

8 1/4"

8 5/8"

9"

4"

72"

13/16"

4 1/16"

5

2 3/4"   7/8"

40 1/4"

1

19"

18 1/8"

NOTE: TOP OF DADOES FROM
BOTTOM – 5 5/16", 14 7/8", 24 1/16",
32 7/8", 41 5/16", 49 1/4", 56 13/16", 64"

NOTE: FACE FRAMES (ALL 13/16" THICK)
TOP   1 1/4" × 39 1/2"
BOTTOM   1 1/4" × 39 1/2"
MIDDLE (7) 13/16" × 39 1/2"
DIVIDER   1" × 13 15/16"

Front, side and top views of the ten-drawer dresser.

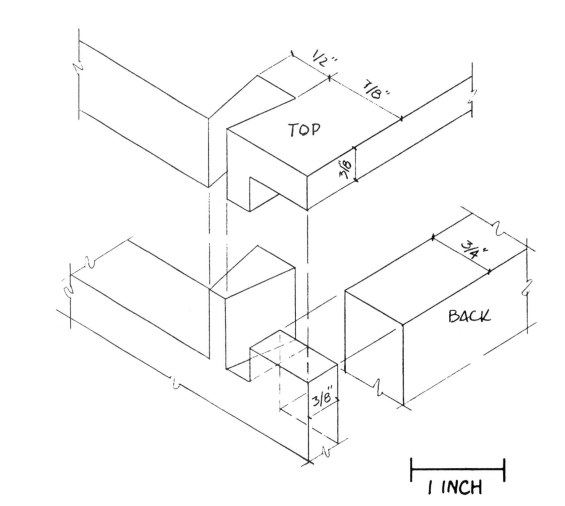

Detail 1: Corner.

TOP

1/2"

7/8"

3/8

BACK

3/4"

3/8"

1 INCH

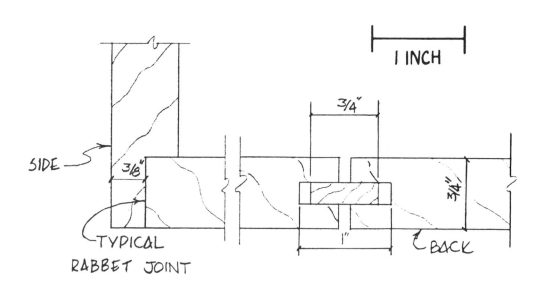

1 INCH

SIDE

3/8"

3/4"

3/4"

1"

TYPICAL
RABBET JOINT

BACK

Detail 4: Back cross section.

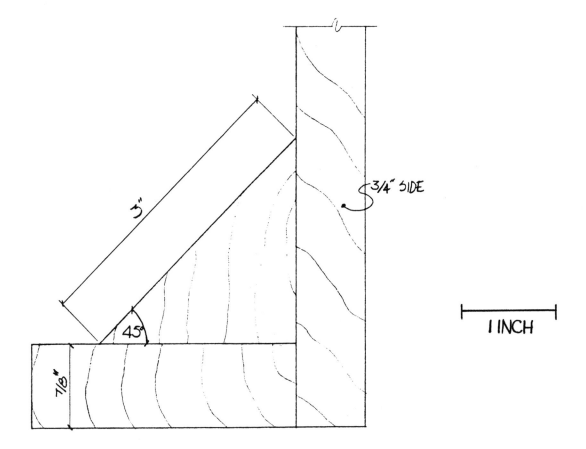

3/4" SIDE

5"

45°

7/8"

1 INCH

Detail 5: Foot.

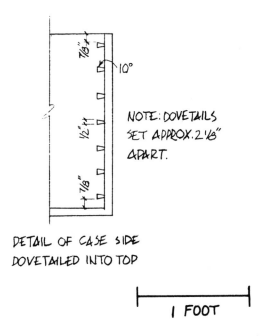

7/8"

10°

1/2"

7/8"

NOTE: DOVETAILS
SET APPROX. 2 1/8"
APART.

DETAIL OF CASE SIDE
DOVETAILED INTO TOP

1 FOOT

Detail 10: Dovetail layout.

Five-Drawer Dresser

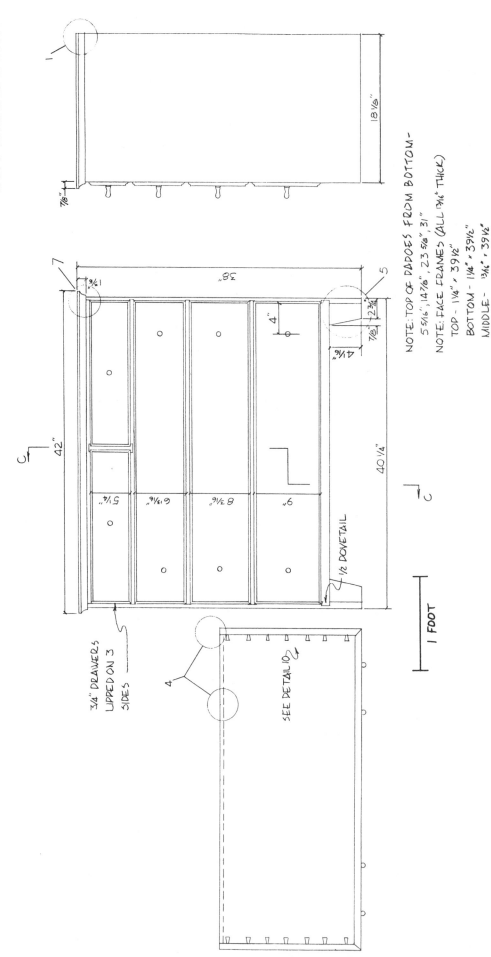

NOTE: TOP OF DADOES FROM BOTTOM—
5 5/16", 14 7/8", 23 5/8", 31"

NOTE: FACE FRAMES (ALL 13/16" THICK)
TOP – 1 1/4" × 39 1/2"
BOTTOM – 1 1/4" × 39 1/2"
MIDDLE – 13/16" × 39 1/2"
DIVIDER – 1" × 5 3/4"

18 1/8"

7/8"

7

1 5/16"

42"

40 1/4"

38"

4"

4 1/16"

2 3/4"

7/8"

5

5 1/4"

6 13/16"

8 3/16"

9"

1/2 DOVETAIL

3/4" DRAWERS
LIPPED ON 3
SIDES

C

C

1 FOOT

4

SEE DETAIL 10

Front, side and top views of the five-drawer dresser. See the photograph on the following page, and the perspective on page 174.

The five-drawer dresser is the most popular of the dressers we've built in that it allows for adequate storage space without taking up too much wall space. Unlike the ten-drawer dresser, there is room to place a mirror or lamp on the top of the dresser.

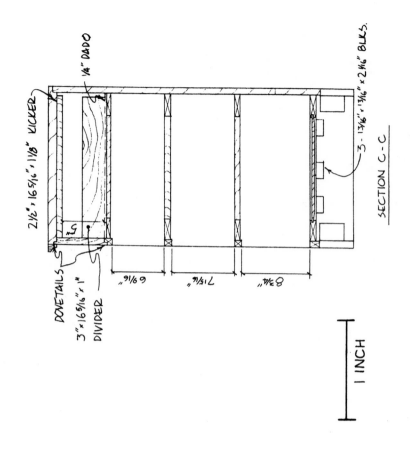

SECTION C-C

1 INCH

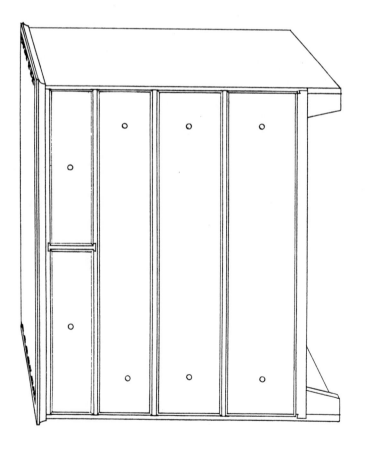

Perspective of the five-drawer dresser.

Seven-Drawer Dresser

The seven-drawer dresser is a compromise between the two previous dressers, taking up optimum wall space. Since its top is almost five feet from the floor, it is too high to allow the use of a mirror; however, it can accommodate a variety of small items. I use a dresser of this size in my bedroom.

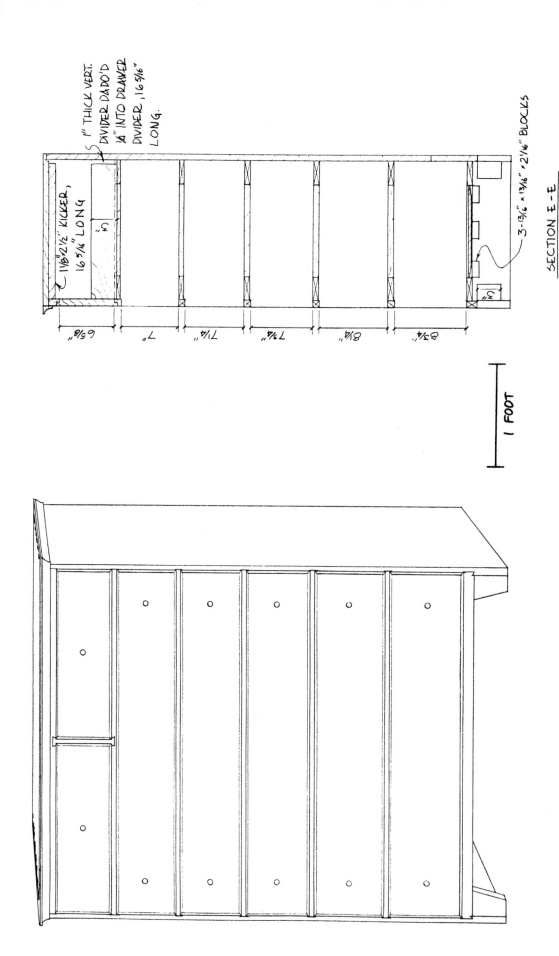

SECTION E-E

1" THICK VERT.
DIVIDER DADO'D
¼" INTO DRAWER
DIVIDER, 16 5/16"
LONG.

1 1/16"·2½" KICKER,
16 5/16" LONG

3-13/16" × 13/16" ·2 1/16" BLOCKS

6 5/8"

7"

7 1/4"

7 3/4"

8 1/4"

8 3/4"

1 FOOT

Perspective of the seven-drawer dresser.

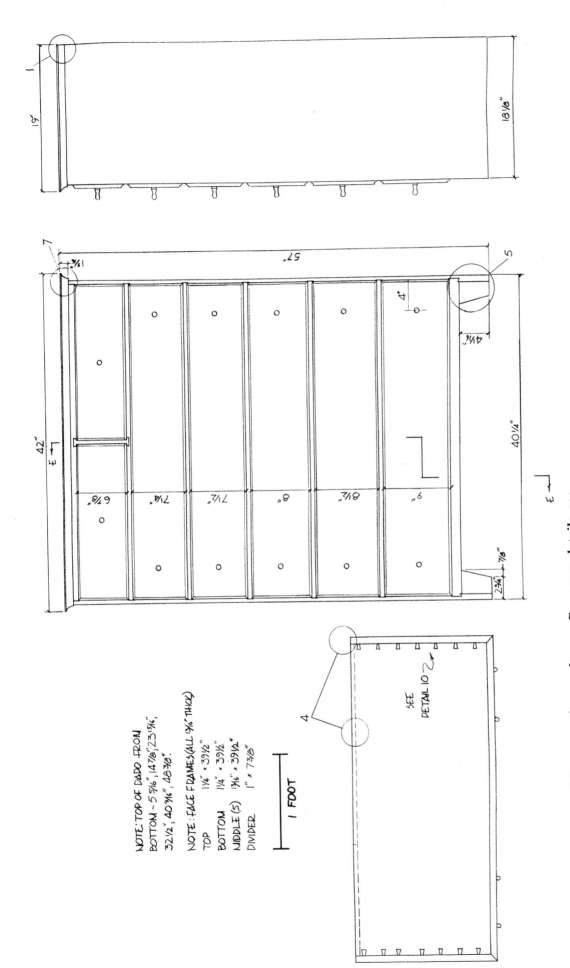

NOTE: TOP OF DADO FROM
BOTTOM — 5 5/16", 14 7/8", 23 15/16",
32 1/2", 40 9/16", 48 3/8".

NOTE: FACE FRAMES (ALL 9/16" THICK)

TOP	1 1/4"	× 39 1/2"
BOTTOM	1 1/4"	× 39 1/2"
MIDDLE (5)	1 9/16"	× 39 1/2"
DIVIDER	1"	× 7 3/8"

1 FOOT

SEE
DETAIL 10

Front, side and top views of the seven-drawer dresser. For more details, see the ten-drawer dresser, pages 170 and 171.

Eight-Drawer Sidechest

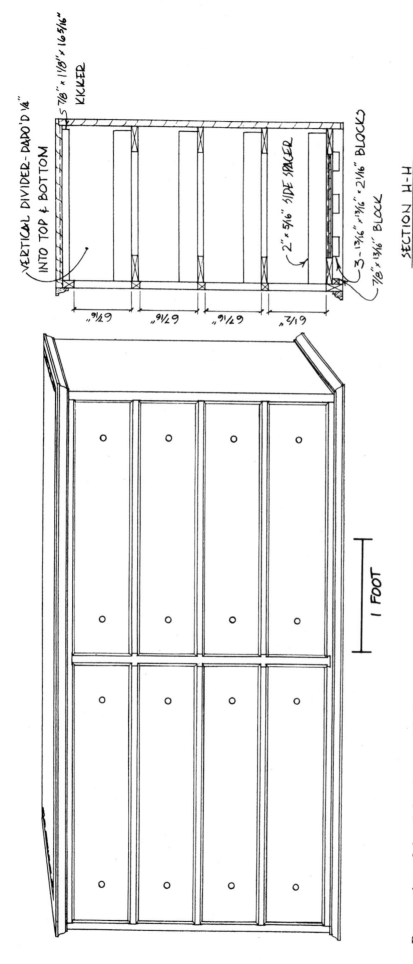

VERTICAL DIVIDER - DADO'D ¼"
INTO TOP & BOTTOM

5 7/8" × 1 1/8" × 16 5/16"
KICKER

3 - 13/16" × 13/16" × 2 1/16" BLOCKS

2" × 5/16" SIDE SPACER

7/8" × 13/16" BLOCK

SECTION H-H

6 7/16"
6 7/16"
6 7/16"
6 1/2"

1 FOOT

Perspective of the eight-drawer sidechest. See the photograph on the
following page.

When wall space is at a premium, in the case of a bedroom that has **knee** walls or where there are windows interrupting the wall surface, the eight–drawer sidechest offers a very low profile. It has a cubic capacity similar to the seven-drawer dresser, yet with only 32 inches (.81 m) of overall height. This height allows the sidechest to fit under most modern windowsills, and offers a good height for lamps and various accouterments.

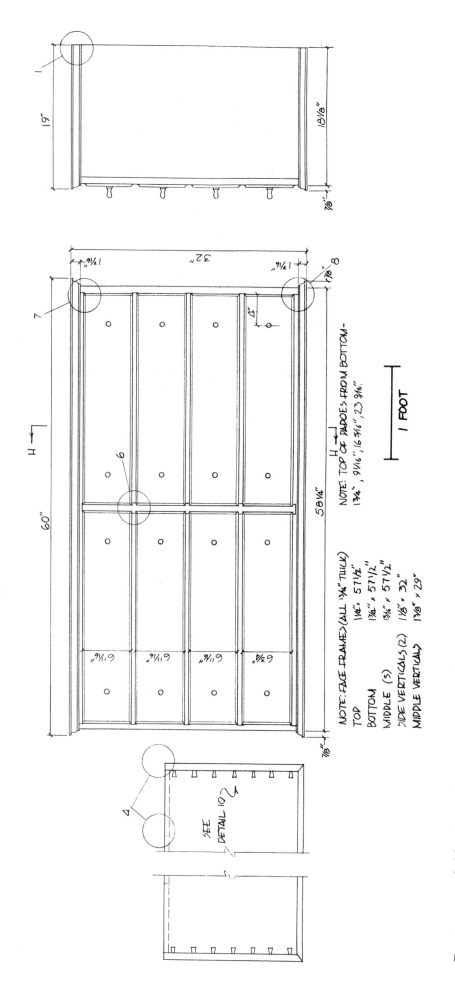

NOTE: FACE FRAME (ALL ¹³/₁₆" THICK)
TOP   1⅛" × 57½"
BOTTOM   1¾" × 57½"
MIDDLE (3)   1⁵/₁₆" × 57½"
SIDE VERTICALS (2)   1⅛" × 32"
MIDDLE VERTICAL   1⅝" × 29"

NOTE: TOP OF DADOES FROM BOTTOM—
1¾", 9¹/₁₆", 16⁵/₁₆", 23 ⁹/₁₆".

1 FOOT

Front, top and side views of the eight-drawer sidechest.

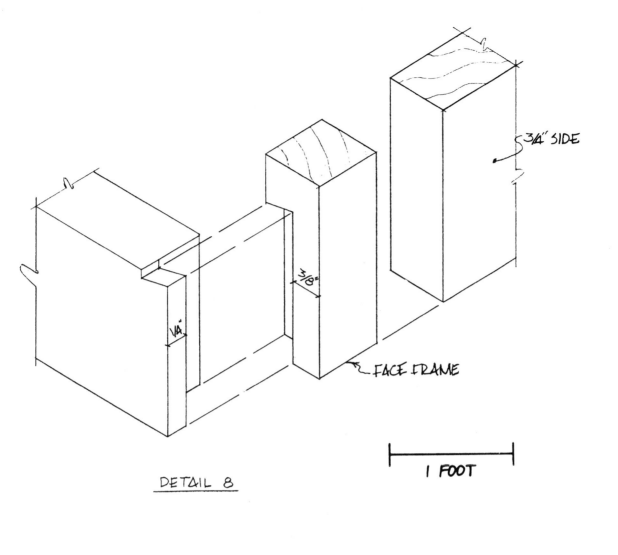

3/4" SIDE

3/8"

1/4"

FACE FRAME

1 FOOT

DETAIL 8

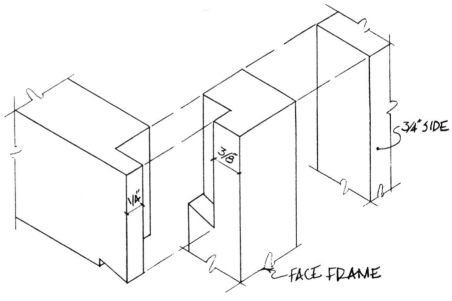

3/4" SIDE

3/8"

1/4"

FACE FRAME

DETAIL 7

Detail 7: Bottom face frame. Detail 8: Top face frame.

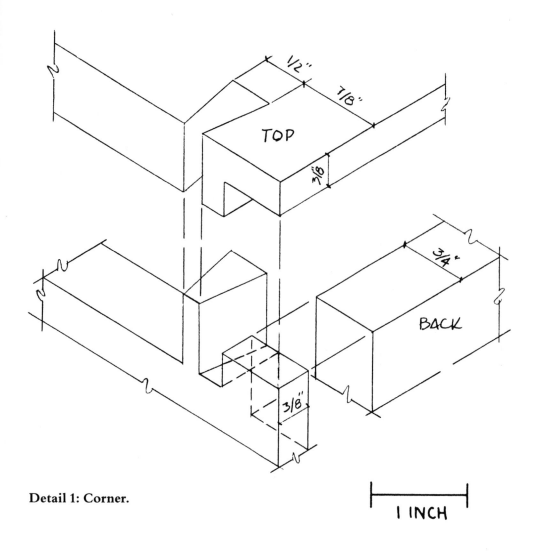

Detail 1: Corner.

1/2"

7/8"

TOP

3/8"

3/4"

BACK

3/8"

1 INCH

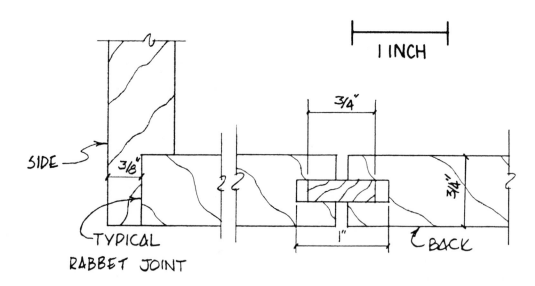

1 INCH

3/4"

3/4"

SIDE

3/8"

TYPICAL
RABBET JOINT

1"

BACK

Detail 4: Back cross section.

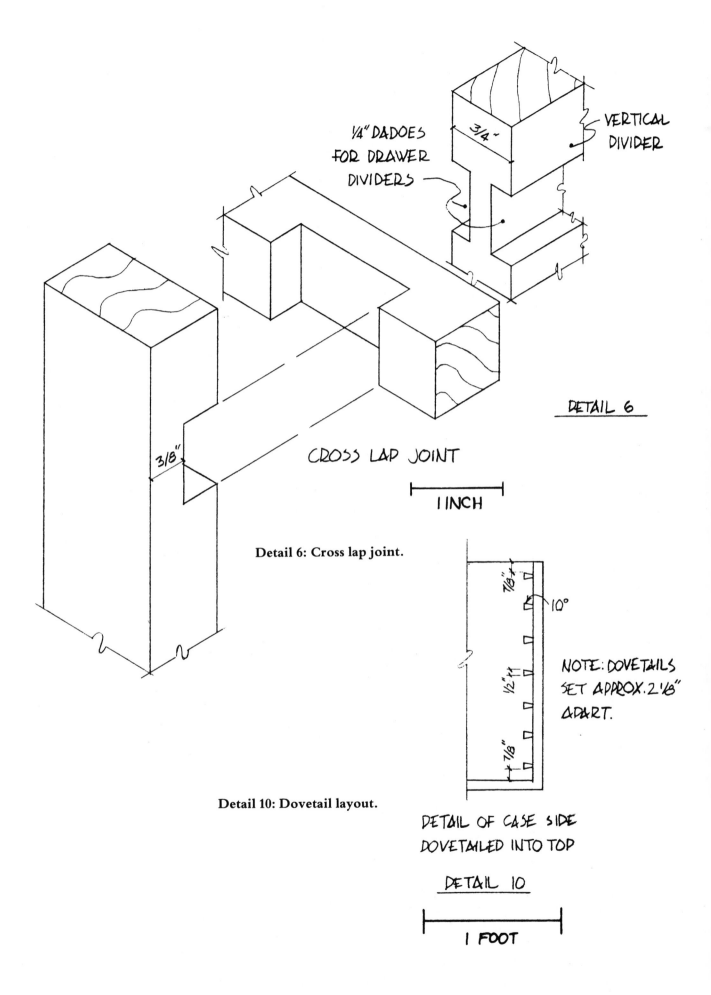

¼" DADOES
FOR DRAWER
DIVIDERS

VERTICAL
DIVIDER

¾"

DETAIL 6

CROSS LAP JOINT

1 INCH

Detail 6: Cross lap joint.

3/8"

7/8"

10°

½"

NOTE: DOVETAILS
SET APPROX. 2⅛"
APART.

7/8"

Detail 10: Dovetail layout.

DETAIL OF CASE SIDE
DOVETAILED INTO TOP

DETAIL 10

1 FOOT

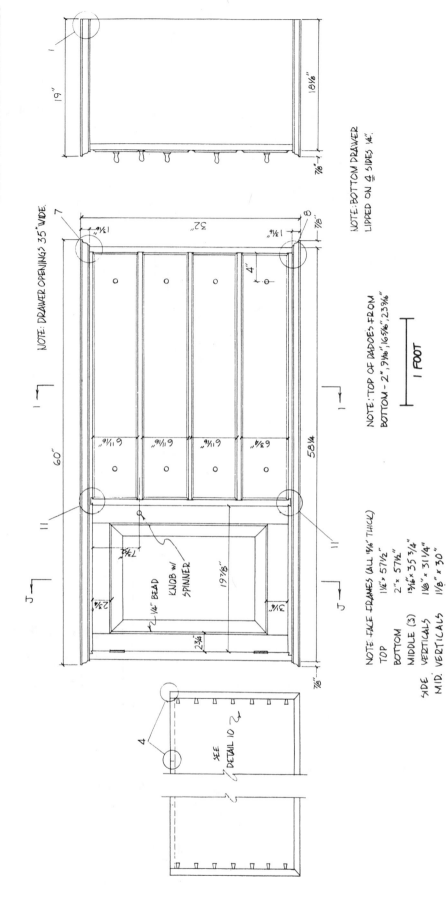

NOTE: BOTTOM DRAWER
LIPPED ON 4 SIDES ¼".

NOTE: DRAWER OPENINGS 35" WIDE.

NOTE: TOP OF DADOES FROM
BOTTOM - 2", 9⁹⁄₁₆", 16⁵⁄₈", 23⁹⁄₁₆"

1 FOOT

NOTE: FACE FRAMES (ALL ¹¹⁄₁₆" THICK)
TOP	1¼" x 57½"
BOTTOM	2" x 57½"
MIDDLE (3)	1⁹⁄₁₆" x 35 ¾"
SIDE VERTICALS	1⅛" x 31¼"
MID. VERTICALS	1⅛" x 30"

KNOB w/
SPINNER

¼" BEAD

SEE
DETAIL 10

**Front, side and top views of the four-drawer sidechest. For the photograph
and perspective, see the following page.**

The four-drawer sidechest can be used either in the bedroom or in the dining room. In the bedroom, in addition to holding folded clothing, its cupboard compartment is useful for storing ski boots, hats, or any objects that are too bulky to fit in a drawer. When the sidechest is used in a dining room, the drawers are ideal for linens and silverware, and the cupboard compartment offers good space for serving pieces, vases, and any objects that are tall. As in all case interiors, the shelf height is adjustable.

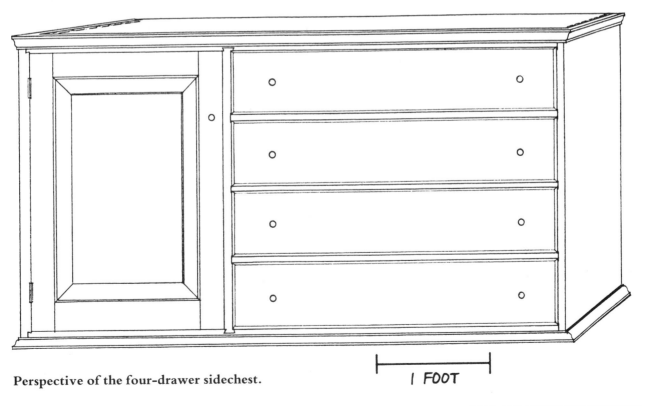

I FOOT

Perspective of the four-drawer sidechest.

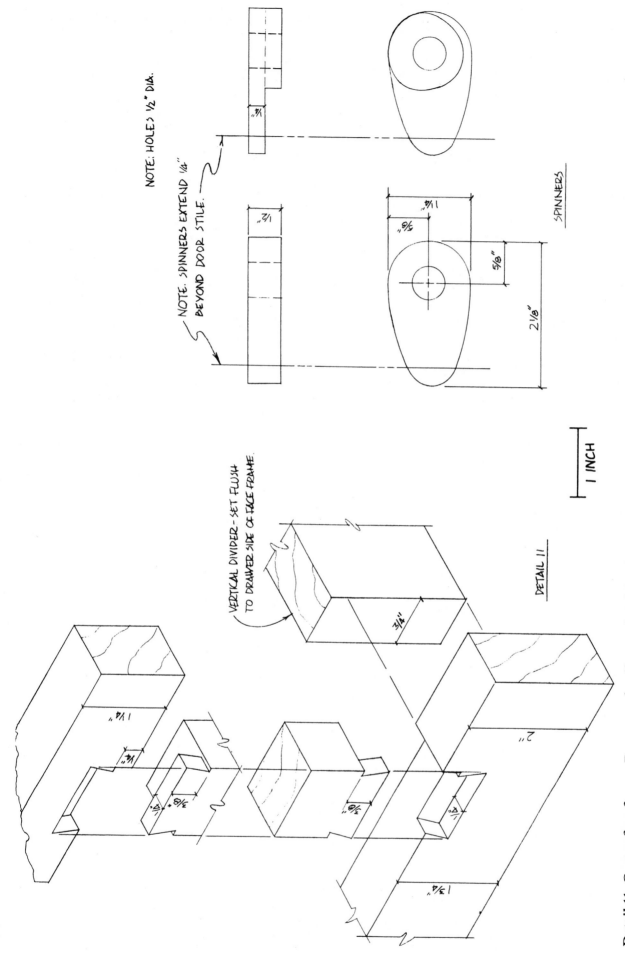

NOTE: HOLES ½" DIA.

NOTE: SPINNERS EXTEND ¼" BEYOND DOOR STILE.

¼"

½"

1¼"

5/8"

5/8"

2⅛"

SPINNERS

1 INCH

VERTICAL DIVIDER - SET FLUSH TO DRAWER SIDE OF FACE FRAME.

¾"

DETAIL 11

1¼"

¼"

½"

3/8"

3/8"

¼"

2"

1¾"

Detail 11: Center face frame. For more details, see the eight-drawer sidechest, pages 181 and 183.

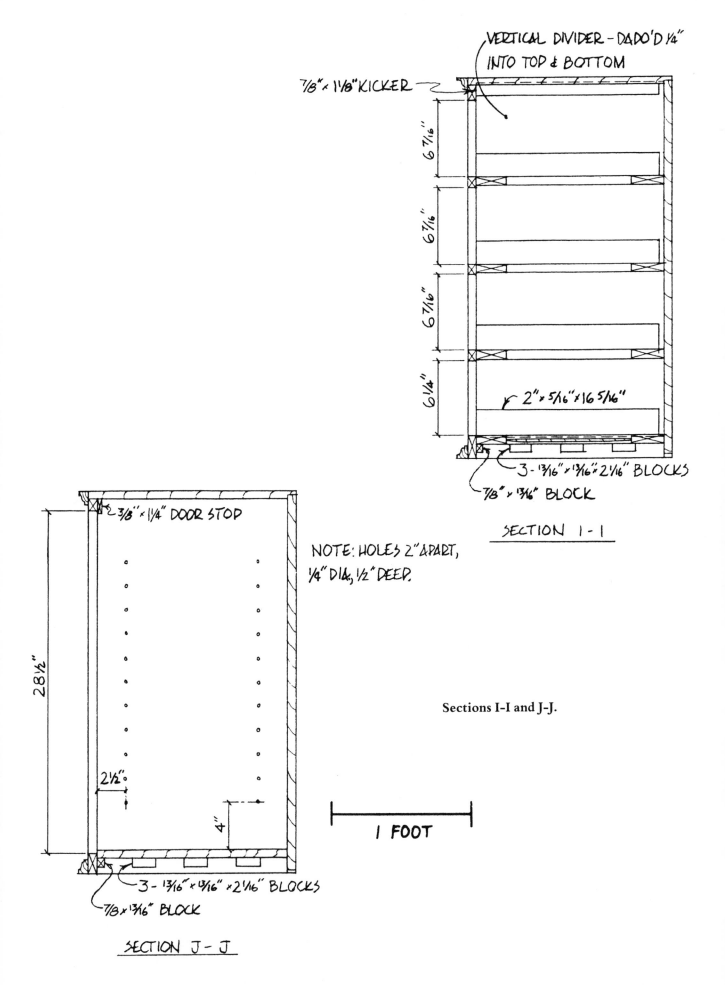

VERTICAL DIVIDER - DADO'D ¼"
INTO TOP & BOTTOM

⅞" × 1⅛" KICKER

6 7/16"

6 7/16"

6 7/16"

6¼"

2" × 5/16" × 16 5/16"

3 - 13/16" × 13/16" × 2 1/16" BLOCKS

⅞" × 13/16" BLOCK

SECTION I-I

⅜" × 1¼" DOOR STOP

NOTE: HOLES 2" APART,
¼" DIA., ½" DEEP.

28½"

2½"

4"

Sections I-I and J-J.

I FOOT

3 - 13/16" × 13/16" × 2 1/16" BLOCKS

⅞ × 13/16" BLOCK

SECTION J-J

Six-Drawer Sidechest

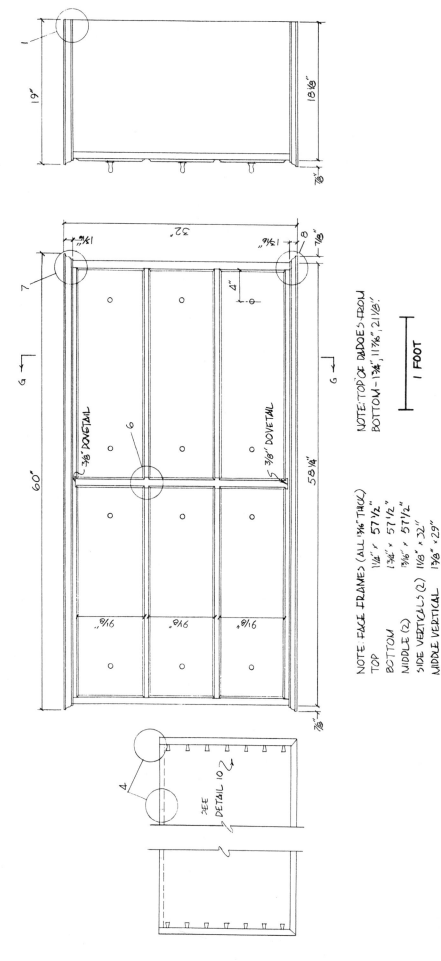

NOTE: FACE FRAMES (ALL ¹³⁄₁₆" THICK)

TOP	1¼" ×	57½"
BOTTOM	1¾" ×	57½"
MIDDLE (2)	¹³⁄₁₆" ×	57½"
SIDE VERTICALS (2)	1⅛" × 32"	
MIDDLE VERTICAL	1⅜" × 29"	

NOTE: TOP OF DADOES FROM
BOTTOM — 1¾", 11¹⁵⁄₁₆", 21⅛".

1 FOOT

Front, top and side views of the six-drawer sidechest. See the photograph and perspective on the following page.

The origin of this design is to be found in a 19th-century Shaker design. A case similar to this was used by the Shakers as a sewing chest, and had a top which folded out to provide more surface space.

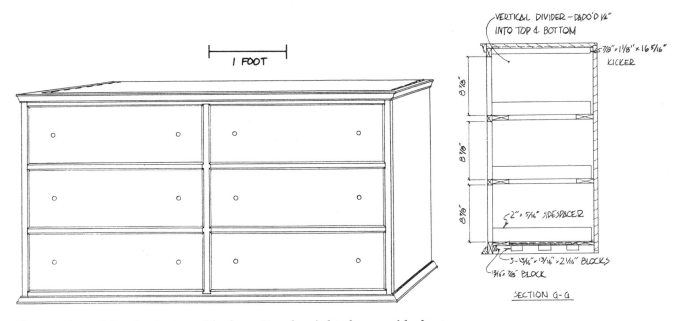

1 FOOT

VERTICAL DIVIDER—DADO'O ¼"
INTO TOP & BOTTOM

5⅞" × 1⅛" × 16⁵⁄₁₆"
KICKER

8⅞"

8⅞"

8⅞"

2" × ⁵⁄₁₆" SIDESPACER

3—1³⁄₁₆" × 1³⁄₁₆" × 2⁷⁄₁₆" BLOCKS
1³⁄₁₆" ⅞" BLOCK

SECTION G-G

Perspective of the six-drawer sidechest. See the eight-drawer sidechest (pages 182 and 183) for further details.

Dr. White's Chest

The first chest of this sort was built by us for a friend and customer named **Dr. White.** Its origin is found in a Shaker piece that dates from around 1830, but we have re-designed it to provide more than ample storage space.
We've often shipped this piece to customers without telling them about the secret compartment and they have later discovered it, much to their joy.

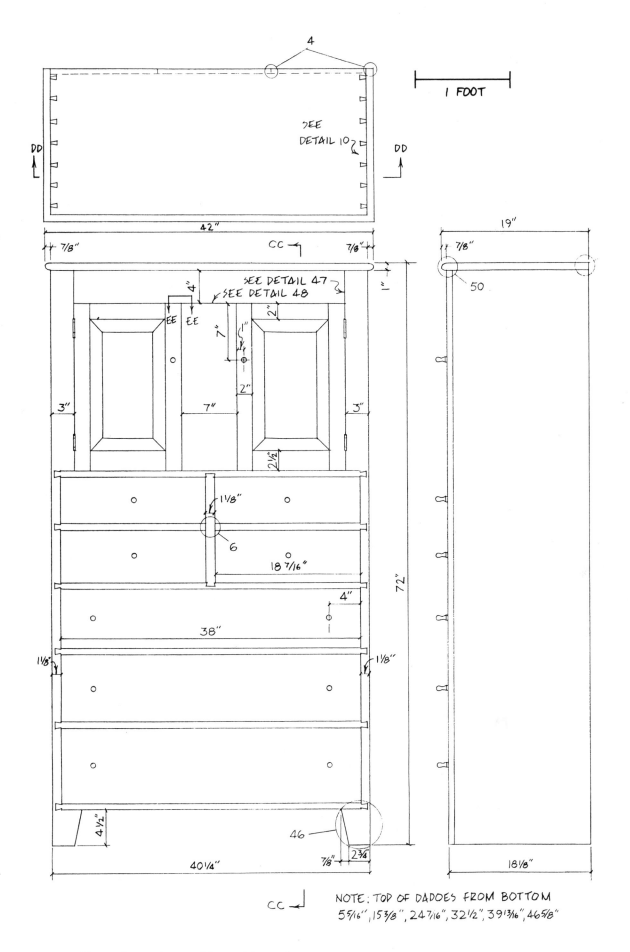

Front, side and top views of Dr. White's chest.

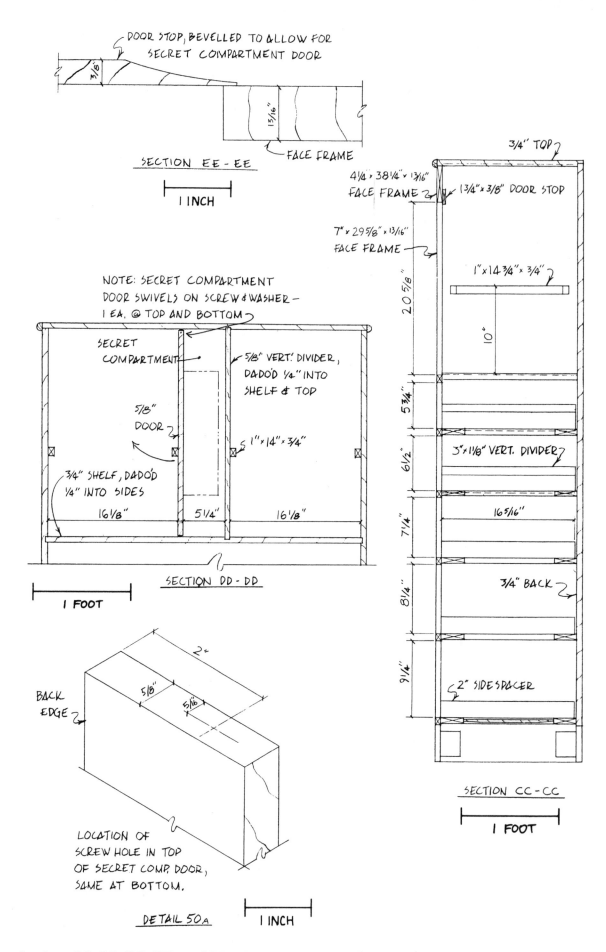

DOOR STOP, BEVELLED TO ALLOW FOR
SECRET COMPARTMENT DOOR

3/8"

15/16"

FACE FRAME

SECTION EE-EE

1 INCH

NOTE: SECRET COMPARTMENT
DOOR SWIVELS ON SCREW & WASHER —
1 EA. @ TOP AND BOTTOM

SECRET
COMPARTMENT

5/8" VERT. DIVIDER,
DADO'D 1/4" INTO
SHELF & TOP

5/8"
DOOR

1" x 14" x 3/4"

3/4" SHELF, DADO'D
1/4" INTO SIDES

16 1/8"

5 1/4"

16 1/8"

SECTION DD-DD

1 FOOT

BACK
EDGE

2"

5/8"

5/16"

LOCATION OF
SCREW HOLE IN TOP
OF SECRET COMP. DOOR,
SAME AT BOTTOM.

DETAIL 50A

1 INCH

3/4" TOP

4 1/4" x 38 1/4" x 13/16"
FACE FRAME

1 3/4" x 3/8" DOOR STOP

7" x 29 5/8" x 13/16"
FACE FRAME

1" x 14 3/4" x 3/4"

20 5/8"

10"

5 3/4"

3" x 1 1/8" VERT. DIVIDER

6 1/2"

16 5/16"

7 1/4"

3/4" BACK

8 1/4"

9 1/4"

2" SIDE SPACER

SECTION CC-CC

1 FOOT

Sections CC-CC, DD-DD, and EE-EE (secret compartment).

192   DR. WHITE'S CHEST

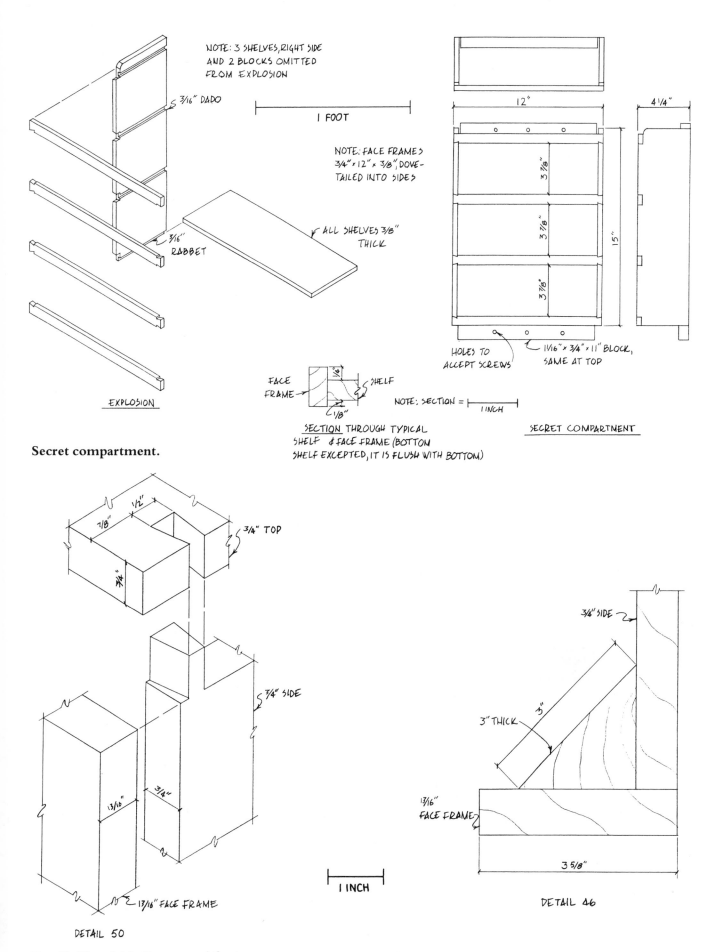

NOTE: 3 SHELVES, RIGHT SIDE AND 2 BLOCKS OMITTED FROM EXPLOSION

3/16" DADO

1 FOOT

NOTE: FACE FRAMES 3/4" x 12" x 3/8", DOVE-TAILED INTO SIDES

3/16" RABBET

ALL SHELVES 3/8" THICK

12"

4 1/4"

3/8"

3/8"

3/8"

15"

HOLES TO ACCEPT SCREWS

11/16" x 3/4" x 11" BLOCK, SAME AT TOP

EXPLOSION

FACE FRAME

1/4"

SHELF

1/8"

NOTE: SECTION = 1 INCH

SECTION THROUGH TYPICAL SHELF & FACE FRAME (BOTTOM SHELF EXCEPTED, IT IS FLUSH WITH BOTTOM)

SECRET COMPARTMENT

Secret compartment.

1/2"

7/8"

3/4" TOP

3/4"

3/4" SIDE

3/4" SIDE

3/4"

3" THICK

3"

13/16"

13/16" FACE FRAME

1 INCH

13/16" FACE FRAME

3 5/8"

DETAIL 50

DETAIL 46

Details 50 and 46: Corner and foot.

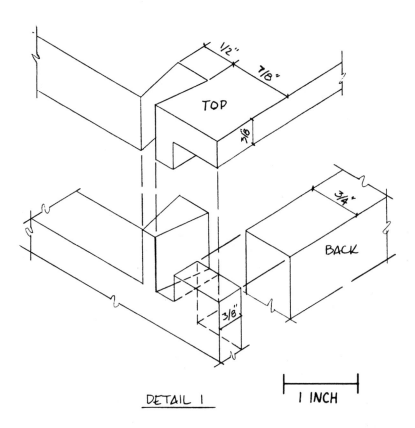

½" ⅞"

TOP

3/16

3/4"

BACK

3/8"

DETAIL 1

1 INCH

Detail 1: Corner.

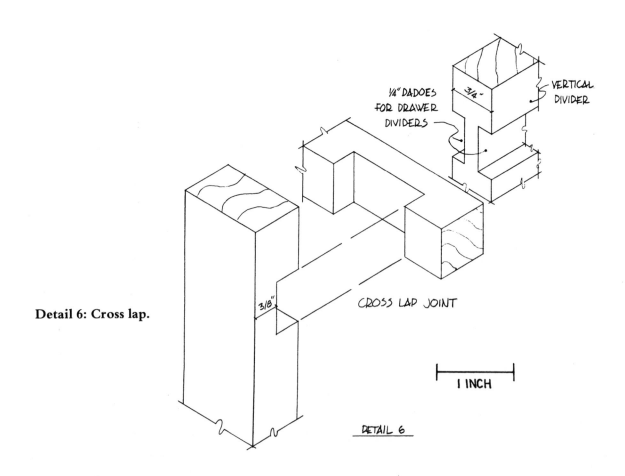

Detail 6: Cross lap.

¼" DADOES
FOR DRAWER
DIVIDERS

3/4"

VERTICAL
DIVIDER

CROSS LAP JOINT

3/8"

1 INCH

DETAIL 6

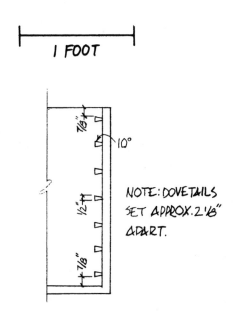

1 FOOT

NOTE: DOVETAILS SET APPROX. 2 1/8" APART.

7/8"

10°

1/2"

7/8"

DETAIL OF CASE SIDE
DOVETAILED INTO TOP

Detail 10: Dovetail layout.

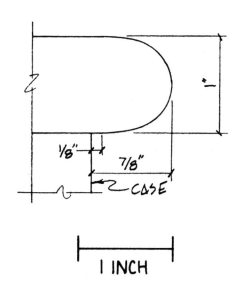

1"

1/8"

7/8"

CASE

1 INCH

Bullnose moulding.

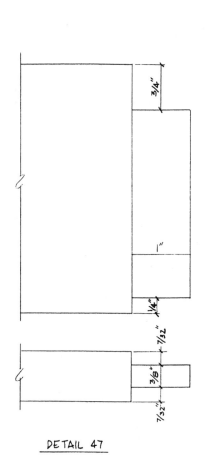

3/4"

1"

1/4"

7/32"

3/8"

7/32"

DETAIL 47

Details 47 and 48: Face frame tenons.

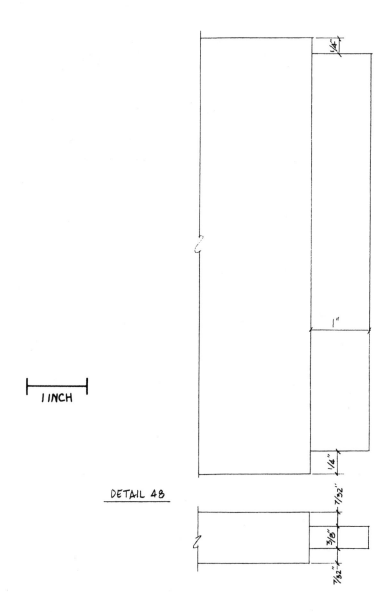

1/4"

1"

1/4"

7/32"

3/8"

7/32"

1 INCH

DETAIL 48

Endchest with Drawers

This small chest of drawers serves well as a bed stand or next to a chair or couch, where a lamp could be placed on it.

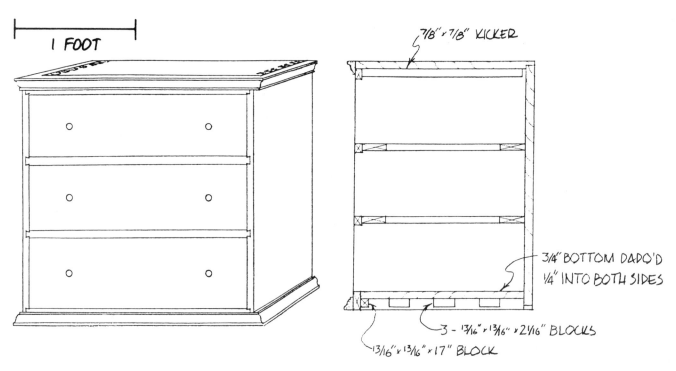

1 FOOT

7/8" x 7/8" KICKER

3/4" BOTTOM DADO'D 1/4" INTO BOTH SIDES

3 - 13/16" x 13/16" x 24/16" BLOCKS

13/16" x 13/16" x 17" BLOCK

SECTION B-B

Perspective of a three-drawer endchest.

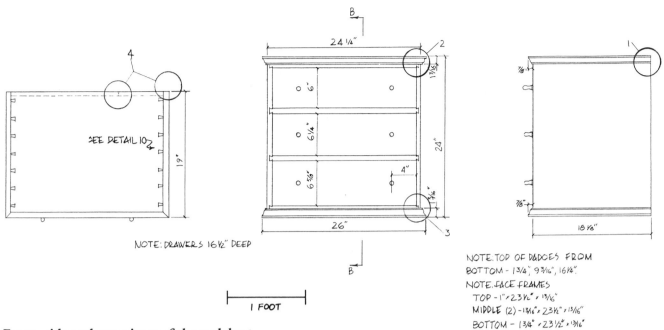

NOTE: DRAWERS 16½" DEEP

1 FOOT

Front, side and top views of the endchest.

NOTE: TOP OF D&DOES FROM
BOTTOM — 1¾", 9³/₁₆", 16¼".
NOTE: FACE FRAMES
 TOP — 1" × 23½" × ¹³/₁₆"
 MIDDLE (2) — 1³/₁₆" × 23½" × ¹³/₁₆"
 BOTTOM — 1¾" × 23½" × ¹³/₁₆"

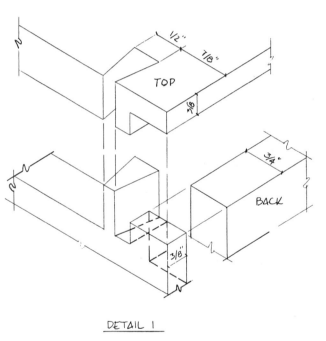

DETAIL 1

Detail 1: Front corner. Detail 2: Back corner.

1 INCH

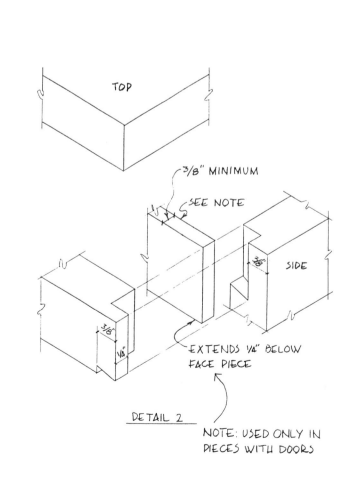

3/8" MINIMUM

SEE NOTE

SIDE

EXTENDS ¼" BELOW
FACE PIECE

DETAIL 2

NOTE: USED ONLY IN
PIECES WITH DOORS

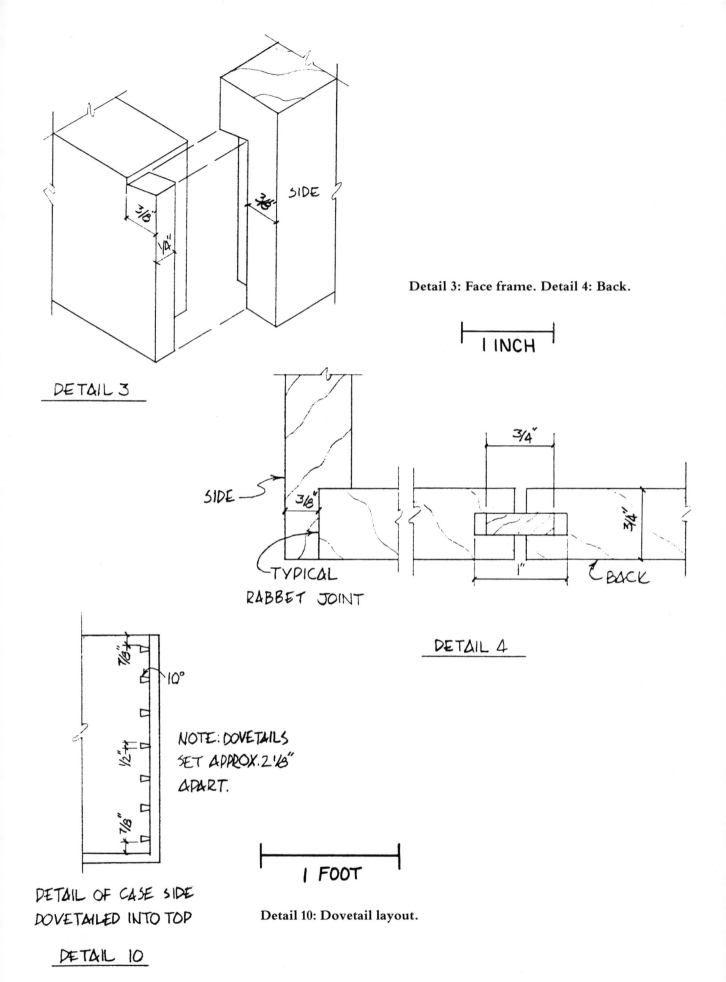

SIDE

3/8"

1/4"

3/8"

SIDE

DETAIL 3

Detail 3: Face frame. Detail 4: Back.

|⊢——————⊣|
I INCH

SIDE

3/8"

TYPICAL
RABBET JOINT

3/4"

3/4"

1"

BACK

DETAIL 4

7/8"

10°

1/2"

NOTE: DOVETAILS
SET APPROX. 2⅛"
APART.

7/8"

|⊢——————⊣|
I FOOT

DETAIL OF CASE SIDE
DOVETAILED INTO TOP

Detail 10: Dovetail layout.

DETAIL 10

Endchest with Doors

The dimensions of this case are identical to the endchest with drawers except, of course, this piece has doors and a single, adjustable shelf inside.

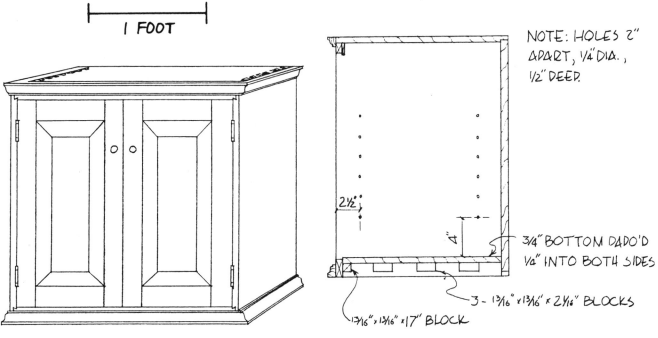

1 FOOT

Perspective of the endchest with two doors.

NOTE: HOLES 2" APART, 1/4" DIA., 1/2" DEEP.

2½"

4"

3/4" BOTTOM DADO'D 1/4" INTO BOTH SIDES

3 - 13/16" x 13/16" x 24/16" BLOCKS

13/16" x 13/16" x 17" BLOCK

SECTION A-A

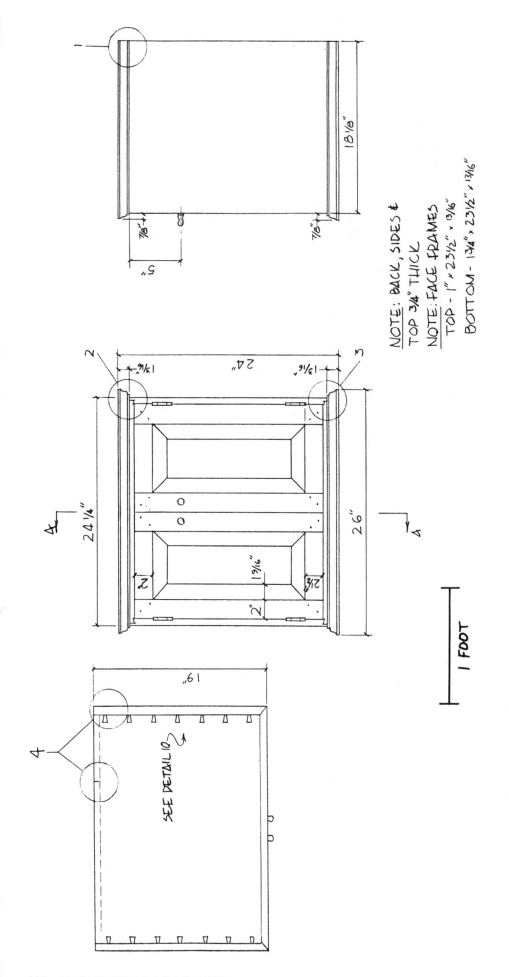

NOTE: BACK, SIDES &
TOP 3/4" THICK

NOTE: FACE FRAMES
TOP - 1" x 23½" x 13/16"
BOTTOM - 1¾" x 23½" x 13/16"

1 FOOT

Front, top and side views of the endchest with doors. For further details, see the endchest with drawers (pages 197 and 198).

Cube

The cube serves the same purpose as the endchest, but in a more contemporary way, with no moulding at the top or the base and no extending knobs. It is very much at home in a contemporary setting. On the bottom right is an exterior look at the endchest. At bottom right is a look at the interior.

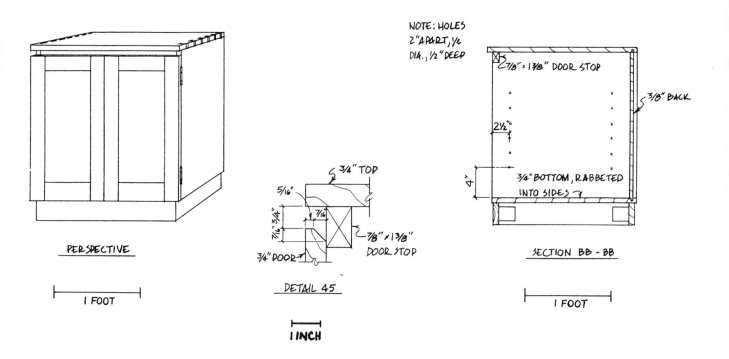

PERSPECTIVE

I FOOT

NOTE: HOLES
2"APART, 1/4
DIA., 1/2"DEEP

3/4" TOP

5/16"

7/16"

7/16" 3/4"

3/4" DOOR

7/8" × 1 3/8"
DOOR STOP

DETAIL 45

I INCH

7/8" × 1 3/8" DOOR STOP

3/8" BACK

2 1/2"

4"

3/4" BOTTOM, RABBETED
INTO SIDES

SECTION BB - BB

I FOOT

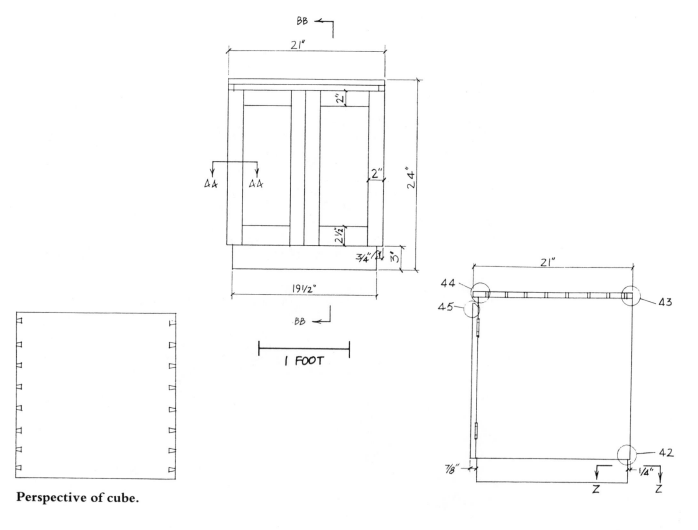

BB

21"

2"

2"

24"

AA   AA

2 1/2"

3/4"   3"

19 1/2"

BB

I FOOT

21"

44   43

45

42

7/8"

1/4"

Z   Z

Perspective of cube.

202 CUBE

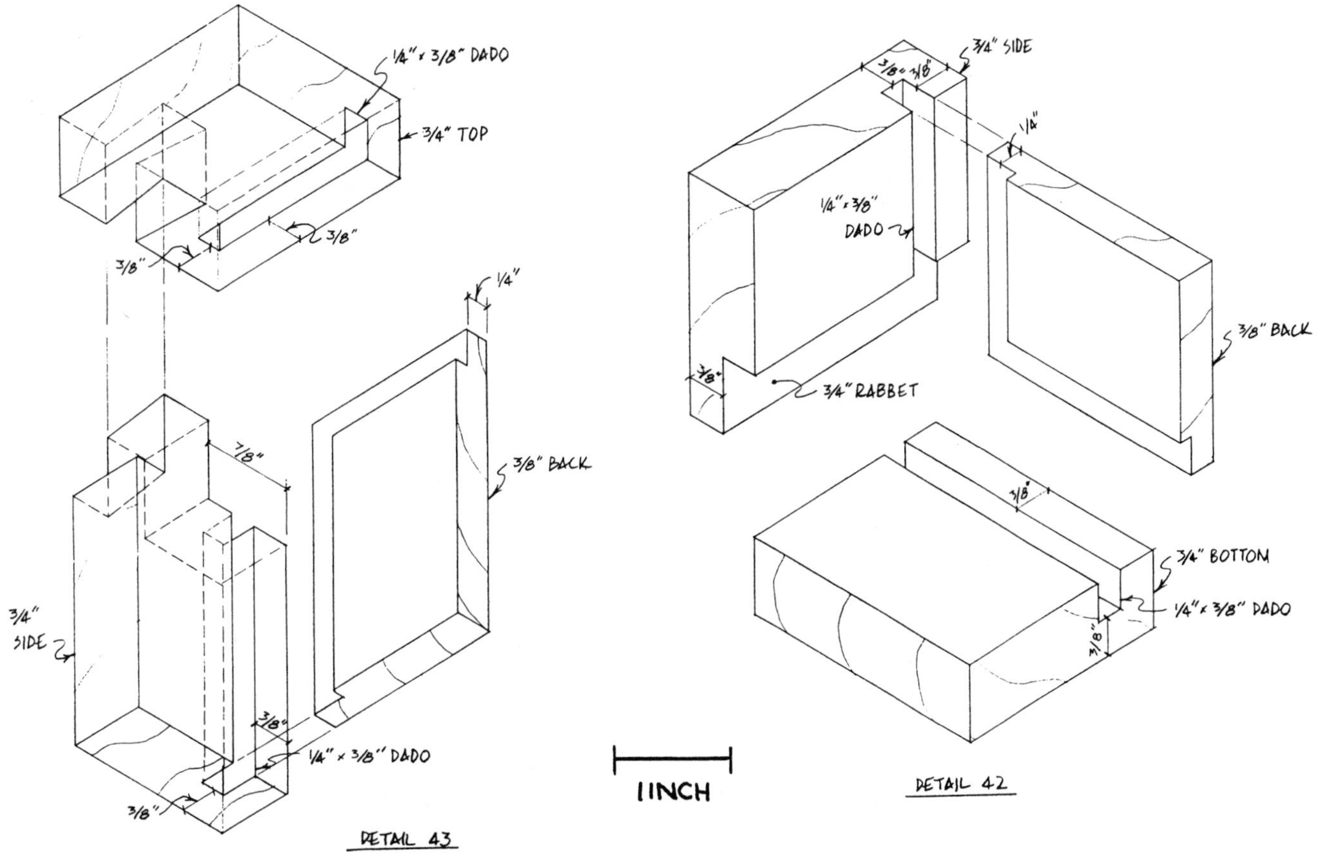
1/4" × 3/8" DADO
3/4" TOP
3/8"
3/8"
1/4"
7/8"
3/8" BACK
3/4" SIDE
3/8"
1/4" × 3/8" DADO
3/8"
DETAIL 43
1 INCH
3/4" SIDE
3/8" 3/8"
1/4"
1/4" × 3/8" DADO
3/8"
3/4" RABBET
3/8" BACK
3/8"
3/4" BOTTOM
1/4" × 3/8" DADO
3/8"
DETAIL 42

Detail 42: Upper corner. Detail 43: Lower corner.

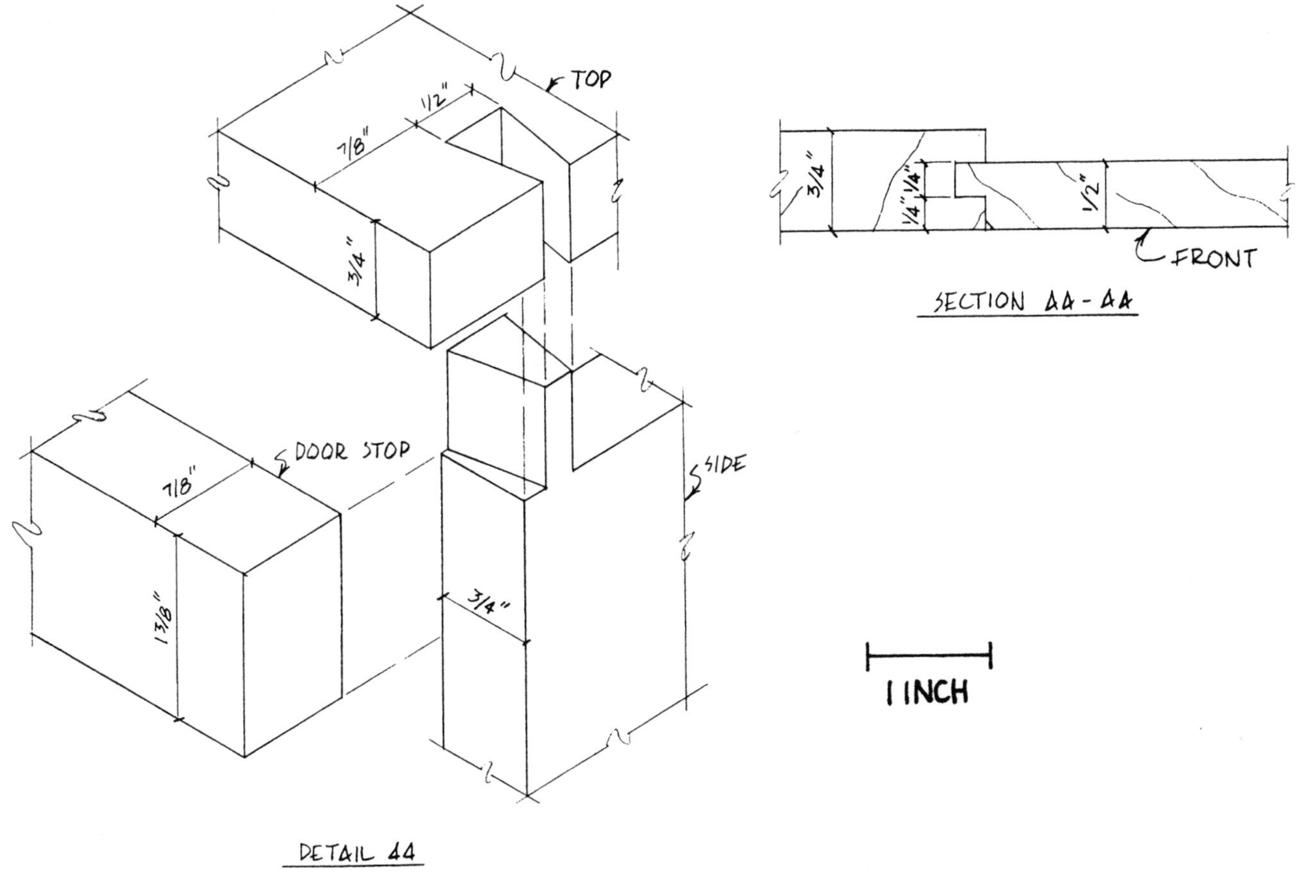
TOP
1/2"
7/8"
3/4"
DOOR STOP
7/8"
13/8"
SIDE
3/4"
3/4"
1/4"
1/4"
1/4"
1/2"
FRONT
SECTION AA-AA
1 INCH
DETAIL 44

Detail 44: Top corner and section AA-AA.

Gates Cabinet

The first of these cabinets was built for a customer of ours—the Gates family—and was intended to house Mrs. Gates' sewing needs. We were so taken with the overall design that we developed the interior to be used in an open fashion, and as a desk. Just recently we built the Gates cabinet in ash, and its interior was designed to hold stemware and other fine glasses. Indeed, the interior of the Gates cabinet can be made to serve any number of functions.

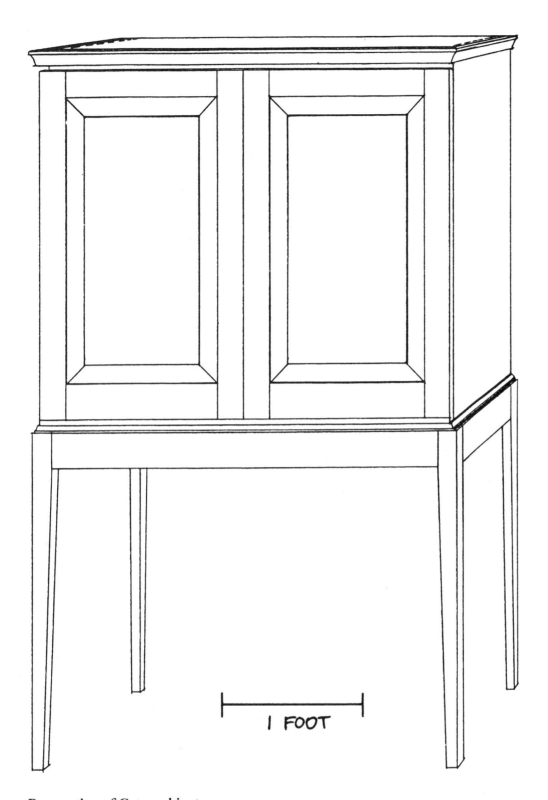

I FOOT

Perspective of Gates cabinet.

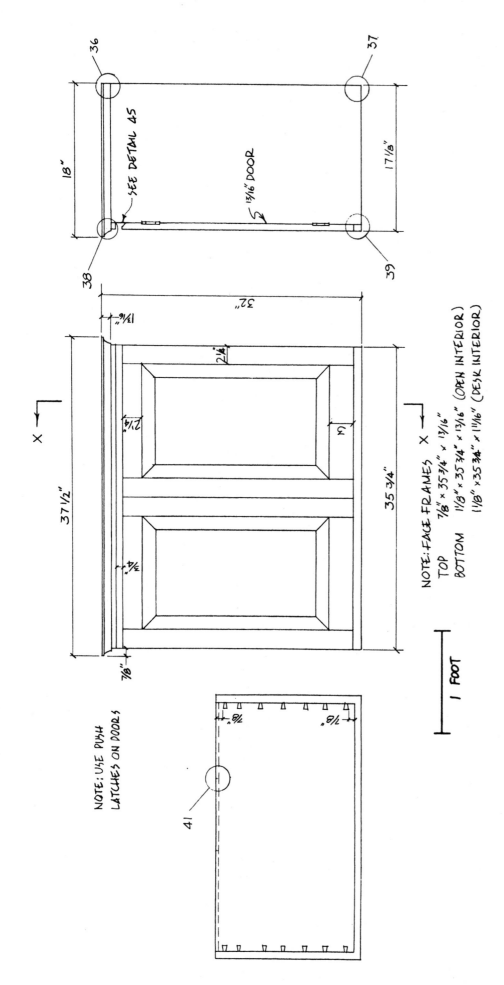

Front, side and top views of the Gates cabinet.

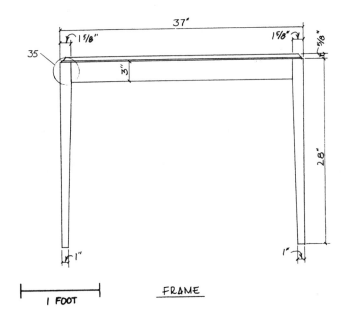

37"

1⁵⁄₈"   1⁵⁄₈"

⁵⁄₈"

35

1⁵⁄₈"

3"

2'8"

1"   1"

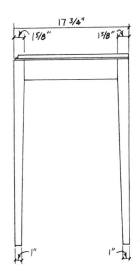

17³⁄₄"

1⁵⁄₈"   1⁵⁄₈"

1"   1"

|—— 1 FOOT ——| FRAME

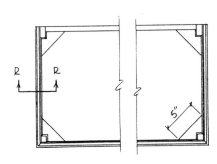

R   R

5"

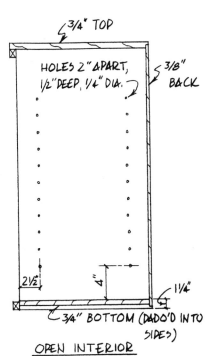

³⁄₄" TOP

HOLES 2" APART,
½" DEEP, ¼" DIA.

³⁄₈"
BACK

2½"   4"   1¼"

³⁄₄" BOTTOM (DADO'D INTO
SIDES)

OPEN INTERIOR

Side, front and top views of the base. Also section X-X—for open interior.

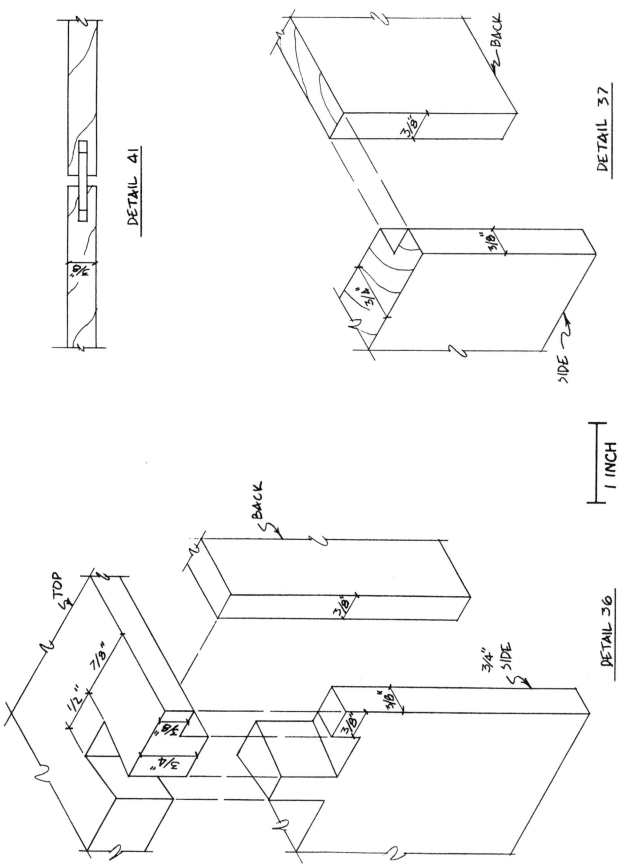

DETAIL 41

DETAIL 37

1 INCH

DETAIL 36

Detail 37: Corner. Detail 36: Back. Detail 41: Spline.

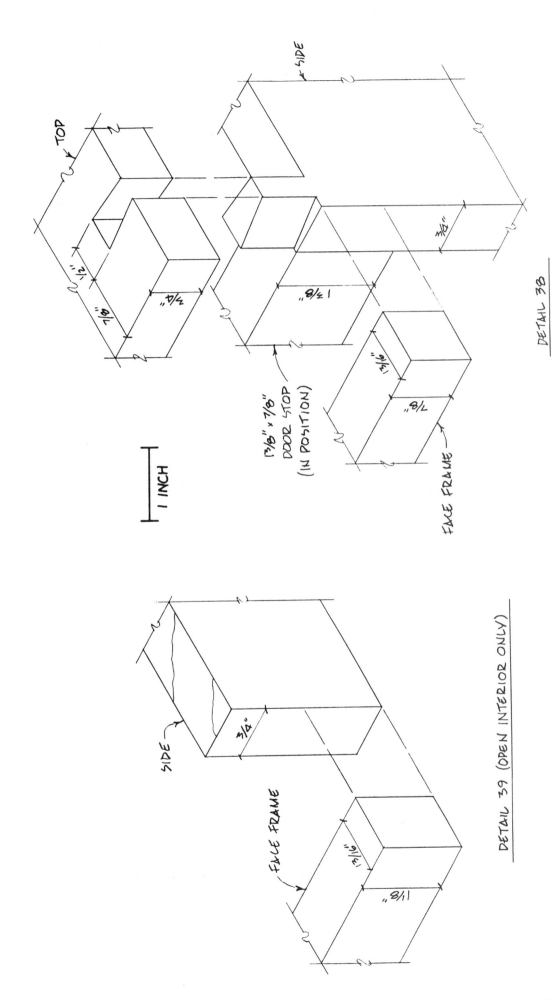

TOP

SIDE

1/2"

7/8"

3/4"

3/8"

1 3/4"

1 3/8"

1 3/4"

7/8"

DETAIL 38

1 3/8" × 7/8"
DOOR STOP
(IN POSITION)

FACE FRAME

1 INCH

SIDE

3/4"

FACE FRAME

1 3/4"

1 1/8"

DETAIL 39 (OPEN INTERIOR ONLY)

Details 38 and 39: Face frames.

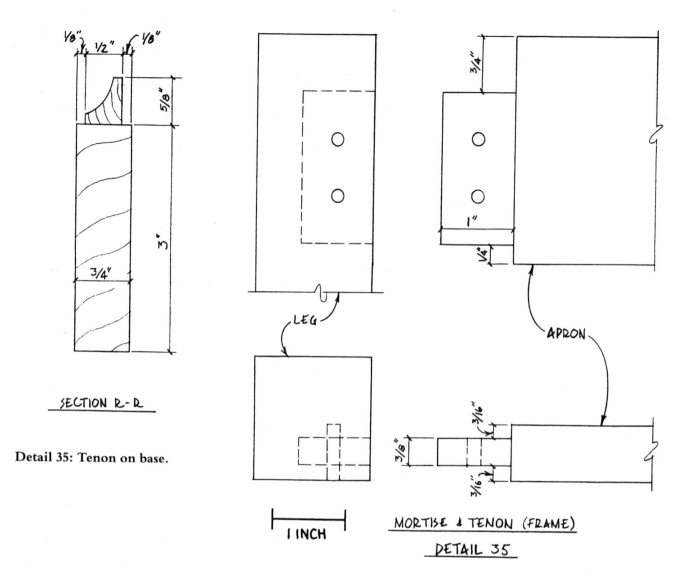

SECTION R-R

Detail 35: Tenon on base.

LEG

1 INCH

APRON

MORTISE & TENON (FRAME)

DETAIL 35

Gates Cabinet (Desk Interior)

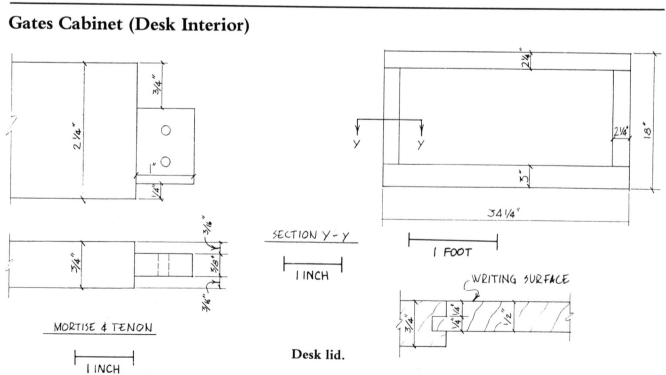

MORTISE & TENON

1 INCH

SECTION Y-Y

1 INCH

1 FOOT

WRITING SURFACE

Desk lid.

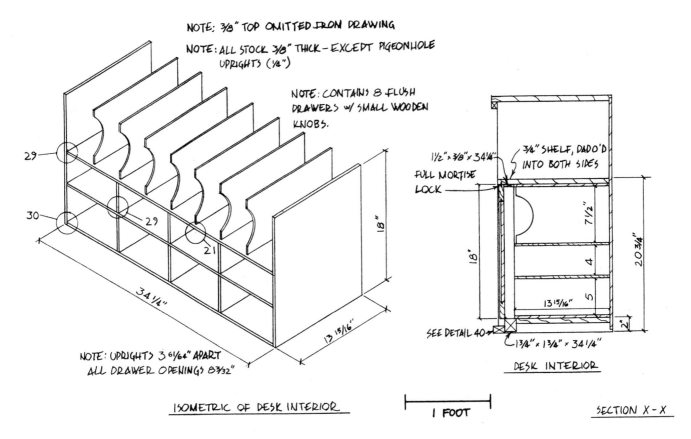

NOTE: 3/8" TOP OMITTED FROM DRAWING

NOTE: ALL STOCK 3/8" THICK — EXCEPT PIGEONHOLE UPRIGHTS (1/4")

NOTE: CONTAINS 8 FLUSH DRAWERS W/ SMALL WOODEN KNOBS.

29

30

29

21

18"

34 1/4"

13 15/16"

NOTE: UPRIGHTS 3 61/64" APART ALL DRAWER OPENINGS 8 3/32"

ISOMETRIC OF DESK INTERIOR

1 FOOT

1 1/2" × 3/8" × 34 1/4"

FULL MORTISE LOCK

3/4" SHELF, DADO'D INTO BOTH SIDES

7 1/2"

18"

4

13 15/16"

5

20 3/4"

2"

SEE DETAIL 40

1 3/4" × 1 3/4" × 34 1/4"

DESK INTERIOR

SECTION X-X

Section X-X for Gates cabinet (desk interior).

Detail 40. For more details, see the Gates cabinet , pages 208 and 209.

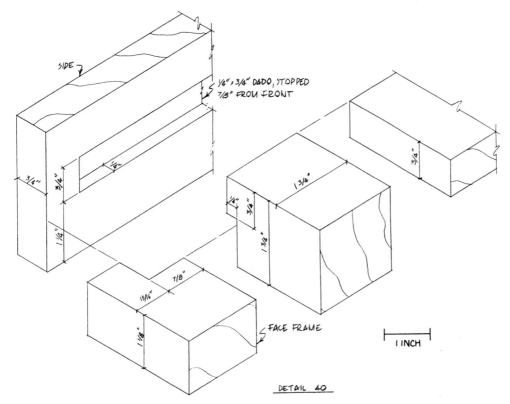

SIDE

1/4" × 3/4" DADO, STOPPED 7/8" FROM FRONT

3/4"

3/4"

1/4"

1/4"

13 3/4"

1/4"

3/4"

13 3/4"

3/4"

13/16"

7/8"

1 1/8"

FACE FRAME

1 INCH

DETAIL 40

Three-Door Sideboard

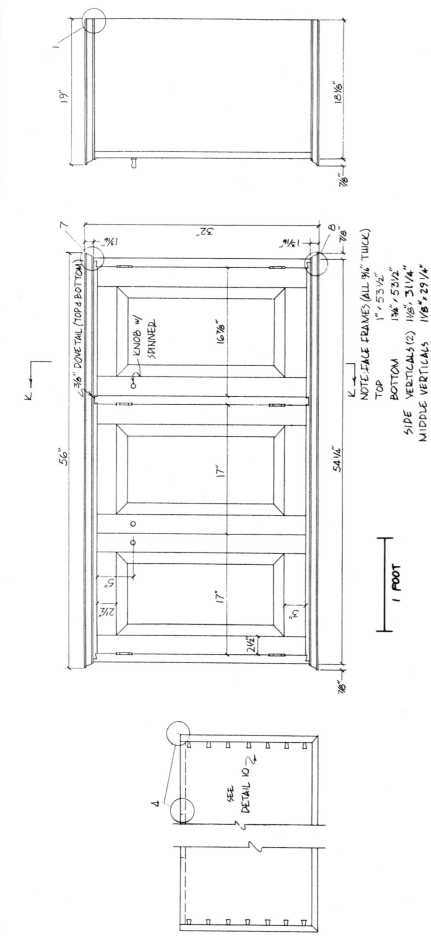

Front, side and top views of the three-door sideboard. See the following page for a perspective and photograph.

NOTE: FACE FRAMES (ALL 9/16" THICK)
TOP   1" × 53½"
BOTTOM   1¾" × 53½"
SIDE VERTICALS (2) 1⅛" × 31¼"
MIDDLE VERTICALS   1⅛" × 29¼"

1 FOOT

KNOB W/ SPINNER

⅜" DOVETAIL (TOP & BOTTOM)

SEE DETAIL 10

The three-door sideboard is slightly narrower than the other sidechests. This ensures as much height in the doors as possible. Behind these doors are two compartments, one 17 inches (43.2 cm) wide and one 34 inches (86.3 cm) wide. With its adjustable shelf, this low cupboard can store a great quantity of household items, and its interior can be fitted with drawer guides for housing files, stereo components or even a television set.

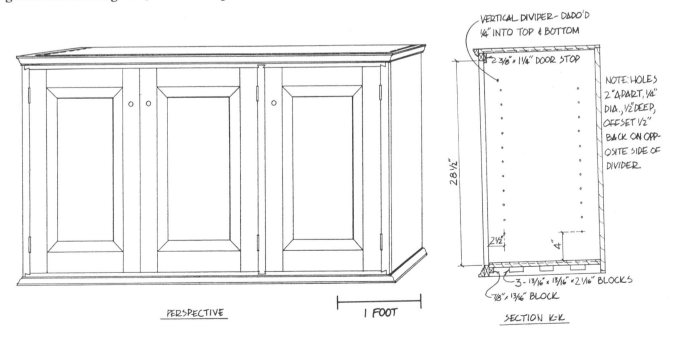

PERSPECTIVE

1 FOOT

VERTICAL DIVIDER - DADO'D 1/4" INTO TOP & BOTTOM

2 3/8" x 1 1/4" DOOR STOP

28 1/2"

NOTE: HOLES 2" APART, 1/4" DIA., 1/2" DEEP, OFFSET 1/2" BACK ON OPPOSITE SIDE OF DIVIDER.

2 1/2"

4"

3 - 13/16" x 13/16" x 2 1/16" BLOCKS

7/8" x 13/16" BLOCK

SECTION K-K

Perspective of the three-door sideboard.

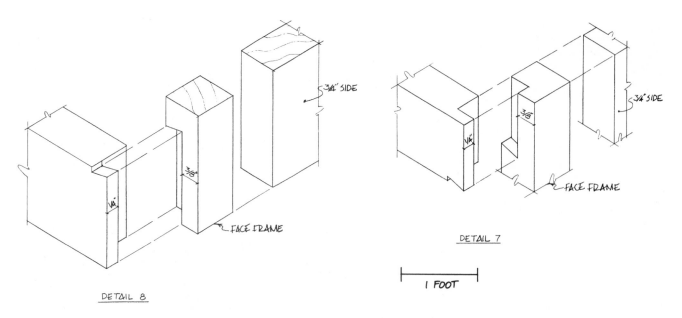

Details 7 and 8: Face frames.

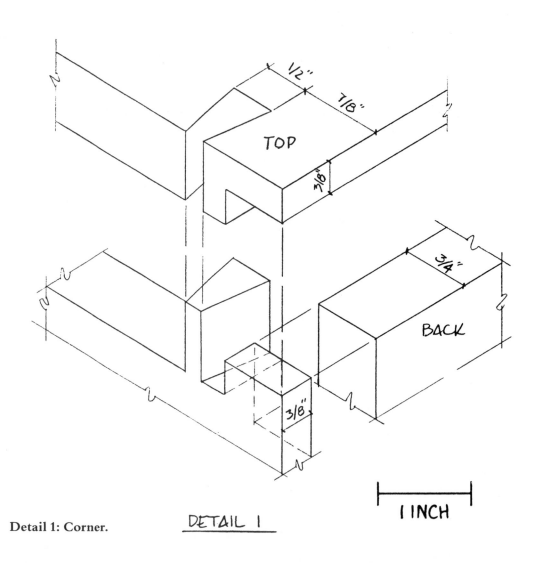

Detail 1: Corner.

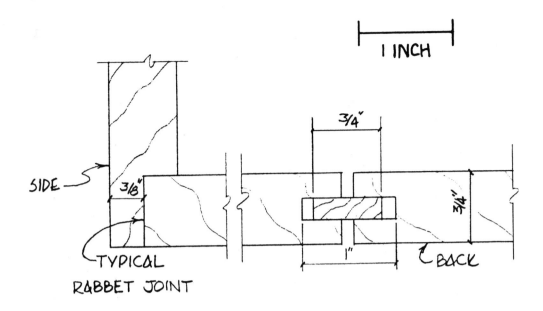

1 INCH

SIDE

3/8"

TYPICAL
RABBET JOINT

3/4"

1"

3/4"

BACK

DETAIL 4

Detail 4: Back.

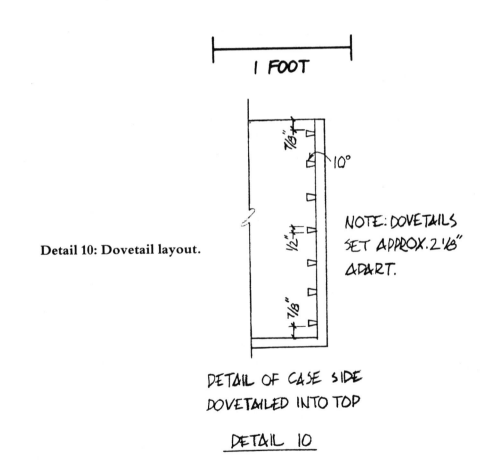

1 FOOT

Detail 10: Dovetail layout.

7/8"

10°

1/2"

7/8"

NOTE: DOVETAILS
SET APPROX. 2 1/8"
APART.

DETAIL OF CASE SIDE
DOVETAILED INTO TOP

DETAIL 10

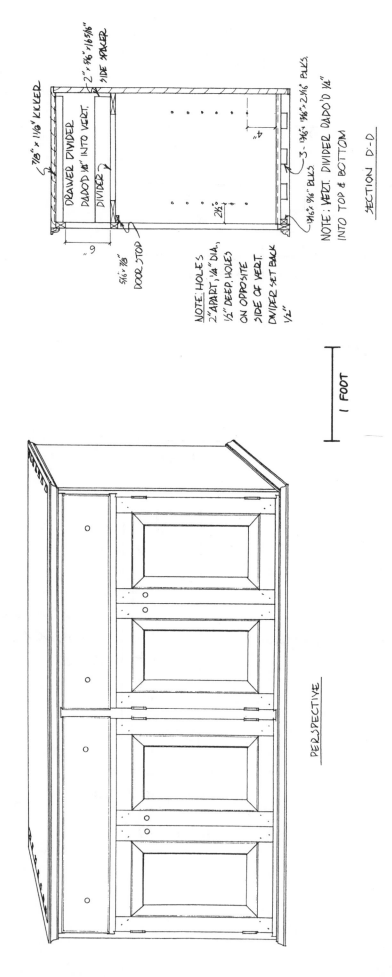

7/8" × 11/8" KICKER

2" × 9/16" × 16 5/16" SIDE SPACER

DRAWER DIVIDER DADO'D 1/4" INTO VERT.

DIVIDER

6"

5/16" 7/8"

DOOR STOP

NOTE: HOLES
2" APART, 1/4" DIA.,
1/2" DEEP, HOLES
ON OPPOSITE
SIDE OF VERT.
DIVIDER SET BACK
1/2"

2 1/2"

4"

3 - 1 7/16" × 9/16" × 2 7/16" PLES.

1 7/16" 9/16" PLES.

NOTE: VERT. DIVIDER DADO'D 1/4"
INTO TOP & BOTTOM

SECTION D-D

1 FOOT

PERSPECTIVE

Perspective of the four-door sideboard. See the following page for the photograph.

This case combines the storage capabilities found in the three-door
sideboard, but also offers two moderately shallow drawers. The four-door
sideboard is at home in either a bedroom or dining room, and can be used
as a credenza behind a desk.

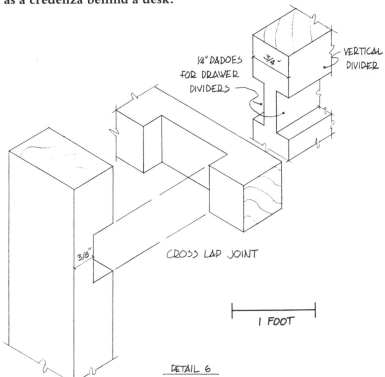

¼" DADOES
FOR DRAWER
DIVIDERS

3/4"

VERTICAL
DIVIDER

3/8"

CROSS LAP JOINT

1 FOOT

DETAIL 6

Detail 6: Cross lap. See the front, side
and top views on the following page.

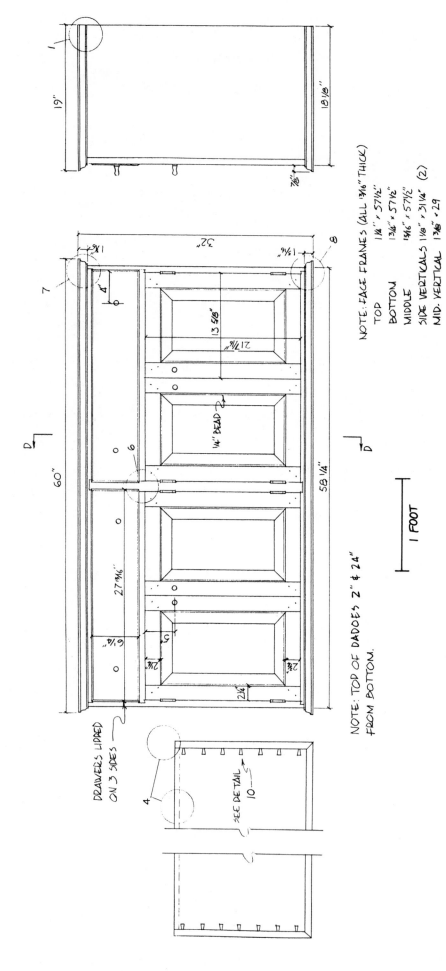

NOTE: FACE FRAMES (ALL 13⁄16" THICK)

TOP   1¼" × 57½"
BOTTOM   3¼" × 57½"
MIDDLE   15⁄16" × 57½"
SIDE VERTICALS 1⅛" × 31¼" (2)
MID. VERTICAL 13⁄8" × 29"

NOTE: TOP OF DADOES 2" & 24"
FROM BOTTOM.

1 FOOT

DRAWERS LIPPED ON 3 SIDES

SEE DETAIL 10

Front, side and top views of the four-door sideboard. For the details, see the three-door sideboard, pages 214 and 215.

Double Cupboard

The double cupboard is patterned after a thin, tall Shaker design which was sometimes called a chimney cupboard because it would fill in the space next to a chimney in some of the early Shaker dwelling places. This cupboard offers a tall, slender form, and is well suited to particular places where vertical storage is desired. The dovetails at the top and step shelf add interest.

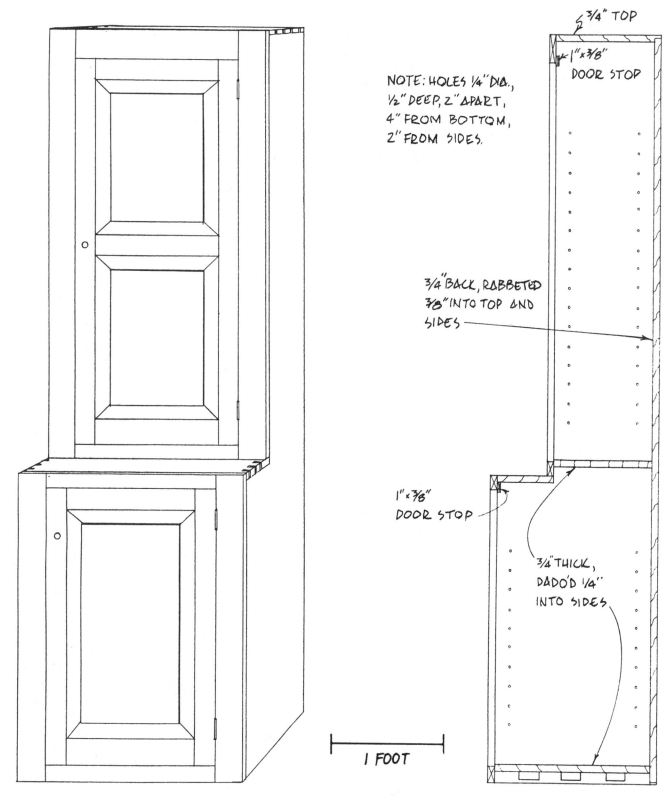

NOTE: HOLES ¼" DIA., ½" DEEP, 2" APART, 4" FROM BOTTOM, 2" FROM SIDES.

¾" TOP

1" x ⅜" DOOR STOP

¾" BACK, RABBETED ⅜" INTO TOP AND SIDES

1" x ⅜" DOOR STOP

¾" THICK, DADO'D ¼" INTO SIDES

1 FOOT

Perspective of the double cupboard.

SECTION CCC - CCC

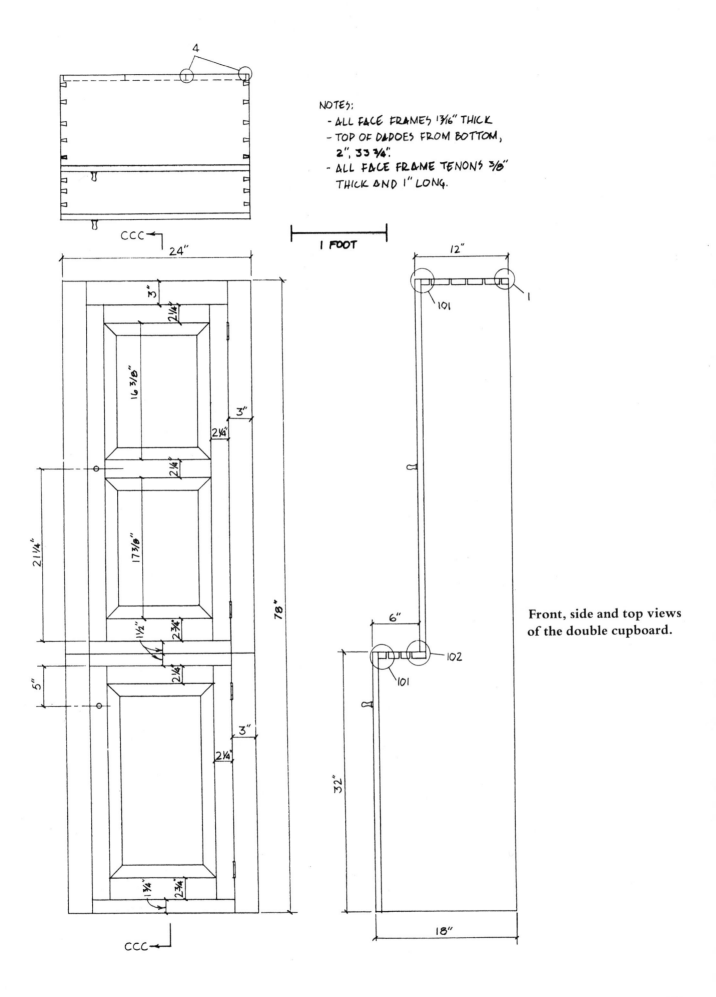

NOTES:
- ALL FACE FRAMES 13/16" THICK
- TOP OF DADOES FROM BOTTOM, 2", 33 3/4".
- ALL FACE FRAME TENONS 3/8" THICK AND 1" LONG.

Front, side and top views of the double cupboard.

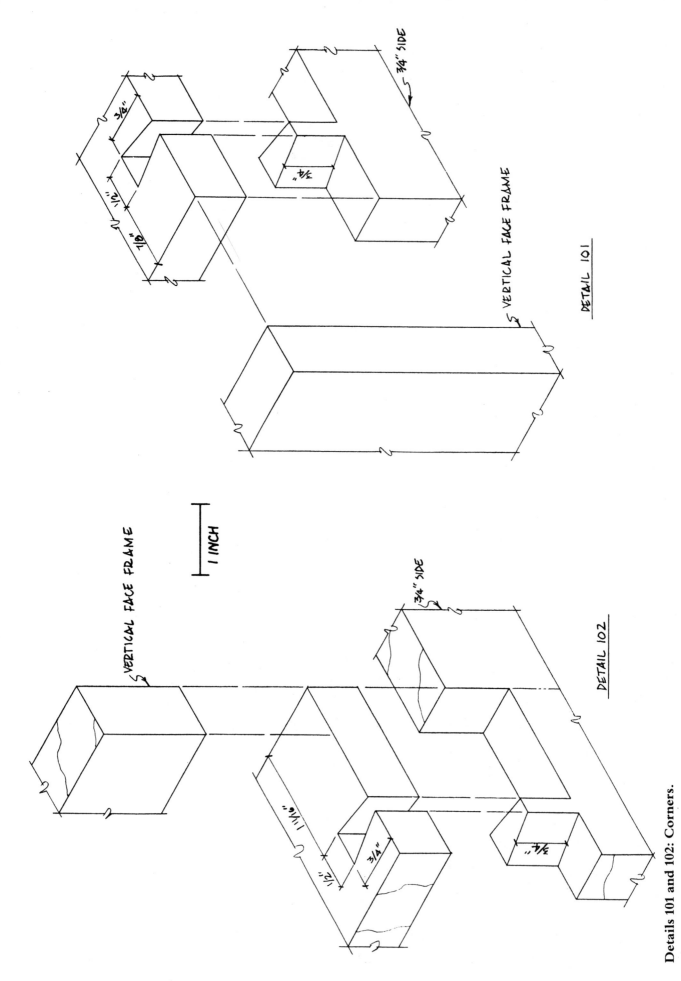

Details 101 and 102: Corners.

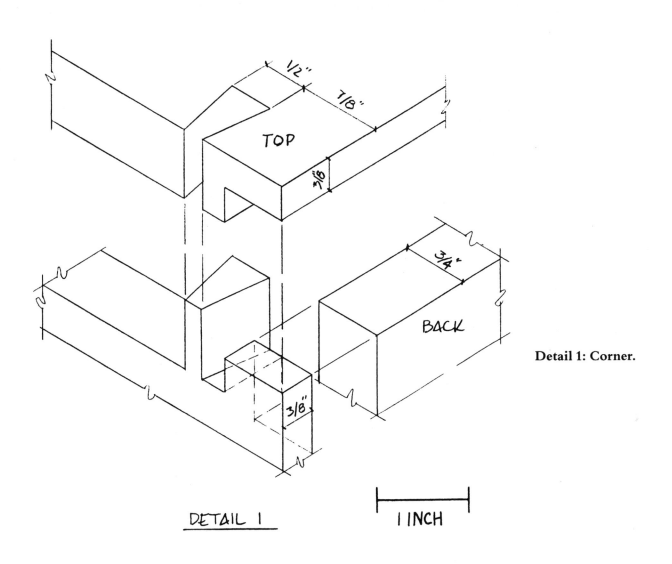

1/2"

7/8"

TOP

3/8

3/4"

BACK

3/8"

Detail 1: Corner.

DETAIL 1

1 INCH

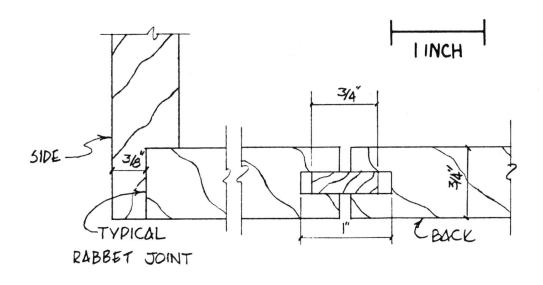

1 INCH

SIDE

3/8"

3/4"

3/4"

1"

BACK

TYPICAL
RABBET JOINT

DETAIL 4

Detail 4: Back.

Corner Cupboard

Perspective of the corner cupboard.

Many dining rooms and living rooms offer limited space for case furniture because of windows and interior doors. The corner cupboard is an ideal solution to providing storage space where only a corner is available. It fits snugly into a wall space of just 26 inches (66.0 cm), and yet offers an overall width of almost 40 inches (1.0 m).

Front, side and top views of the corner cupboard.

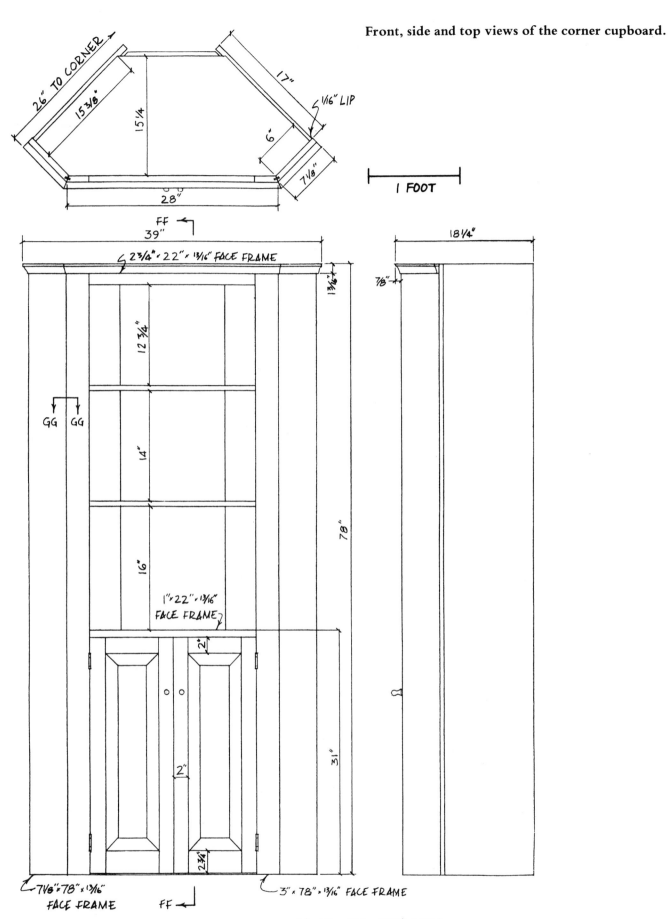

26" TO CORNER

15 3/8"

17"

15 1/4"

1/16" LIP

6"

7 1/8"

28"

1 FOOT

FF

39"

2 3/4" × 22" × 13/16" FACE FRAME

13/16"

18 1/4"

7/8"

12 3/4"

GG GG

14"

78"

16"

1" × 22" × 13/16" FACE FRAME

2"

2"

31"

2 3/4"

7 1/8" × 78" × 13/16" FACE FRAME

FF

3" × 78" × 13/16" FACE FRAME

NOTE: TOP OF DADOES FROM BOTTOM- 2", 18", 31 1/4", 47 3/4", 62 1/2"

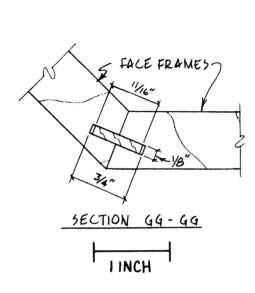

FACE FRAMES

11/16"

1/8"

3/4"

SECTION GG-GG

1 INCH

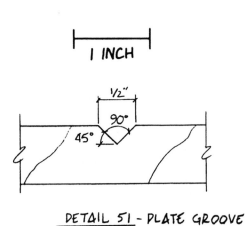

1 INCH

1/2"

90°

45°

DETAIL 51 - PLATE GROOVE

NOTE: GROOVE RUNS ALONG BOTH
SIDES AS WELL AS BACK

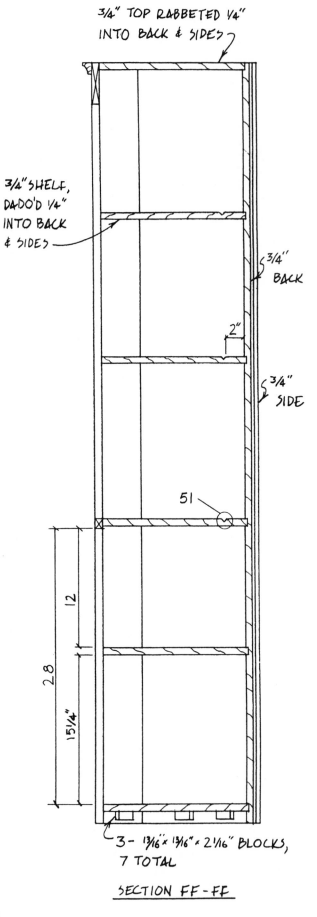

3/4" TOP RABBETED 1/4"
INTO BACK & SIDES

3/4" SHELF,
DADO'D 1/4"
INTO BACK
& SIDES

3/4"
BACK

2"

3/4"
SIDE

51

12

28

15 1/4"

3 - 1 3/16" × 1 3/16" × 2 1/16" BLOCKS,
7 TOTAL

SECTION FF-FF

Detail 51 (groove) and sections FF-FF and GG-GG.

BEDS

Mattress sizes have become standardized. These sizes are outlined in the table on pages 228, 254, and 256 and have to be consulted when designing a bed. One of the frustrations in bed designing is that standards are not always adhered to. It is common to find mattress and foundation combinations measuring from 12 inches (30.5 cm) in overall thickness to 16 inches (40.6 cm). Widths and lengths of mattresses also vary. The dimensions given in the section on beds are such they will accommodate certainly 90 percent of mattresses available. One additional complexity to bed design is the need to make the bed transportable or mobile. By definition, beds must be knocked down. The need for stability in the knock-down joint cannot be ignored.

Pencil-Post Bed (see following page)

The design for the pencil-post bed offers flexibility in that the posts can be topped with finials offering openness, or they can be joined by slats creating a canopy to hold a covering. At 26 inches (66.0 cm), the mattress is quite a bit higher than most modern beds. This bed is designed to house 14 or 15 inches (35.5 to 38.1 cm) of mattress and box spring overall. Occasionally, manufacturers these days are making mattresses 16 to 17 inches (40.6 to 43.2 cm) thick. If the bed is to accommodate such an overstuffed mattress, the headboard would have to be raised slightly so that the bottom of the headboard comes roughly even to the top of the mattress. This allows the bedsheets to be easily made without leaving so much room that the pillow falls through the space between the mattress and the headboard.

This bed is entirely knocked-down and is little more than a bundle of highly engineered sticks until it is bolted together to become a bed. The dimensions given here are for standard-sized mattresses. In almost all cases, manufacturers conform to these dimensions, but it is wise to empirically match a mattress to a bed. The pencil-post bed is not shown in king size because, at that size it is so enormous it loses its gracefulness and becomes almost a parody of itself. If this size is required, just make the headboard; the bed can be set upon a concealed, conventional steel frame.

The pencil-post bed has also been called a tester bed, field bed, canopy bed and a four-poster.

DIMENSIONS

MATTRESS	SIZE	Outside width D3	Shoulder to Shoulder width D4	Outside Length D5	Shoulder to Shoulder Length D6	Inside Length D7	Inside width D8	Mattress Hanger Location D9	Overall length of Canopy D10	Overall width of Canopy D11
39 x 75	TWIN	44½"	39"	81"	75½"	76½"	40"	37¾"	79⅜"	42⅞"
54 x 75	FULL	59½"	54"	81"	75½"	76½"	55"	37¾"	79⅜"	57⅞"
60 x 80	QUEEN	65½"	60"	86"	80½"	81½"	61"	40¼"	84⅜"	63⅞"

OVERALL DIMENSIONS

TWIN	44½" x 81" x 82"
FULL	59½" x 81" x 82"
QUEEN	65½" x 86" x 82"

NOTES:

- SHOWN AS FULL SIZE BED
- SEE DETAIL 170
- INCLUDES 6 MATTRESS HANGERS AND 8 BRASS BEDBOLT COVERS

Dimensions of the pencil-post bed.

Pencil-post bed.

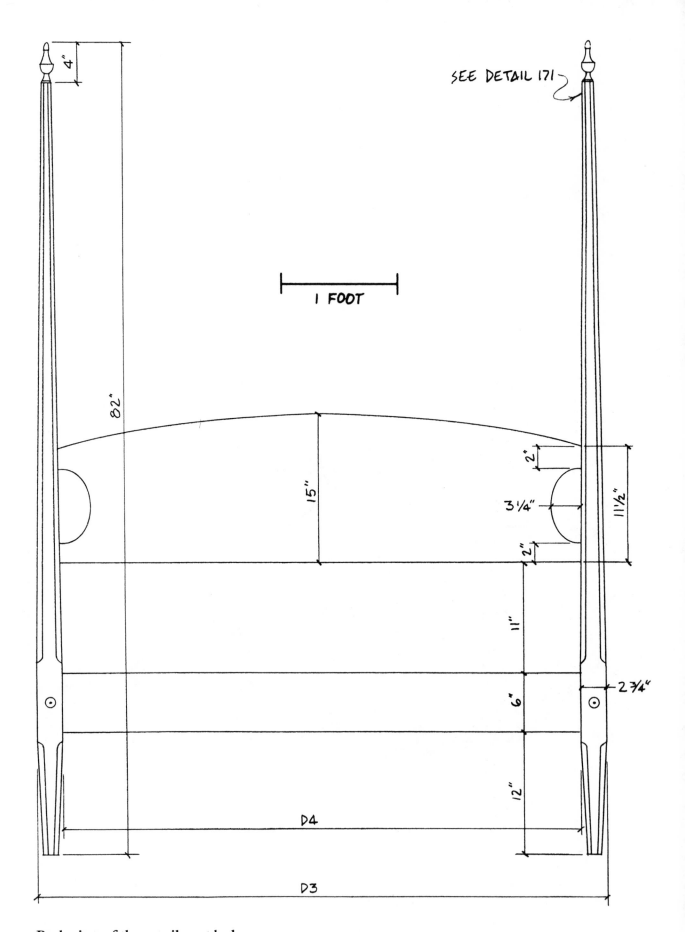

4"

SEE DETAIL 171

1 FOOT

82"

15"

2"

3¼"

11½"

2"

11"

6"

2¾"

12"

D4

D3

Back view of the pencil-post bed.

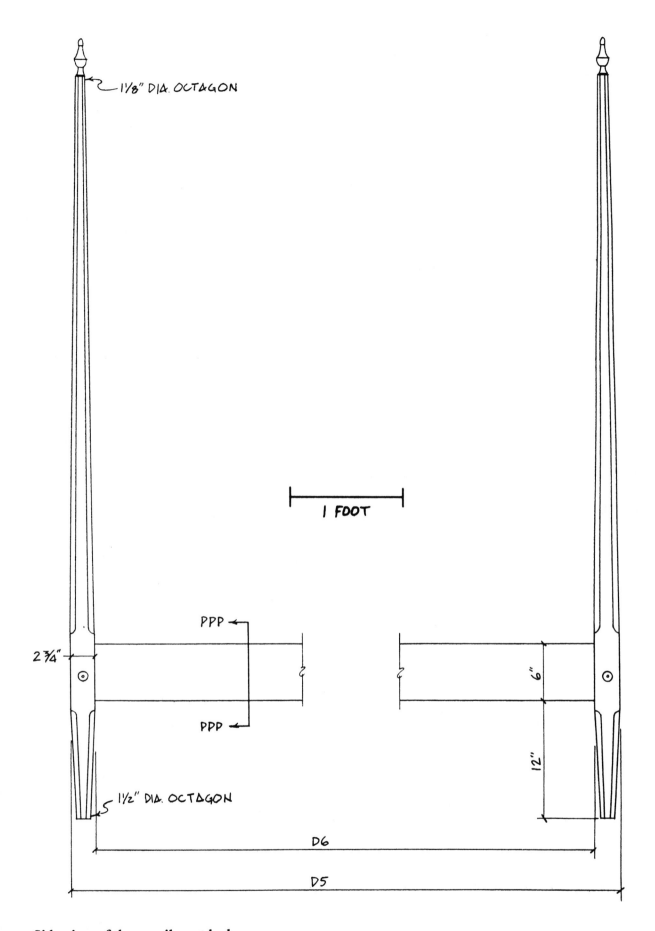

1⅛" DIA. OCTAGON

1 FOOT

PPP ←

2¾"

PPP ←

6"

12"

1½" DIA. OCTAGON

D6

D5

Side view of the pencil-post bed.

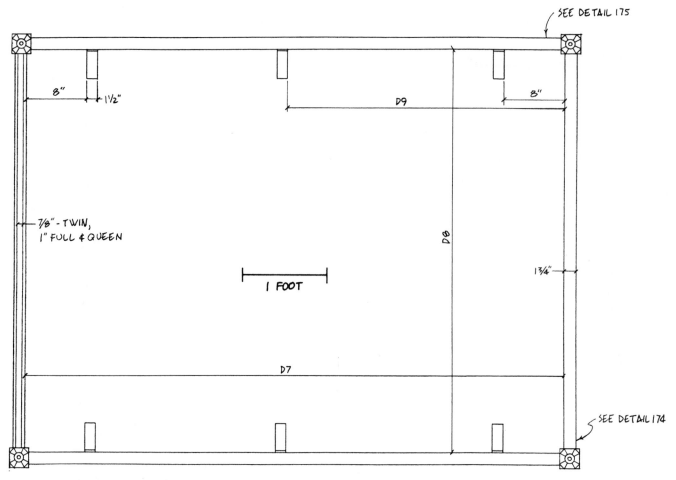

SEE DETAIL 175

8"

1½"

D9

8"

D8

13¾"

⅞" - TWIN,
1" FULL & QUEEN

1 FOOT

D7

SEE DETAIL 174

Top view of the pencil-post bed.

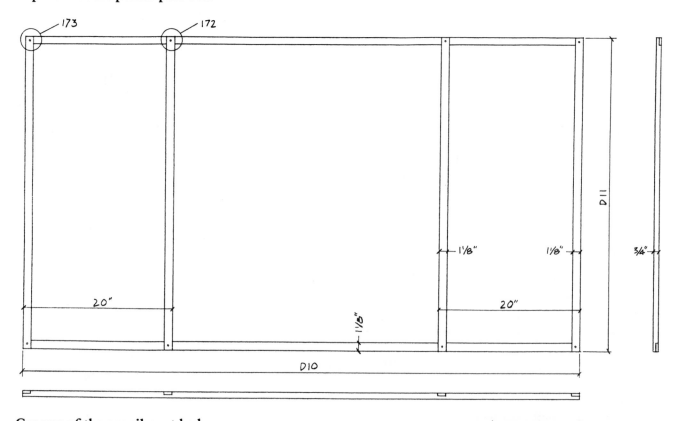

173

172

D11

1⅛"

1⅛"

¾"

20"

20"

1⅛"

D10

Canopy of the pencil-post bed.

1 FOOT

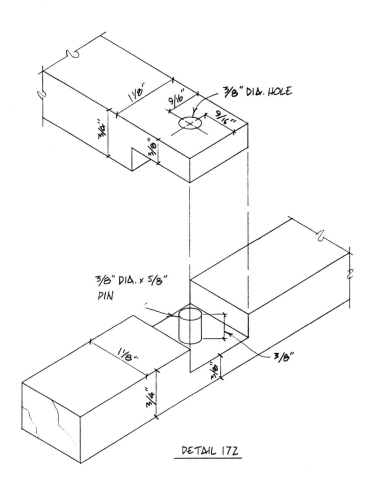

3/8" DIA. HOLE

1⅛"

9/16"

9/16"

3/4"

3/8"

3/8" DIA. × 5/8" PIN

1⅛"

3/4"

3/8"

3/8"

DETAIL 172

├─ 1 INCH ─┤

Details 172 and 173: Canopy.

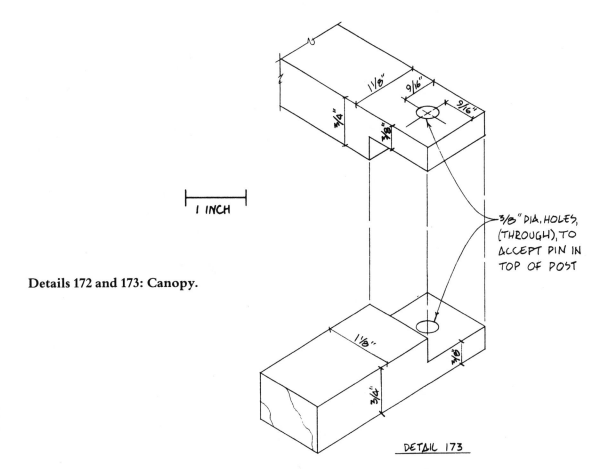

1⅛"

9/16"

9/16"

3/4"

3/8"

3/8" DIA. HOLES, (THROUGH), TO ACCEPT PIN IN TOP OF POST

1⅛"

3/8"

3/4"

DETAIL 173

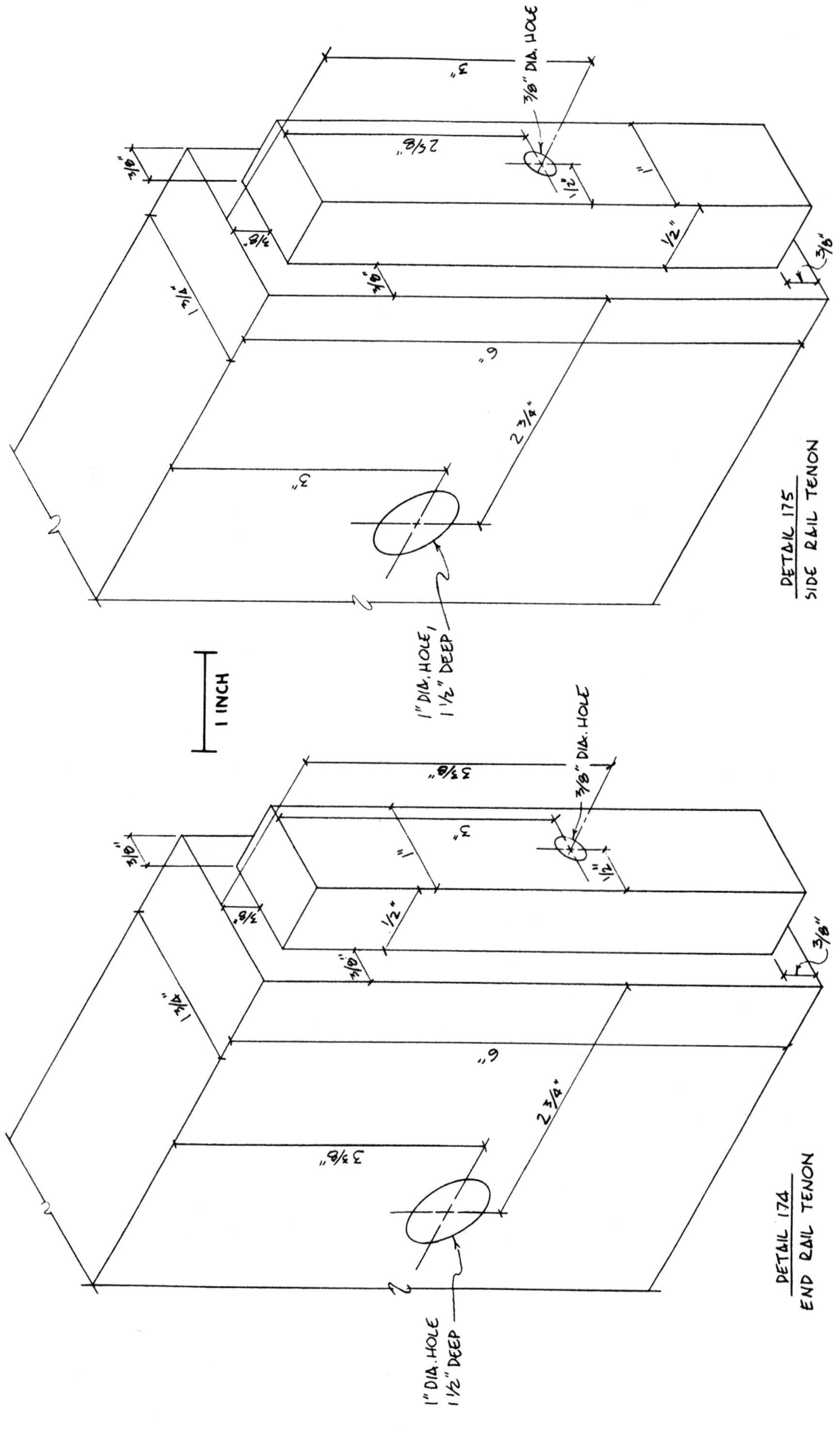

DETAIL 175
SIDE RAIL TENON

DETAIL 174
END RAIL TENON

1 INCH

Rail tenons.

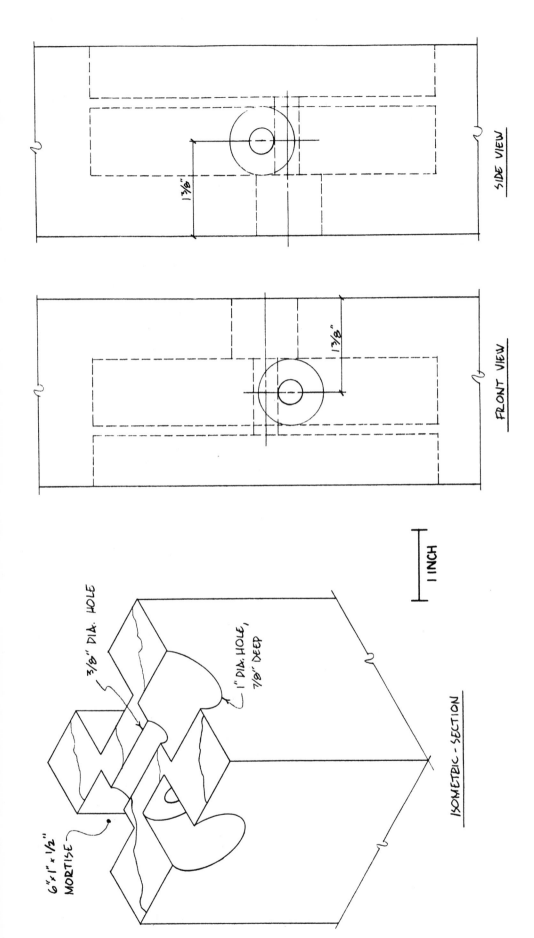

SIDE VIEW

1 3/8"

FRONT VIEW

1 3/8"

1 INCH

3/8" DIA. HOLE

1" DIA. HOLE, 7/8" DEEP

6" x 1" x 1/2" MORTISE

ISOMETRIC - SECTION

Post details.

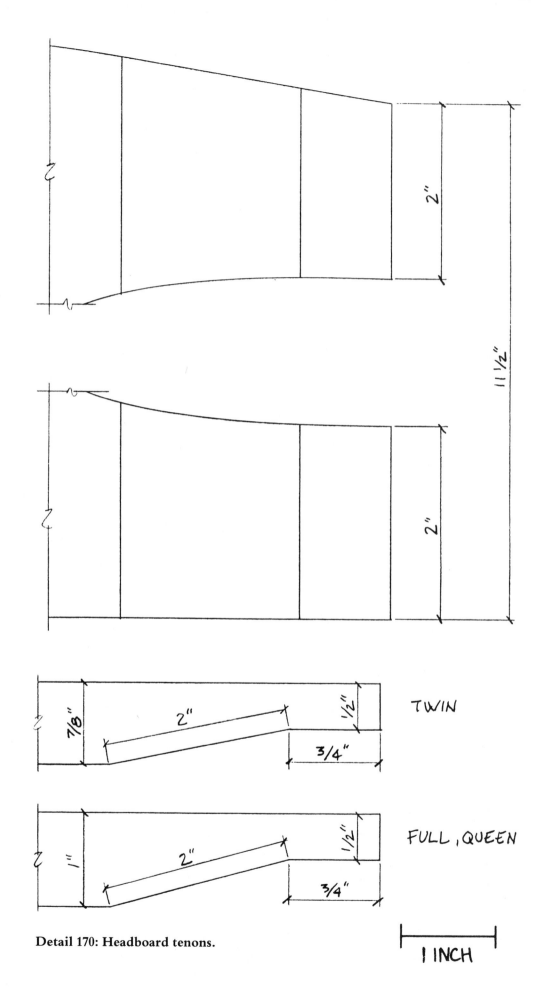

Detail 170: Headboard tenons.

1 INCH

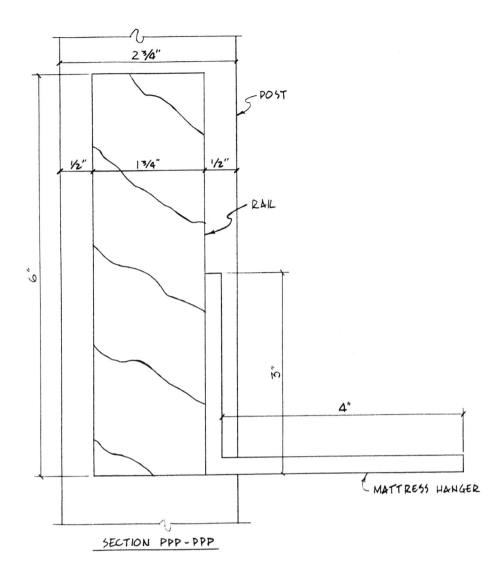

2 3/4"

POST

1/2" · 1 3/4" · 1/2"

RAIL

6"

3"

4"

MATTRESS HANGER

SECTION PPP-PPP

1 INCH

Top of post and section PPP-PPP.

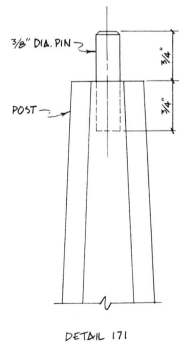

3/8" DIA. PIN

3/4"

POST

3/4"

DETAIL 171

Panel Headboard

The panel headboard is designed to be used with a steel frame, sometimes called a Hollywood frame or Harvard frame. The legs of the headboard are screwed to mounting plates that are permanently attached to the steel frame. The frame carries the bottom of the innerspring foundation to roughly 6 or 7 inches (15.2 or 17.7 cm) from the floor. This, added to the combined mattress and foundation height of 15 inches (38.1 cm), brings the sleeping surface of most contemporary beds to 21 inches (53.3 cm) from the floor. A headboard measuring 38 inches (.96 m) overall leaves plenty of room for pillows to be stacked, enabling one to sit up in bed without leaning against the wall.

Front, top and sides of twin-size panel headboard.

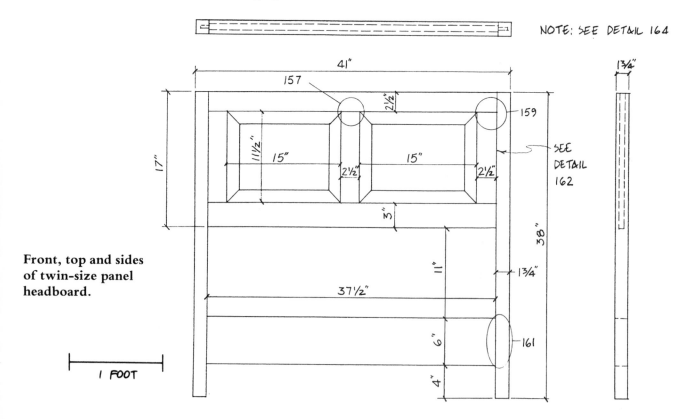

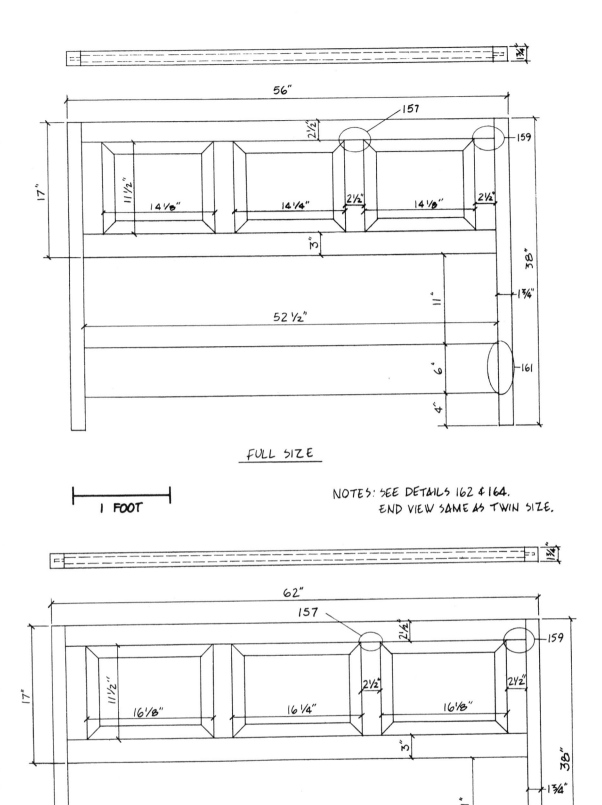

56"

157

2½"

159

17"

11½"

14⅛" 14¼" 2½" 14⅛" 2½"

3"

38"

1¾"

52½"

11"

6"

161

4"

FULL SIZE

|← 1 FOOT →|

NOTES: SEE DETAILS 162 & 164.
END VIEW SAME AS TWIN SIZE.

1¾"

62"

157

2½"

159

17"

11½"

16⅛" 16¼" 2½" 16⅛" 2½"

3"

38"

1¾"

58½"

11"

6"

161

4"

QUEEN SIZE

Full-size and queen-size headboards.

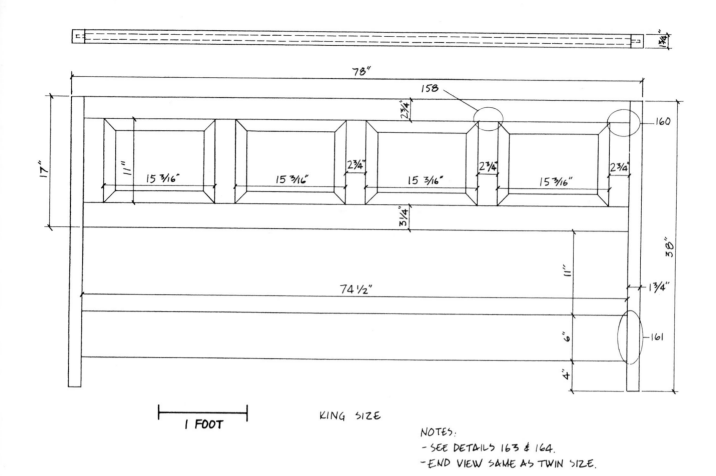

1 FOOT

KING SIZE

NOTES:
- SEE DETAILS 163 & 164.
- END VIEW SAME AS TWIN SIZE.

King-size headboard.

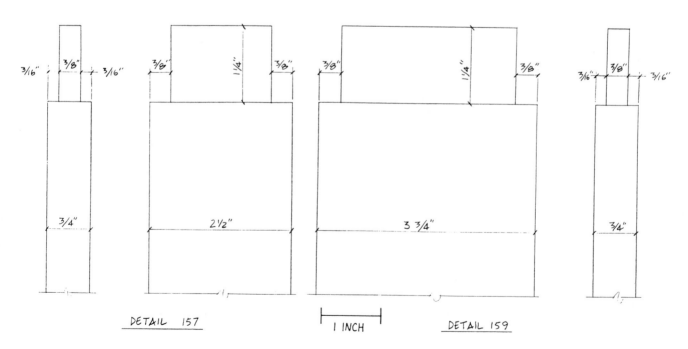

DETAIL 157

1 INCH

DETAIL 159

Stile tenons.

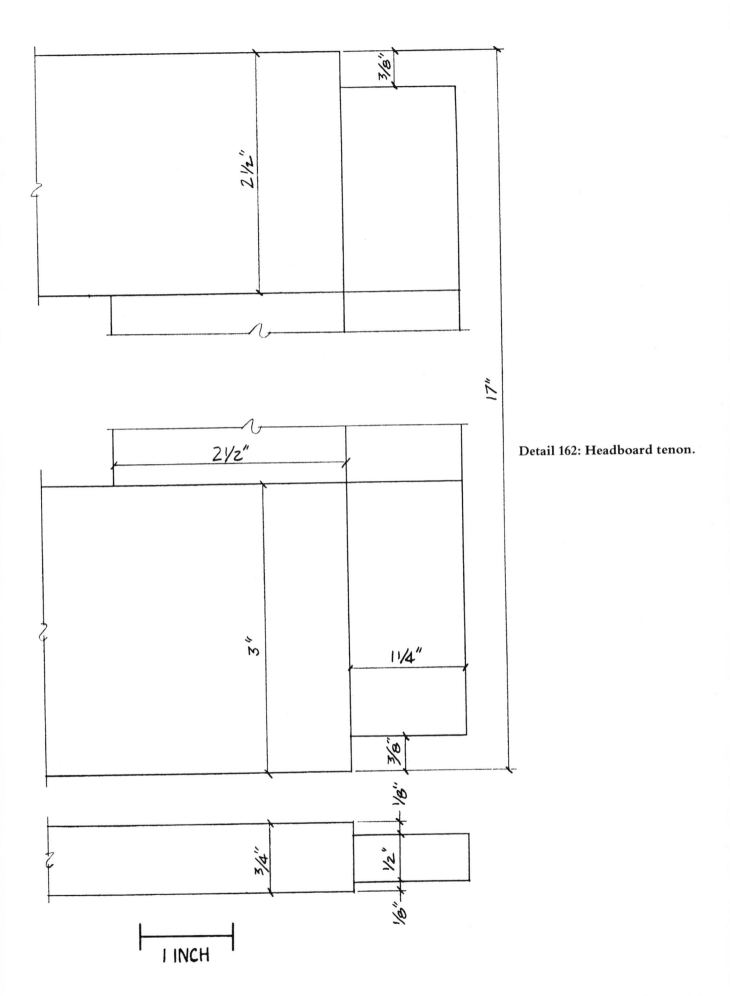

Detail 162: Headboard tenon.

2½"

⅜"

17"

2½"

3"

1¼"

⅜"

⅛"

¾"

½"

⅛"

I INCH

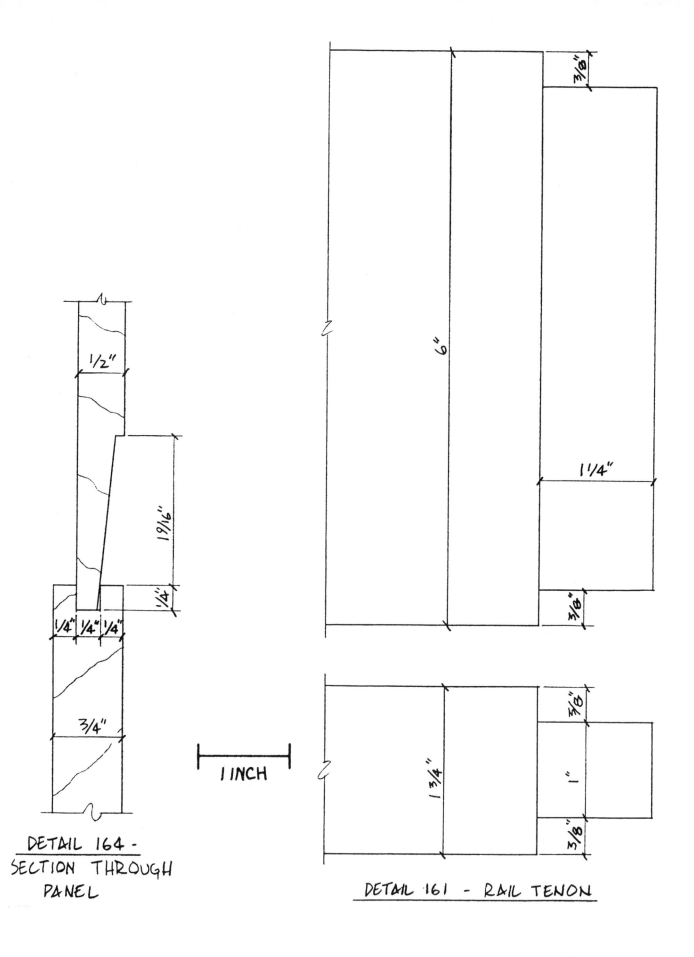

1/2"

19/16"

1/4"

1/4" 1/4" 1/4"

3/4"

DETAIL 164 -
SECTION THROUGH
PANEL

1 INCH

3/8"

6"

1 1/4"

3/8"

3/8"

1 3/4"

1"

3/8"

DETAIL 161 - RAIL TENON

Detail 164: Panel. Detail 161: Rail.

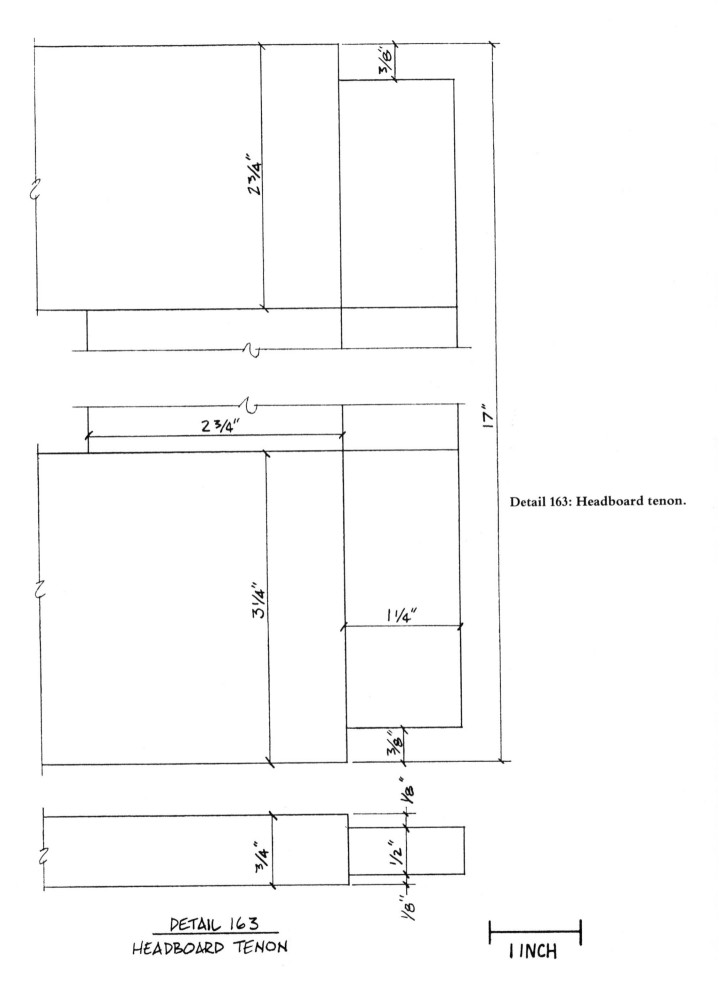

3/8"

2³/4"

17"

2 3/4"

3¹/4"

1¹/4"

3/8"

1/8"

3/4"

1/2"

1/8"

Detail 163: Headboard tenon.

DETAIL 163
HEADBOARD TENON

1 INCH

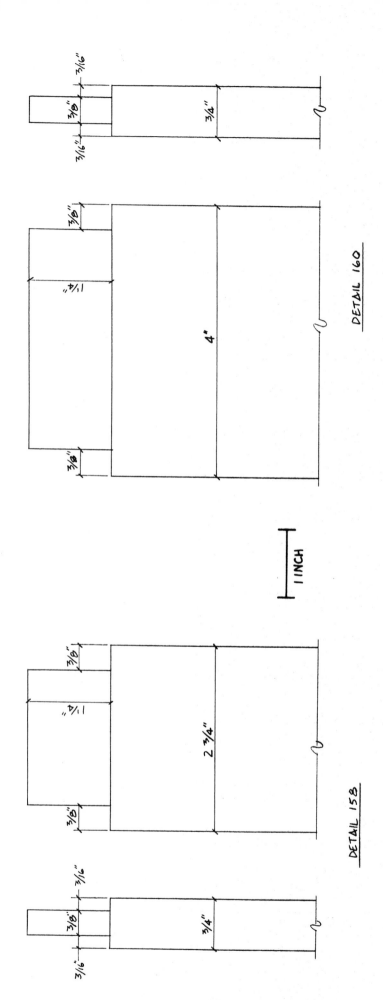

DETAIL 160

DETAIL 158

1 INCH

Details 158 and 160: Stile tenons.

Spindle Headboard

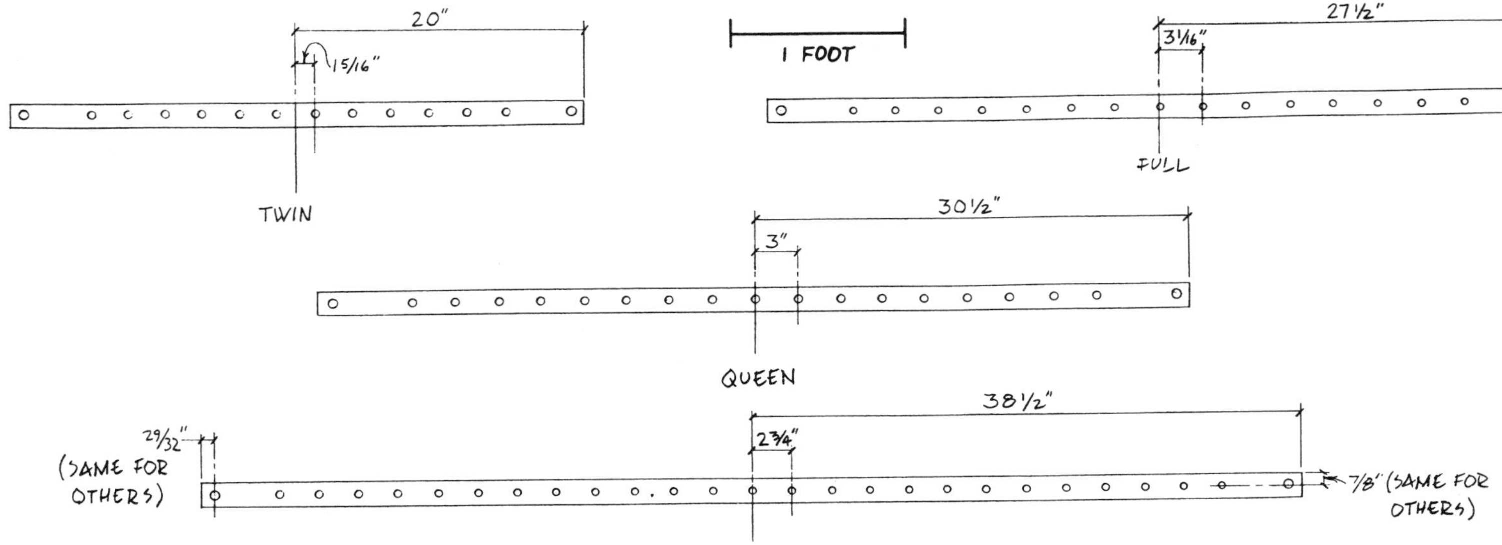

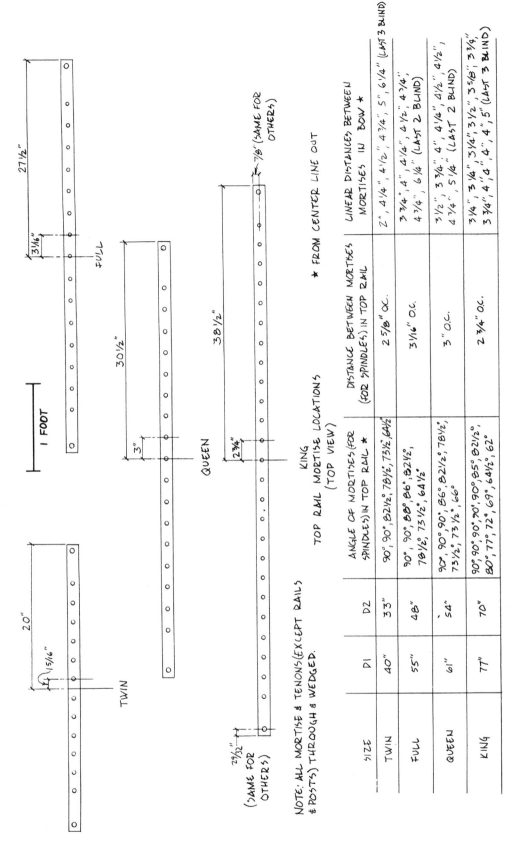

20"
15/16"
TWIN
1 FOOT
27½"
3¹⁄₁₆"
FULL
30½"
3"
QUEEN
38½"
2¾"
29/32"
(SAME FOR OTHERS)
7/8" (SAME FOR OTHERS)

NOTE: ALL MORTISE & TENONS (EXCEPT RAILS & POSTS) THROUGH & WEDGED.

KING

TOP RAIL MORTISE LOCATIONS (TOP VIEW)

★ FROM CENTER LINE OUT

SIZE	D1	D2	ANGLE OF MORTISES (FOR SPINDLES) IN TOP RAIL ★	DISTANCE BETWEEN MORTISES (FOR SPINDLES) IN TOP RAIL	LINEAR DISTANCES BETWEEN MORTISES IN BOW ★
TWIN	40"	33"	90°, 90°, 82½°, 78½°, 73½°, 64½°	2 5/8" O.C.	2", 4¼", 4½", 4¾", 5", 6¼" (LAST 3 BLIND)
FULL	55"	48"	90°, 90°, 88°, 86°, 82½°, 78½°, 73½°, 64½°	3¹⁄₁₆" O.C.	3¾", 4", 4¼", 4½", 4¾", 4¾", 6¼" (LAST 2 BLIND)
QUEEN	61"	54"	90°, 90°, 90°, 86°, 82½°, 78½°, 73½°, 73½°, 66°	3" O.C.	3½", 3¾", 4", 4¼", 4½", 4½", 4¾", 5¼" (LAST 2 BLIND)
KING	77"	70"	90°, 90°, 90°, 90°, 90°, 85°, 82½°, 80°, 77°, 72°, 69°, 64½°, 62°	2¾" O.C.	3¼", 3¼", 3¼", 3½", 3⅝", 3¾", 3¾", 4", 4", 4", 4", 5" (LAST 3 BLIND)

The spindle headboard incorporates many building techniques found in Windsor chairs. The curved portion of the headboard is made of nine to twelve strips laminated together and shaped while the spindles are turned in ash. This design is a good example of how a technique (the laminate curve) can be adapted to different uses. Here are the dimensions and drilling patterns for the spindle headboard. For the front, side and top views see the following page.

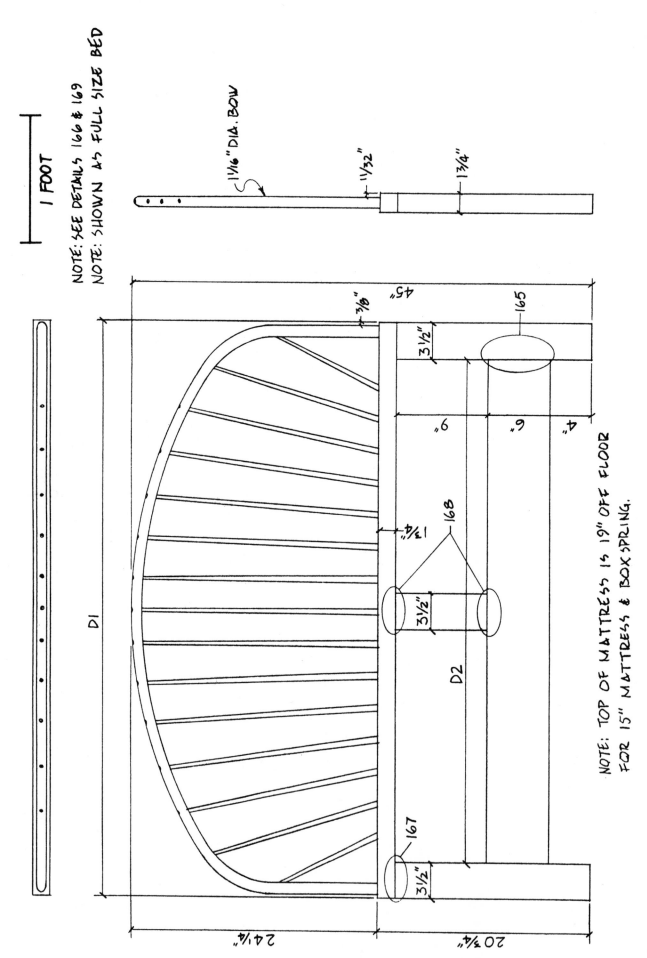

NOTE: SEE DETAILS 166 & 169

NOTE: SHOWN AS FULL SIZE BED

1 FOOT

1 1/16" DIA. BOW

1 1/32"

1 3/4"

45"

3/8"

165

3 1/2"

6"

6"

4"

168

1 3/4"

3 1/2"

D2

D1

167

3 1/2"

24 1/4"

20 3/4"

NOTE: TOP OF MATTRESS IS 19" OFF FLOOR FOR 15" MATTRESS & BOX SPRING.

Spindle headboard. For width (DI), consult table on page 245.

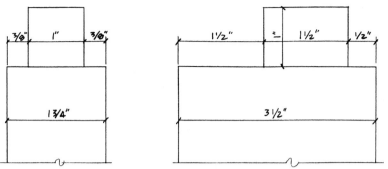

DETAIL 167 - POST TENON

1 INCH

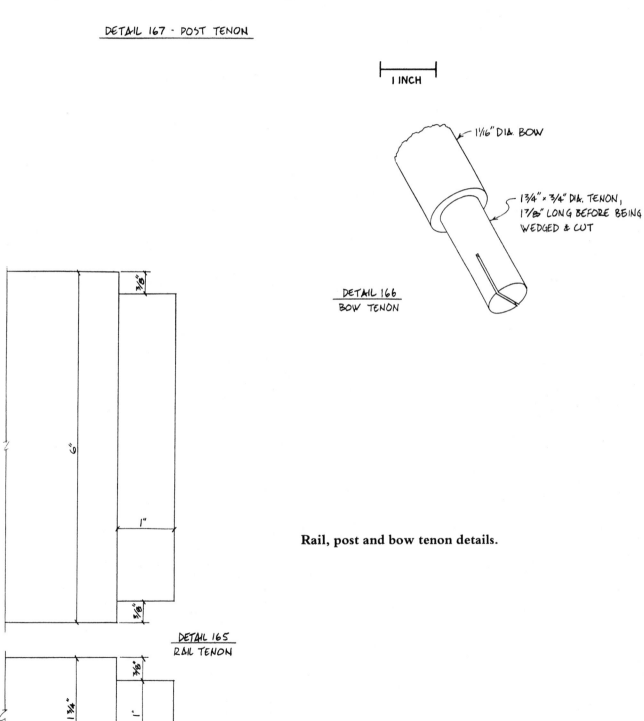

1¹/₁₆″ DIA. BOW

1³/₄″ × ³/₄″ DIA. TENON,
1⁷/₈″ LONG BEFORE BEING
WEDGED & CUT

DETAIL 166
BOW TENON

DETAIL 165
RAIL TENON

Rail, post and bow tenon details.

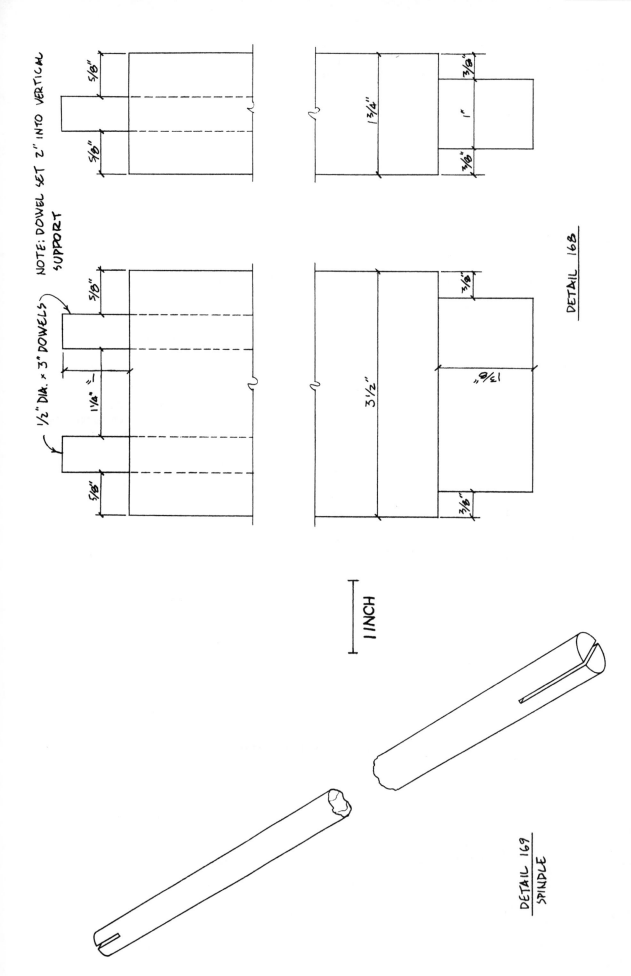

NOTE: DOWEL SET 2" INTO VERTICAL SUPPORT

5/8"

5/8"

1 3/4"

3/8"

1"

3/8"

DETAIL 168

1/2" DIA. × 3" DOWELS

5/8"

1 1/4"

5/8"

3 1/2"

3/8"

1 3/8"

3/8"

1 INCH

DETAIL 169
SPINDLE

Detail 168: Support. Detail 169: Support.

Spindle Bed

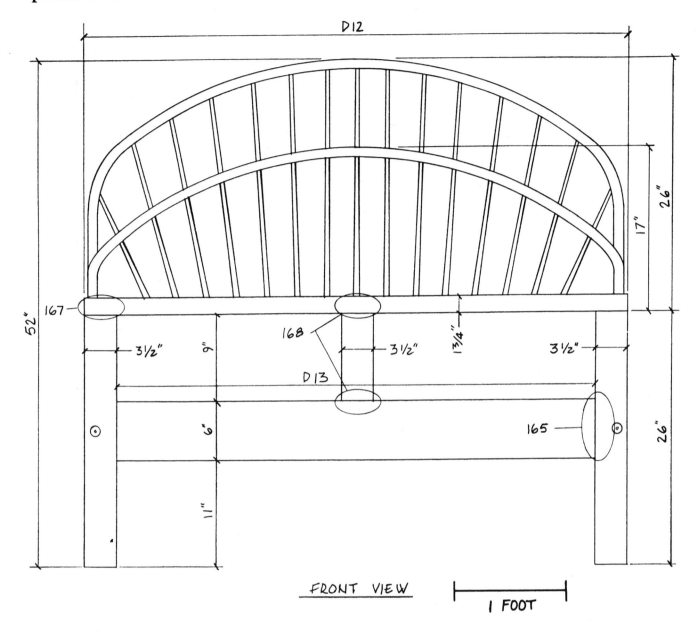

FRONT VIEW

1 FOOT

If a footboard is desired, it can be joined to the headboard with side rails that would also support the mattress in the conventional way. When wood-framed foundation box springs are used in the bed, then steel mattress hangers, three on a side, are usually sufficient to support the foundation. When a mattress is used without a foundation, then it is necessary to put plywood across the base to support the mattress. There were a number of other arrangements we have followed in supporting a mattress, but we have concluded that one-quarter-inch steel mattress hangers without bed boards are the best approach.

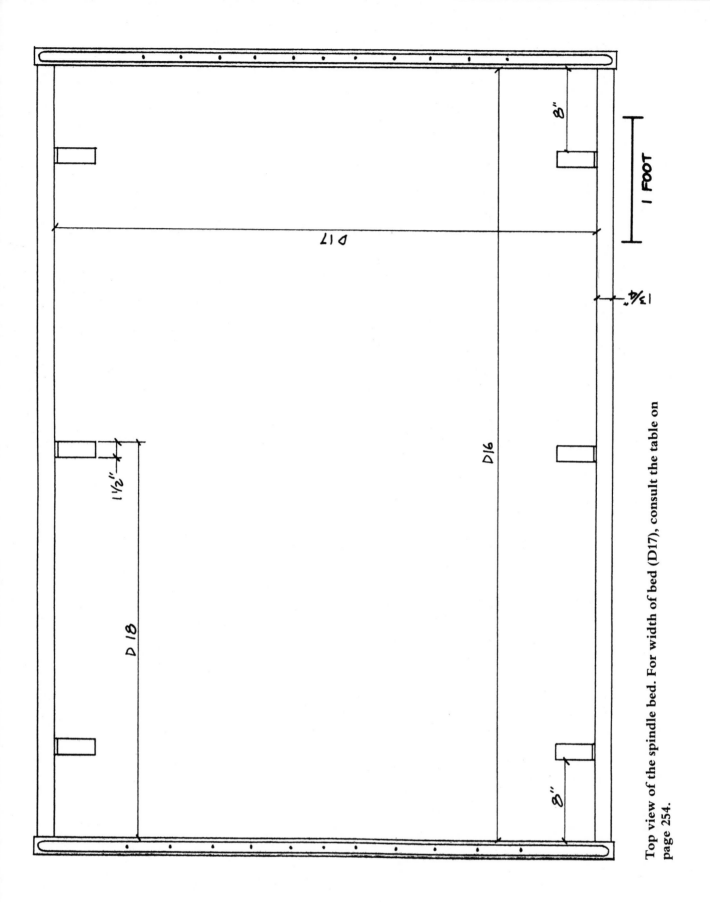

8"

1 FOOT

D17

1¾"

D16

1½"

D18

8"

Top view of the spindle bed. For width of bed (D17), consult the table on page 254.

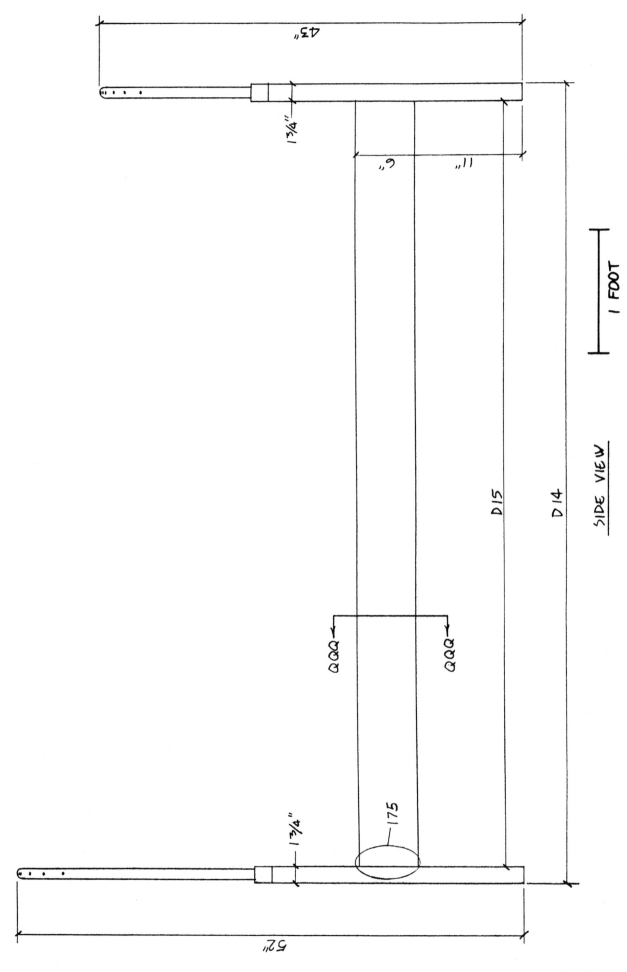

Side view of the spindle bed.

SPINDLE BED 251

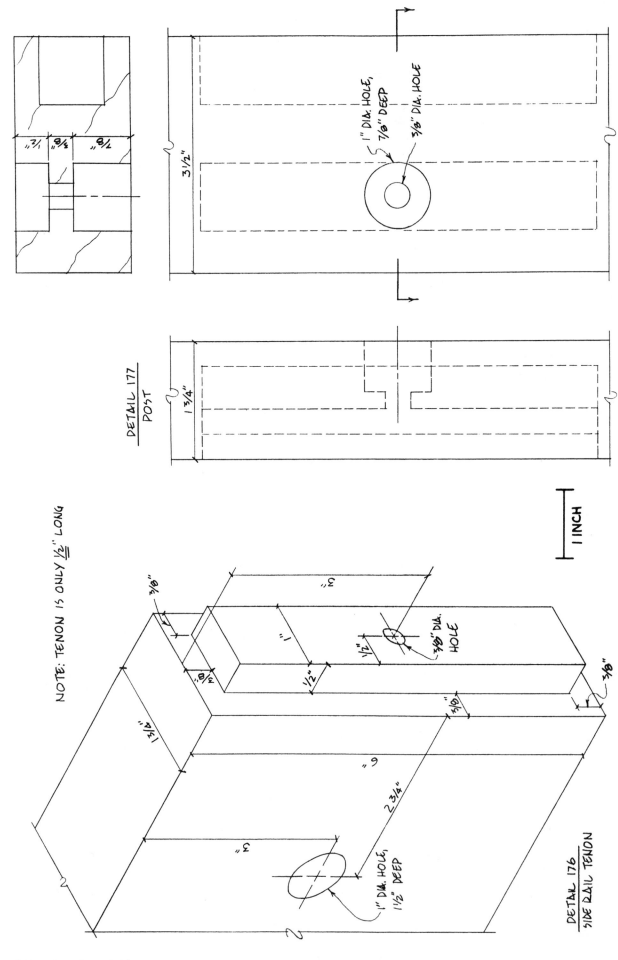

1/2" 3/4" 7/8"

3 1/2"

1" DIA. HOLE, 7/8" DEEP

5/8" DIA. HOLE

DETAIL 177
POST

1 3/4"

1 INCH

NOTE: TENON IS ONLY 1/2" LONG

3/8"

3"

1"

3/4"

1/2"

1/2"

5/8" DIA. HOLE

5/8"

1 3/4"

3/8"

6"

2 3/4"

3"

1" DIA. HOLE, 1 1/2" DEEP

DETAIL 176
SIDE RAIL TENON

Detail 176: Rail tenon. Detail 177: Post.

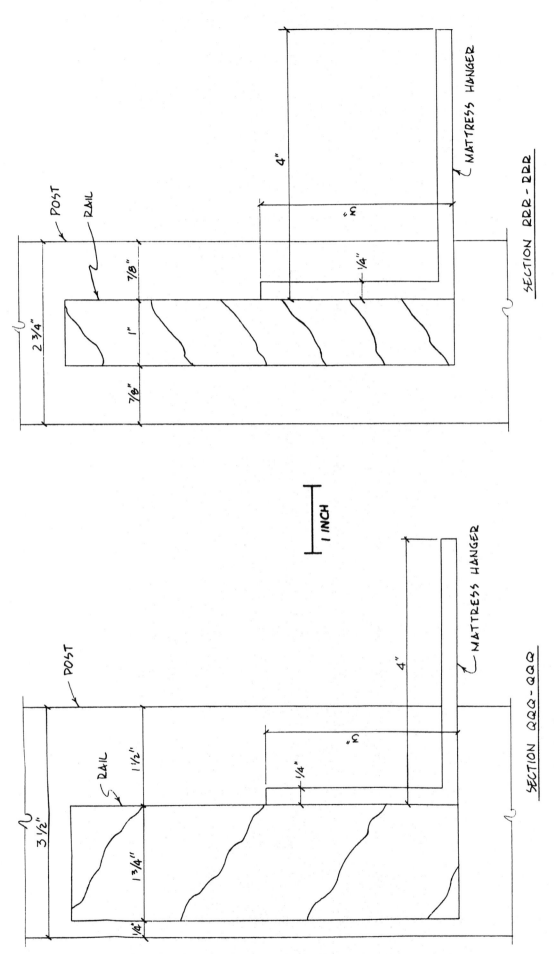

POST

RAIL

2 3/4"

7/8"

1"

7/8"

4"

3"

1/4"

MATTRESS HANGER

<u>SECTION RRR - RRR</u>

1 INCH

POST

RAIL

3 1/2"

1 1/2"

1 3/4"

1/4"

1/4"

4"

3"

MATTRESS HANGER

<u>SECTION QQQ - QQQ</u>

Sections QQQ-QQQ and RRR-RRR.

DIMENSIONS

Mattress Size	SIZE	Outside width D12	Shoulder to shoulder Rail Length D13	Outside Length D14	Shoulder to shoulder Side Rail D15	Inside Length D16	Inside width D17	Mattress Hanger Location D18
39 x 75	TWIN	44"	37"	79"	75½"	75½"	40"	37 3/8"
54 x 75	FULL	59"	52"	79"	75½"	75½"	55"	37 3/8"
60 x 80	QUEEN	65"	58"	84"	80½"	80½"	61"	40 7/8"

OVERALL DIMENSIONS: TWIN - 44" × 79" × 52", FULL - 59" × 79" × 52", QUEEN - 65" × 84" × 52"

SIZE	DISTANCE BETWEEN TOP RAIL SPINDLE MORTISES*	ANGLES OF TOP RAIL SPINDLE MORTISES*†	LINEAR DISTANCES BETWEEN BOW MORTISES - HEADBOARD†	LINEAR DISTANCES BETWEEN BOW MORTISES - FOOTBOARD†
TWIN	2 3/4" O.C.	90°, 90°, 82½°, 78½°, 73½°, 64½°		(LAST 3 BLIND
FULL	3 3/16" O.C.	90°, 90°, 88°, 86°, 82½°, 78½°, 73½°, 64½°		(LAST 2 BLIND)
QUEEN	3 1/8" O.C.	90°, 90°, 90°, 86°, 82½°, 78½°, 73½°, 73½°, 66°	3 3/4", 3 7/8", 4 1/8", 4 3/8", 4 3/8", 4 3/8", 4½", 6"	3 5/8", 3 3/4", 4", 4 1/4", 4", 4", 3 3/4", 3½" (LAST 2 BLND)

* SAME FOR HEADBOARD & FOOTBOARD
† FROM CENTER LINE OUT

NOTES:
- SEE DETAILS 166 & 169
- SHOWN AS FULL SIZE BED
- BOTH BOWS 1 1/16" DIA.
- INCLUDES 6 MATTRESS HANGERS
- TWIN AND FULL SIZE BEDS DO NOT HAVE CENTER SUPPORT IN HEADBOARD OR FOOTBOARD

Drilling patterns for the spindle bed.

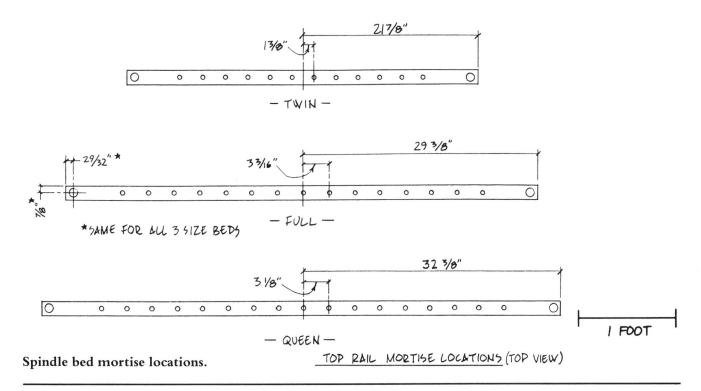

$2 1/8''$

$1 3/8''$

— TWIN —

$29 3/8''$

$29/32'' ★$

$3 3/16''$

$7/8''$

*SAME FOR ALL 3 SIZE BEDS

— FULL —

$32 3/8''$

$3 1/8''$

— QUEEN —

1 FOOT

Spindle bed mortise locations.

TOP RAIL MORTISE LOCATIONS (TOP VIEW)

Low-Post Bed

By definition, the low-post bed presents a low profile in a bedroom, but offers more interest than a mattress and foundation on a steel frame. This bed is designed to be knocked down, in that the headboard and footboard are separate assemblies held together by rails. The low-post bed functions well as a twin-, full-, queen- or king-size bed frame. As in all the pencil-post and spindle beds, bed bolts are used to attach the legs to the side rails.

SIZE

		TWIN	FULL	QUEEN
OUTSIDE WIDTH	D 19	43 3/4"	58 3/4"	64 3/4"
SH. TO SH. LENGTH	D 20	38 1/4"	53 1/4"	59 1/4"
SH. TO SH. HDBD. LENGTH	D 21	38 3/8"	53 3/8"	59 3/8"
INSIDE LENGTH	D 22	77 1/4"	77 1/4"	82 1/4"
SIDE RAIL SH. TO SH. LENGTH	D 23	75 1/2"	75 1/2"	80 1/2"
OUTSIDE LENGTH	D 24	81"	81"	86"
INSIDE WIDTH	D 25	40"	55"	61"
MATTRESS HANGER LOC.	D 26	37 1/8"	37 1/8"	39 5/8"

NOTES:
- SEE DETAILS 178, 179, 180
- SHOWN AS FULL SIZE BED
- INCLUDES 6 MATTRESS HANGERS
- END RAIL TENON SAME AS SIDE RAIL TENON (178), EXCEPT FOR NO BEDBOLT HOLES.

OVERALL DIMENSIONS
TWIN   43 3/4" × 81" × 39"
FULL   58 3/4" × 81" × 39"
QUEEN   64 3/4" × 86" × 39"

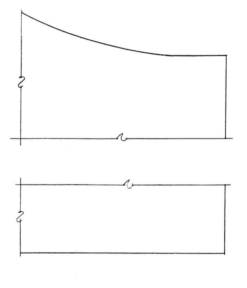

NOTE: TENON ACCEPTED BY 3/4" DEEP MORTISE

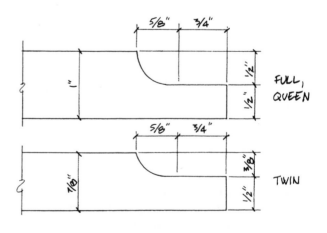

DETAIL 180
HEADBOARD TENON

Dimensions of the low-post bed. Also, the headboard tenon.

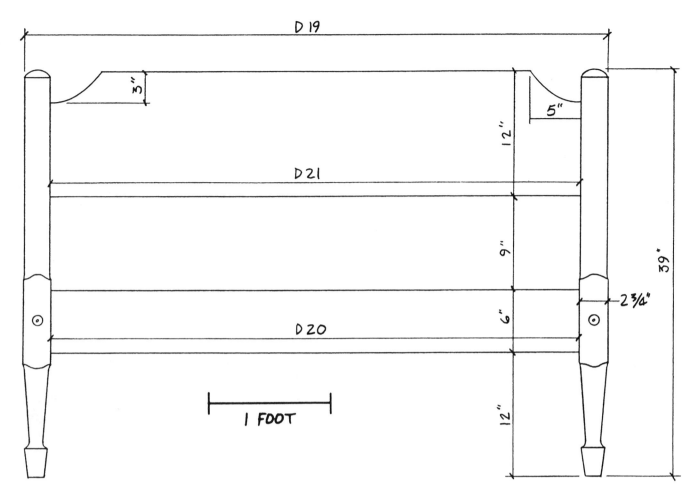

Back view of the low-post bed.

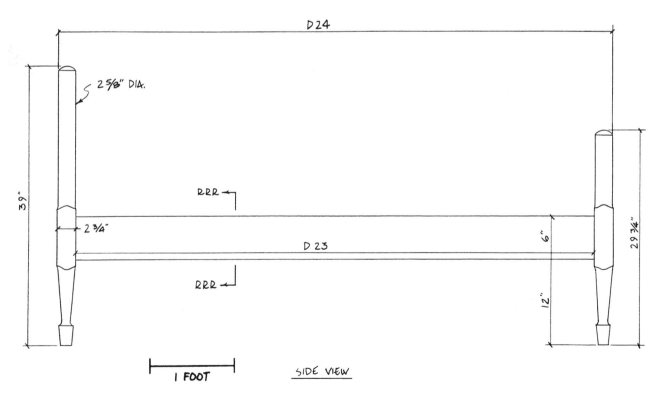

Side view of the low-post bed.

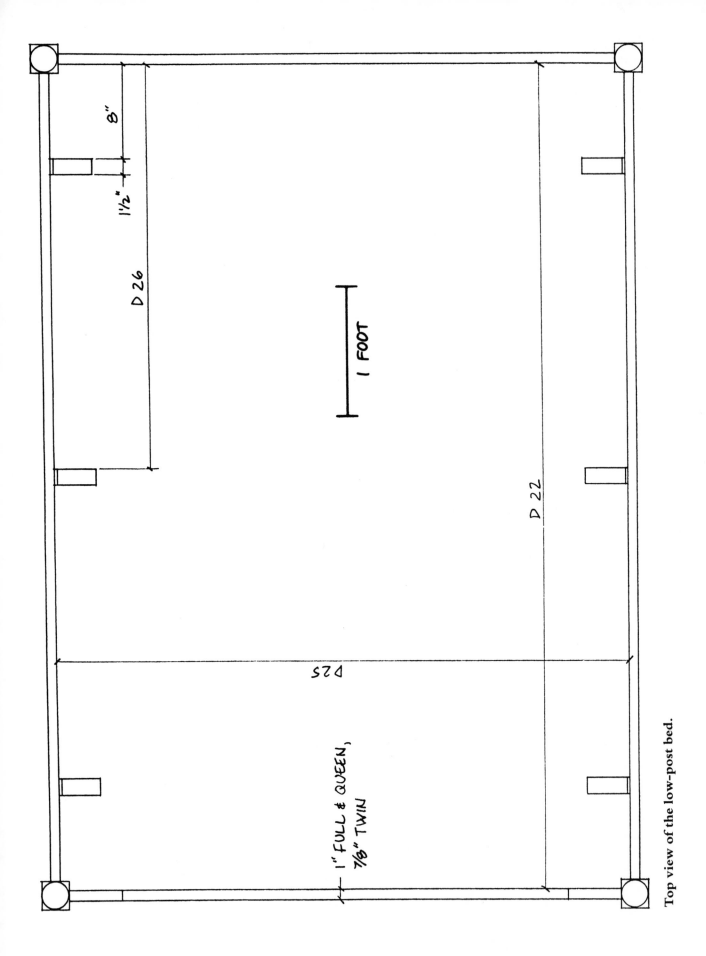

8″

1½″

▷ 26

1 FOOT

▷ 22

▷ 25

1″ FULL & QUEEN,
7/8″ TWIN

Top view of the low-post bed.

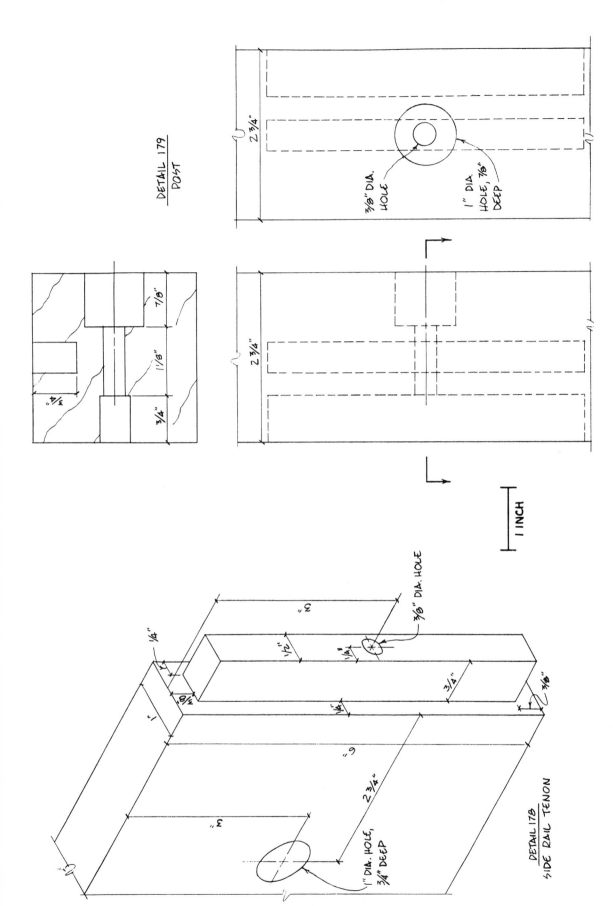

3/8" DIA.
HOLE

1" DIA.
HOLE, 7/8"
DEEP

2 3/4"

7/8"

1 1/8"

3/4"

3/4"

2 3/4"

1 INCH

3"

1/2"

1/4"

3/8" DIA. HOLE

1/4"

3/4"

3/4"

1/4"

1

3/4"

6"

2 3/4"

3"

3/4"

1" DIA. HOLE,
3/4" DEEP

DETAIL 178
SIDE RAIL TENON

Detail 178: Rail tenon. Detail 179: Post.

MISCELLANEOUS PIECES

Wall Clock

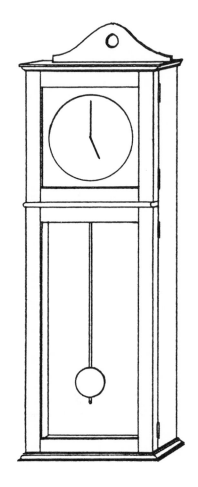

PERSPECTIVE

1 FOOT

In the early 19th century, the Shakers built a great variety of clocks. This wall clock is a synthesis of several early Shaker models. It exists with virtually no ornamentation except the mechanism itself, that is, the pendulum and dial. The clear-glass lower panel offers a full view of the pendulum in motion, reminding us that time is motion. See the photograph on the following page.

Wall clock.

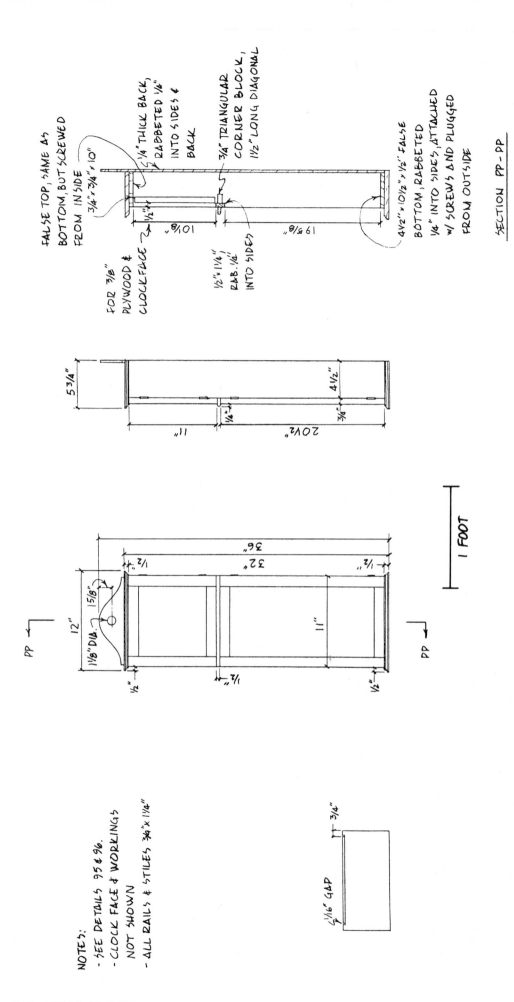

SECTION PP-PP

FALSE TOP, SAME AS BOTTOM, BUT SCREWED FROM INSIDE 3/4" × 3/4" × 10"

1/4" THICK BACK, RABBETED 1/4" INTO SIDES & BACK

3/4" TRIANGULAR CORNER BLOCK, 11/2" LONG DIAGONAL

FOR 3/8" PLYWOOD & CLOCKFACE

1/2" 11/4" RAB. 1/4" INTO SIDES

4 1/2" × 10 1/2" × 1/2" FALSE BOTTOM, RABBETED 1/4" INTO SIDES, ATTACHED W/ SCREWS AND PLUGGED FROM OUTSIDE

10 1/8"

19 5/8"

5 3/4"

11"

20 1/2"

1/4"

4 1/2"

3/4"

1 FOOT

PP

PP

12"

15/8"

1 1/8" DIA.

36"

32"

1/2"

1/2"

11"

1/2"

1/2"

PP

3/4"

1/16" GAP

NOTES:
- SEE DETAILS 95 & 96.
- CLOCK FACE & WORKINGS NOT SHOWN
- ALL RAILS & STILES 3/4" × 11/4"

Top, front and side views of the wall clock, and section PP-PP.

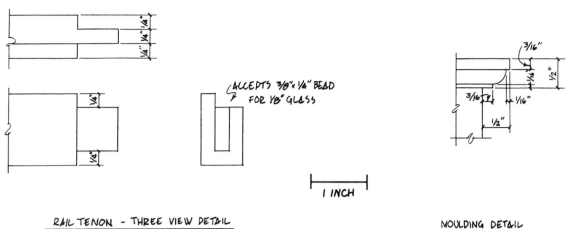

ACCEPTS 3/8" x 1/4" BEAD
FOR 1/8" GLASS

1 INCH

RAIL TENON - THREE VIEW DETAIL

MOULDING DETAIL

Moulding and door details.

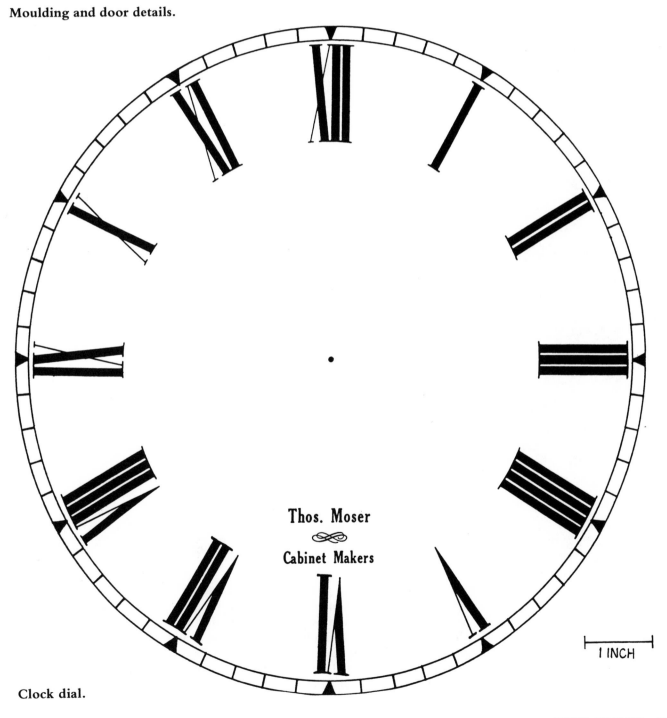

Thos. Moser

Cabinet Makers

1 INCH

Clock dial.

Tall Clock

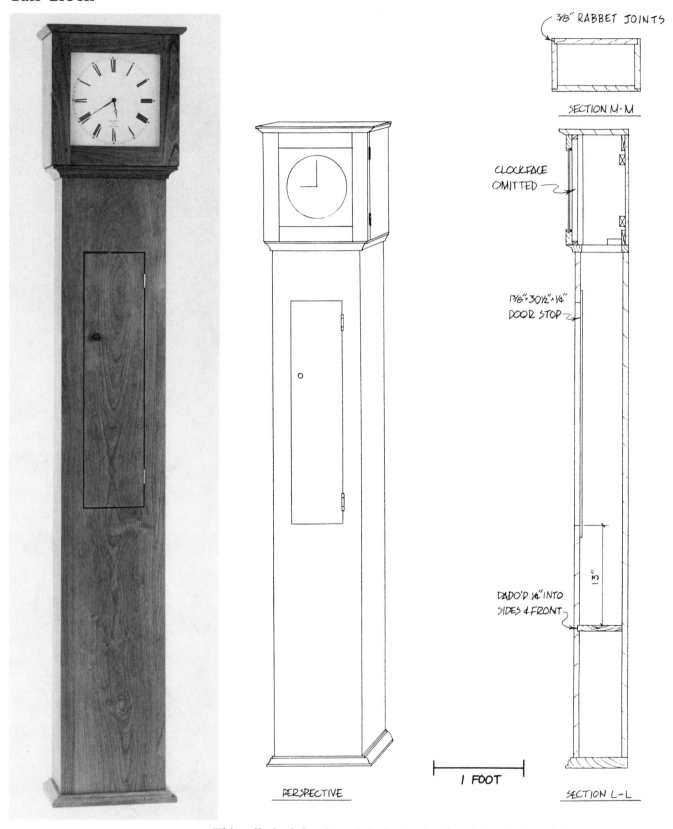

SECTION M-M

⅜" RABBET JOINTS

CLOCKFACE
OMITTED

1⅜" 30½" × ¼"
DOOR STOP

13"

DADO'D ¼" INTO
SIDES & FRONT

PERSPECTIVE

1 FOOT

SECTION L-L

This tall clock has its origin in England, where clocks of this sort stood in hallways and were high not only to provide a better view of the dial, but also to house the 30-inch (76.2-cm) pendulum and massive weight and chain mechanism needed to drive the movement. The 30-inch pendulum produced a one-second interval between "tick" and "tock." At right is the perspective of the tall clock.

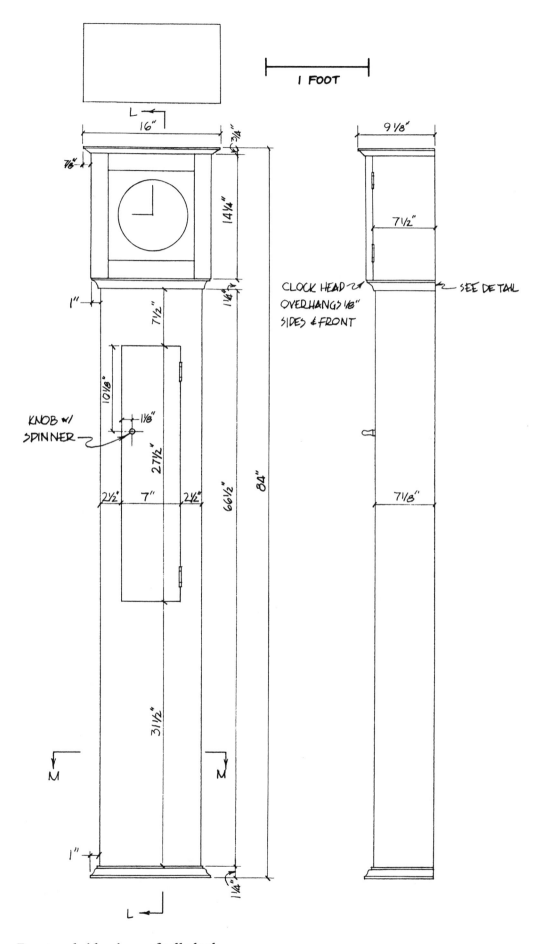

1 FOOT

16"

2 3/4"

7/8"

14 1/4"

1"

1 1/4"

7 1/2"

9 1/8"

7 1/2"

CLOCK HEAD
OVERHANGS 1/8"
SIDES & FRONT

SEE DETAIL

10 1/8"

KNOB w/
SPINNER

1 1/8"

27 1/2"

2 1/2"   7"   2 1/2"

66 1/2"

84"

7 1/8"

M

M

31 1/2"

1"

1 1/4"

L

L

Front and side views of tall clock.

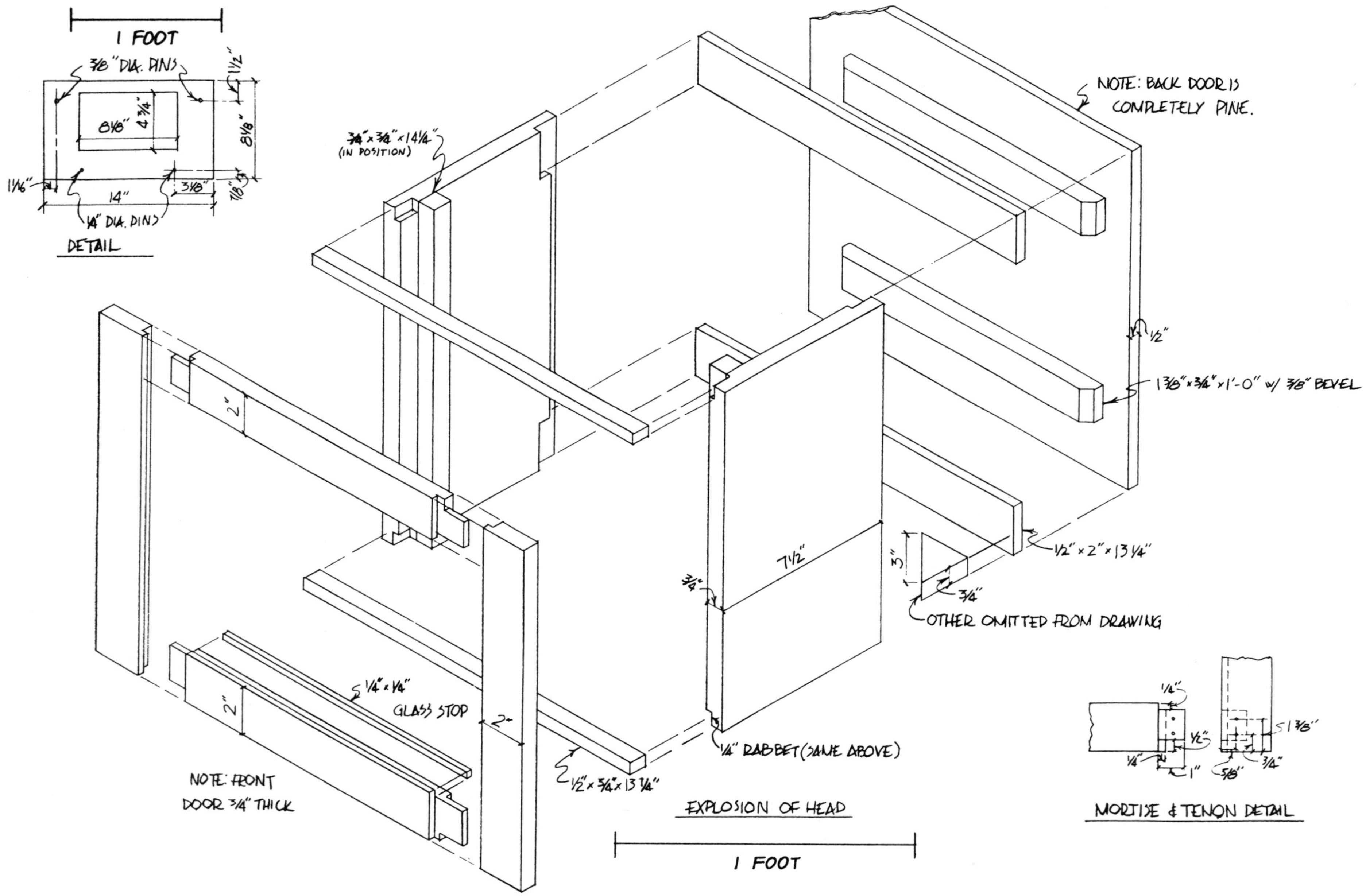
1 FOOT
3/8" DIA. PINS
1 1/2"
8 1/8"
4 3/4"
8 1/8"
1 1/16"
14"
3 1/8"
7/8"
1/4" DIA. PINS
DETAIL
3/4" x 3/4" x 14 1/4" (IN POSITION)
NOTE: BACK DOOR IS COMPLETELY PINE.
1/2"
1 3/8" x 3/4" x 1'-0" w/ 3/8" BEVEL
2"
7 1/2"
3/4"
3"
3/4"
1/2" x 2" x 13 1/4"
OTHER OMITTED FROM DRAWING
1/4" x 1/4"
GLASS STOP
NOTE: FRONT DOOR 3/4" THICK
1/2" x 3/4" x 13 1/4"
1/4" RABBET (SAME ABOVE)
EXPLOSION OF HEAD
1 FOOT
1/4"
1/2"
1/4"
1"
5/8"
3/4"
1 3/8"
MORTISE & TENON DETAIL

Exploded bonnet.

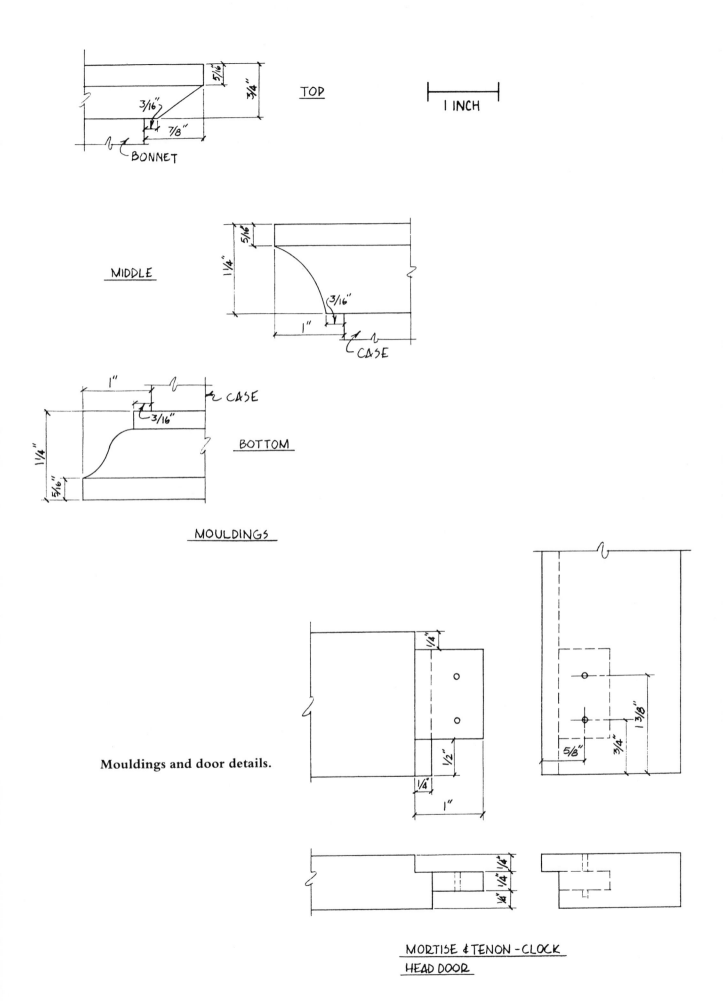

TOP

1 INCH

MIDDLE

BOTTOM

MOULDINGS

Mouldings and door details.

MORTISE & TENON - CLOCK
HEAD DOOR

Tall clock dial.

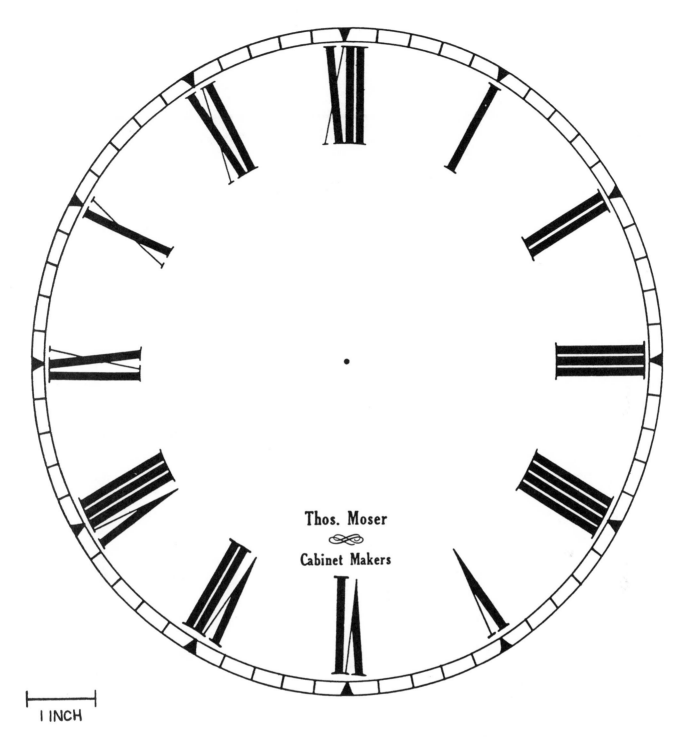

Thos. Moser
Cabinet Makers

⊢——⊣
I INCH

Perspective of the tall clock dial.

Sidestand

Measuring 18″ × 18″ × 27″ (45.7 × 45.7 × 68.5 cm), the sidestand is one of the most universal pieces of furniture. It can be used in several places: next to a reading chair or couch; in a hallway to hold a lamp; or next to a bed to hold the alarm clock. With its small drawer, it even offers some storage space.

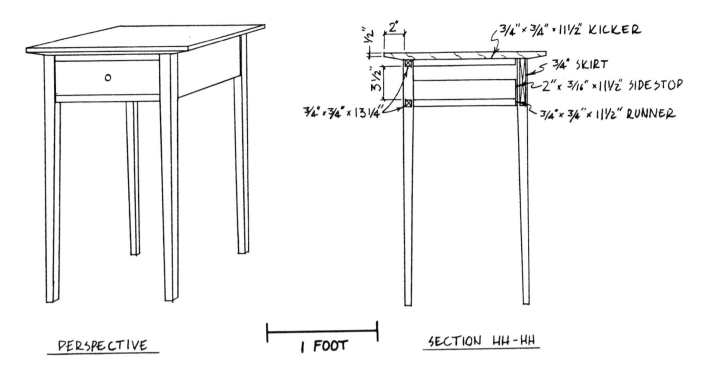

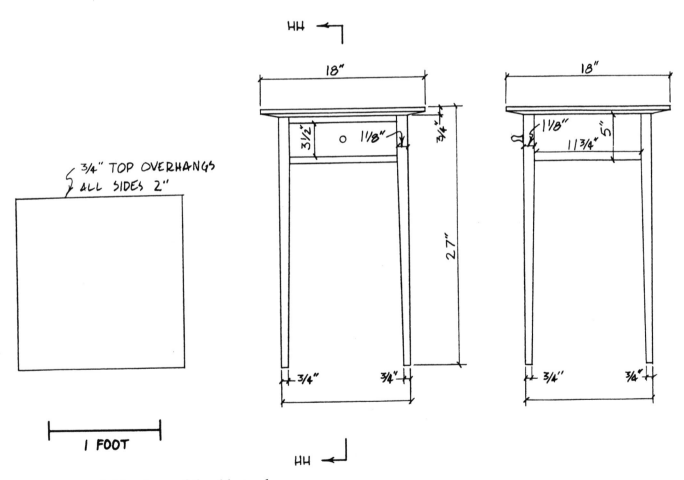

PERSPECTIVE

|—— 1 FOOT ——|

SECTION HH-HH

3/4" × 3/4" × 11 1/2" KICKER

3/4" SKIRT

2" × 3/16" × 11 1/2" SIDESTOP

3/4" × 3/4" × 11 1/2" RUNNER

3/4" × 3/4" × 13 1/4"

1/2"

2"

3 1/2"

Perspective of the sidestand and section HH-HH.

HH ←

3/4" TOP OVERHANGS
ALL SIDES 2"

|—— 1 FOOT ——|

18"

3 1/2"

1 1/8"

3/4"

2 7"

3/4"   3/4"

18"

1 1/8"

5"

1 3/4"

3/4"   3/4"

HH ←

Front, top and side views of the sidestand.

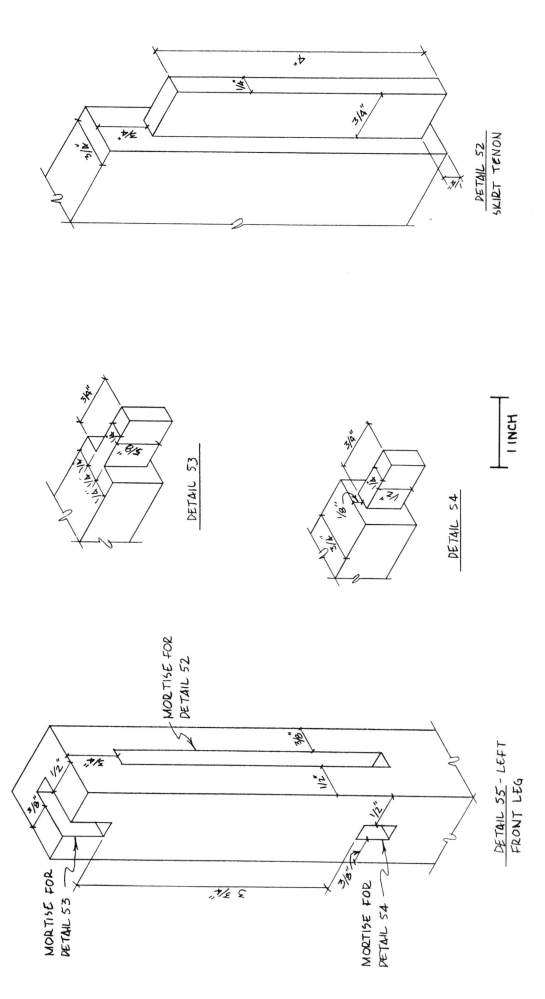

Details 52 and 53: Skirt tenons. Details 54 and 55: Leg.

Roundstand #1

This is a variation of a table that was built by the Shakers in the early 19th century. The use of the quarter-round legs, so far as I know, was unique to the Shaker original. Imagine, a totally contemporary form in 1830!

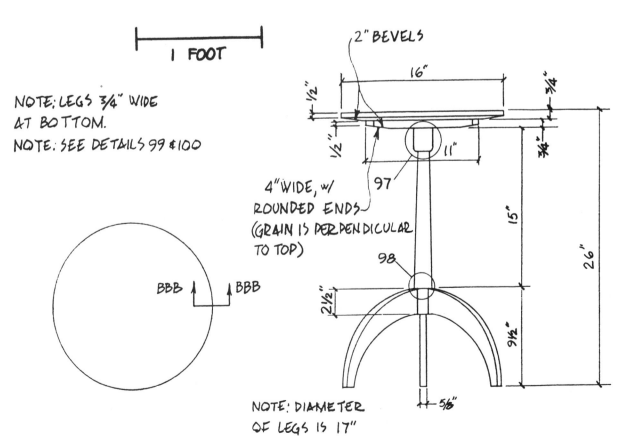

1 FOOT

NOTE: LEGS 3/4" WIDE
AT BOTTOM.
NOTE: SEE DETAILS 99 &100

BBB ↑   ↑ BBB

2" BEVELS

16"

1/2"

3/4"

1/2"

11"

97

3/4"

4" WIDE, w/
ROUNDED ENDS
(GRAIN IS PERPENDICULAR
TO TOP)

15"

26"

98

2½"

9½"

5/8"

NOTE: DIAMETER
OF LEGS IS 17"

Top and side views of roundstand #1.

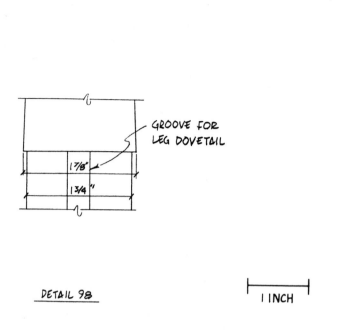

GROOVE FOR
LEG DOVETAIL

1 7/8"

1 3/4"

DETAIL 98

|— 1 INCH

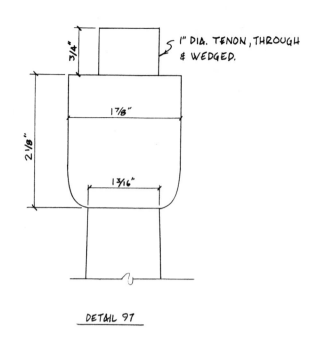

1" DIA. TENON, THROUGH
& WEDGED.

3/4"

2 1/8"

1 7/8"

1 3/16"

DETAIL 97

Details 97 and 98: Turning.

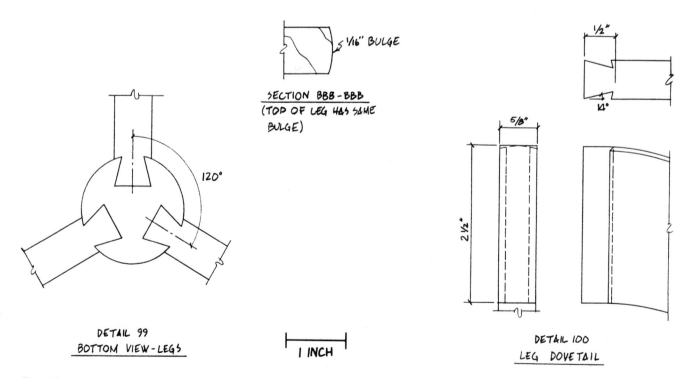

1/16" BULGE

SECTION BBB-BBB
(TOP OF LEG HAS SAME
BULGE)

120°

DETAIL 99
BOTTOM VIEW-LEGS

|— 1 INCH

1/2"

4°

5/8"

2 1/2"

DETAIL 100
LEG DOVETAIL

Details 99 and 100: Leg details.

Roundstand #2

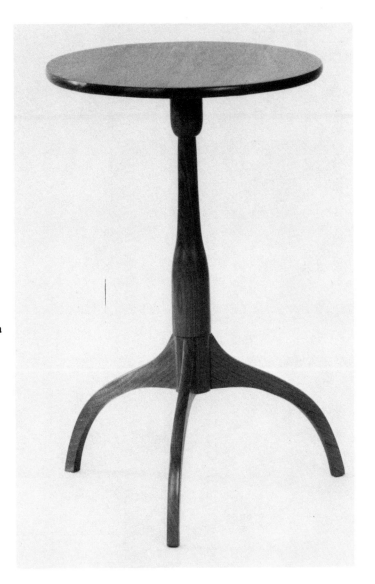

Where a little more surface space is required, the 18-inch (45.7-cm) diameter top of the roundstand #2 can be utilized. This table has also been called a spider table, or spider-leg table, because of the shape of the legs.

NOTE: SEE DETAIL 156

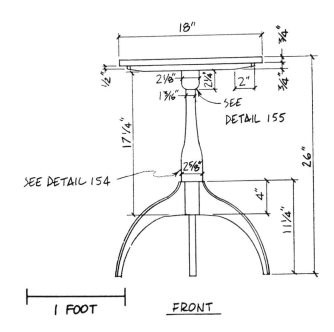

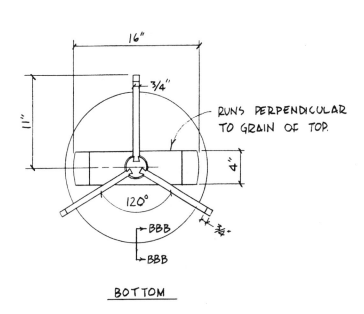

Side and bottom views of the roundstand #2.

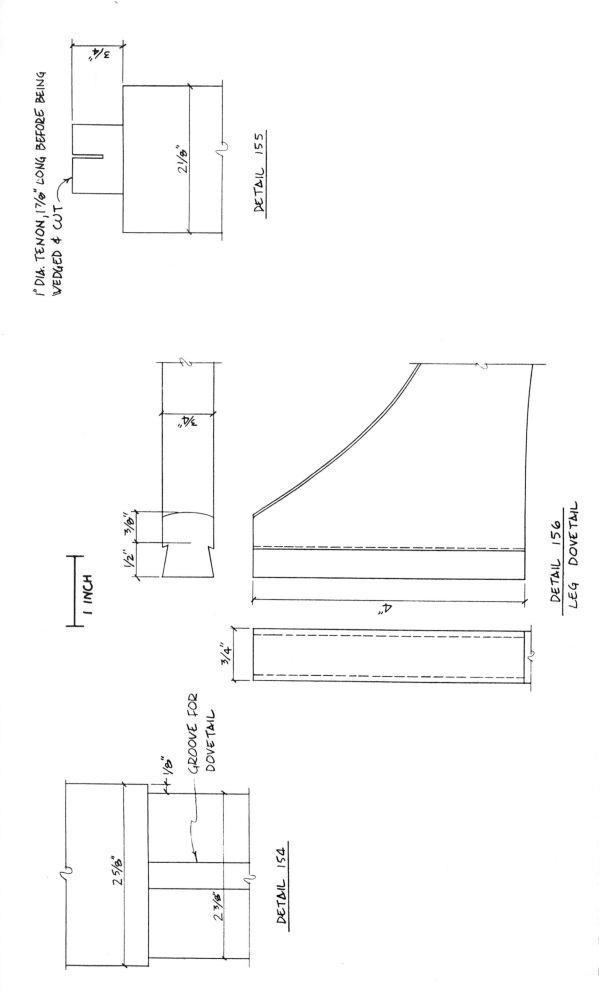

1" DIA. TENON, 1⅞" LONG BEFORE BEING WEDGED & CUT

¾"

2⅛"

DETAIL 155

1 INCH

¾"

½" ⅜"

⅛"

GROOVE FOR DOVETAIL

2⅝"

2⅜"

DETAIL 154

4"

3/4"

DETAIL 156
LEG DOVETAIL

Details 154 and 155: Turning. Detail 156: Leg dovetail.

Stereo Components Cabinet

Having spent the better part of an afternoon in a stereo store measuring components, I noticed that certain universal dimensions began to appear. On the basis of these, this cabinet was designed to house the turntable, with or without changer, amplifier/pre-amplifier combination and tuner and tape deck. The bottom two compartments are for housing tapes and records stored on their edges.

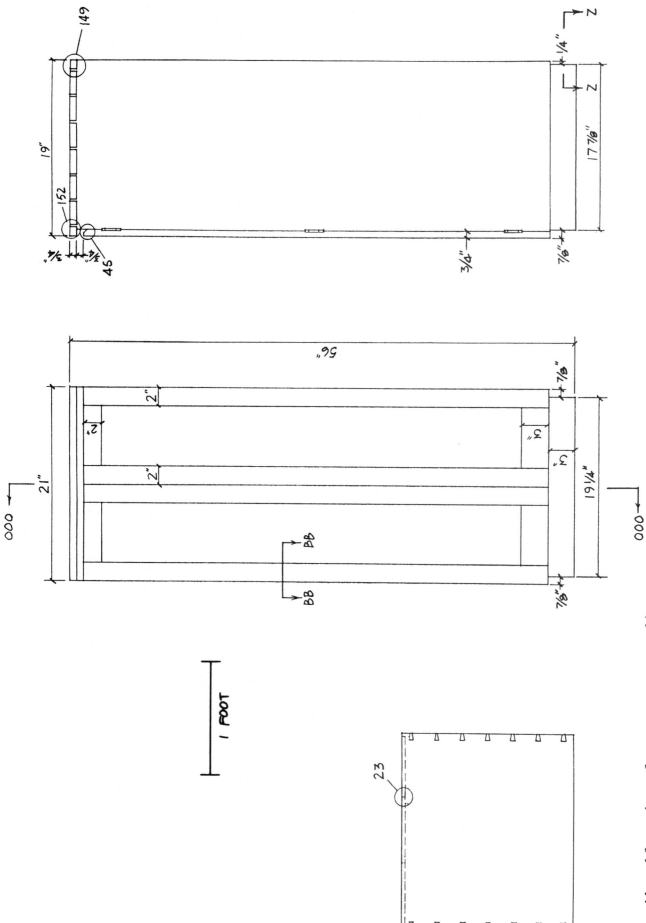

Top, side and front views of stereo components cabinet.

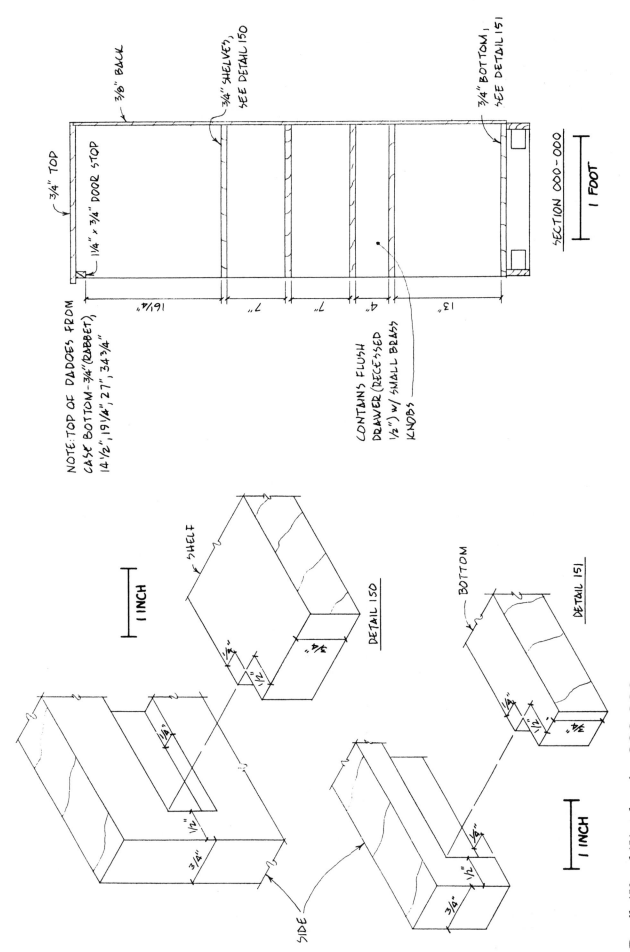

3/8" BACK

3/4" SHELVES,
SEE DETAIL 150

3/4" BOTTOM,
SEE DETAIL 151

3/4" TOP

1/4" x 3/4" DOOR STOP

SECTION OOO-OOO

1 FOOT

NOTE: TOP OF DADOES FROM
CASE BOTTOM—3/4" (RABBET),
14 1/2", 19 1/4", 27", 34 3/4"

19 1/4"

7"

7"

4"

13"

CONTAINS FLUSH
DRAWER (RECESSED
1/2") W/ SMALL BRASS
KNOBS

SHELF

1 INCH

1/2"
1/2"
3/4"

DETAIL 150

1/4"
1/2"
3/4"

SIDE

BOTTOM

1/4"
1/2"
3/4"

DETAIL 151

1 INCH

Details 150 and 151 and section OOO-OOO.

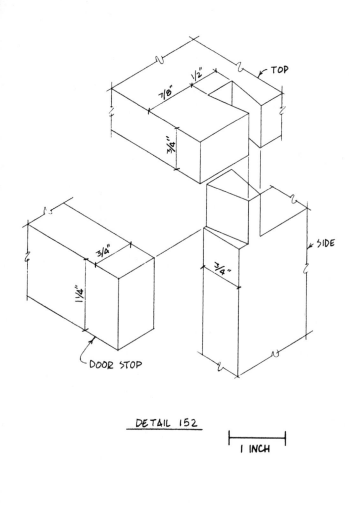

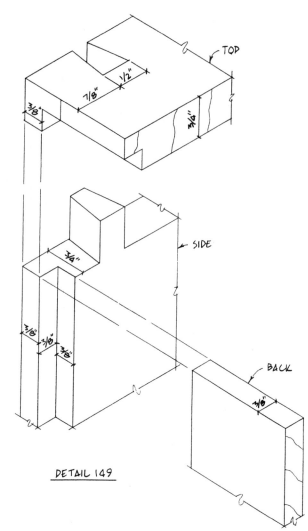

TOP

7/8" 1/2"

3/4"

3/4"

3/4"

SIDE

DOOR STOP

DETAIL 152

1 INCH

BACK

DETAIL 149

Details 149 and 152: Corner joints.

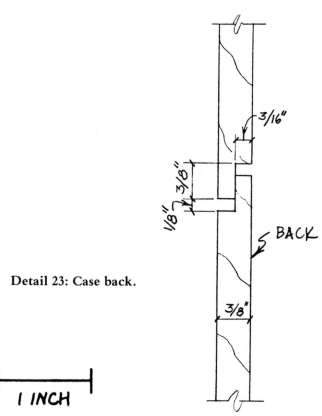

3/16"

3/8"

1/8"

BACK

3/8"

Detail 23: Case back.

1 INCH

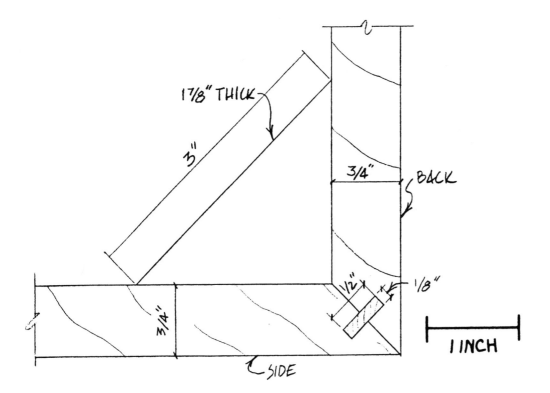

Section Z-Z.

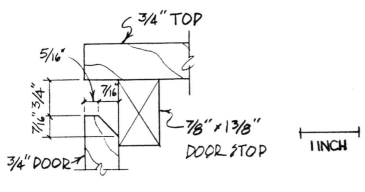

DETAIL 45

Detail 45 (door pull).

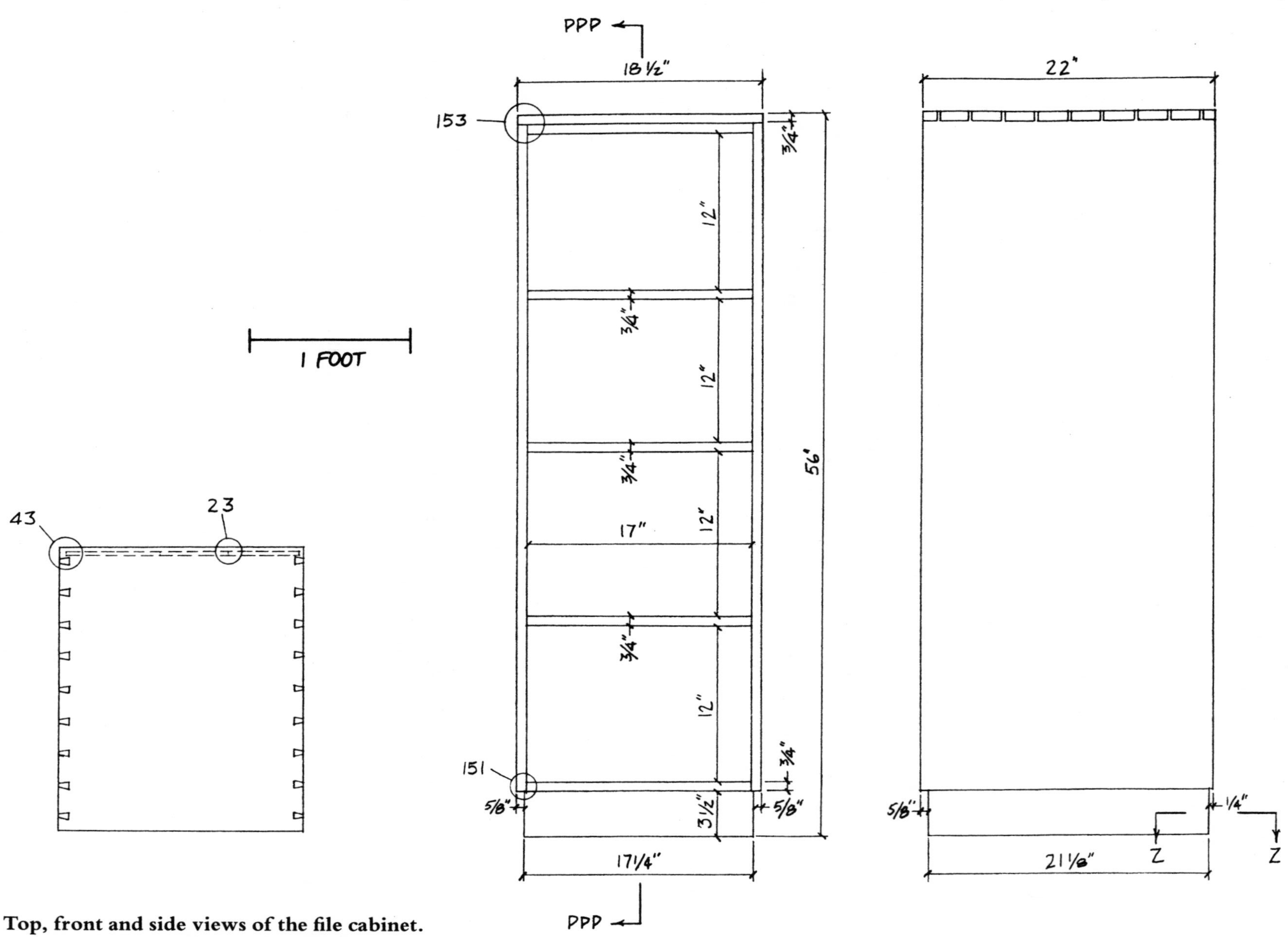

File Cabinet (Four-Drawer)

22"

21⅛"

¼"

Z

Z

⅝"

56"

3¼"

¾"

⅝"

12"

12"

12"

12"

¾"

¾"

¾"

17"

3½"

18½"

17¼"

PPP

PPP

153

151

⅝"

1 FOOT

23

43

Top, front and side views of the file cabinet.

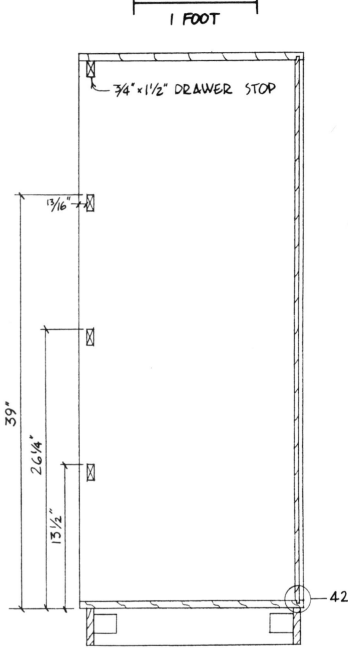

Section PPP-PPP.

Most contemporary filing cabinets are made of steel, and although quite functional they don't offer much in the way of aesthetics. If properly made, a wooden file cabinet can be as utilitarian as one in steel.

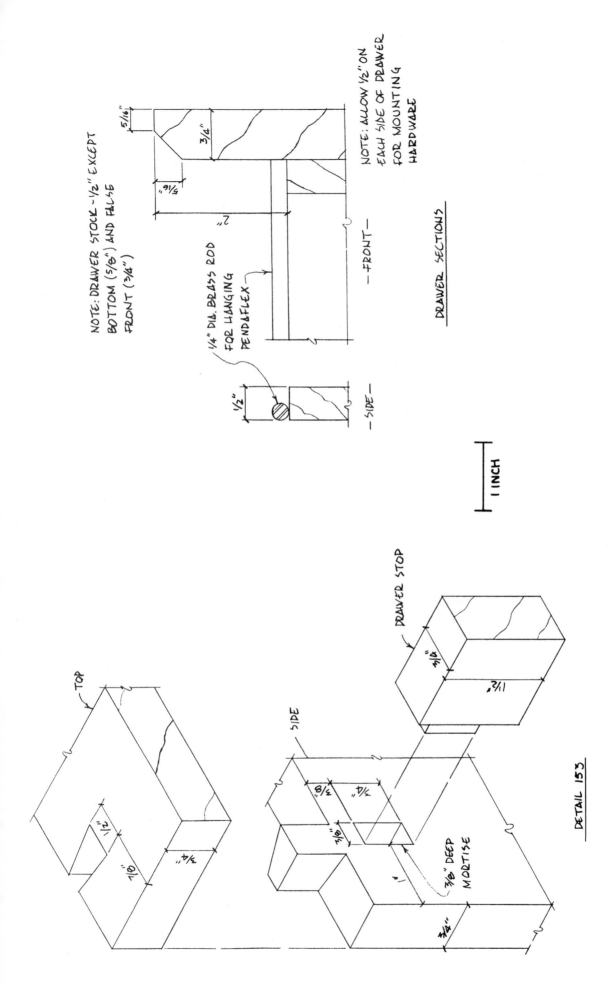

NOTE: DRAWER STOCK - ½" EXCEPT BOTTOM (5/8") AND FALSE FRONT (3/4")

5/16"

3/4"

5/16"

2"

— FRONT —

NOTE: ALLOW ½" ON EACH SIDE OF DRAWER FOR MOUNTING HARDWARE

DRAWER SECTIONS

¼" DIA. BRASS ROD FOR HANGING PENDAFLEX

½"

— SIDE —

1 INCH

TOP

½"

1/10"

3/4"

SIDE

3/8"

½"

3/8"

3/8" DEEP MORTISE

1"

3/4"

DRAWER STOP

3/8"

1/2"

DETAIL 153

Detail 153: Corner and drawer sections.

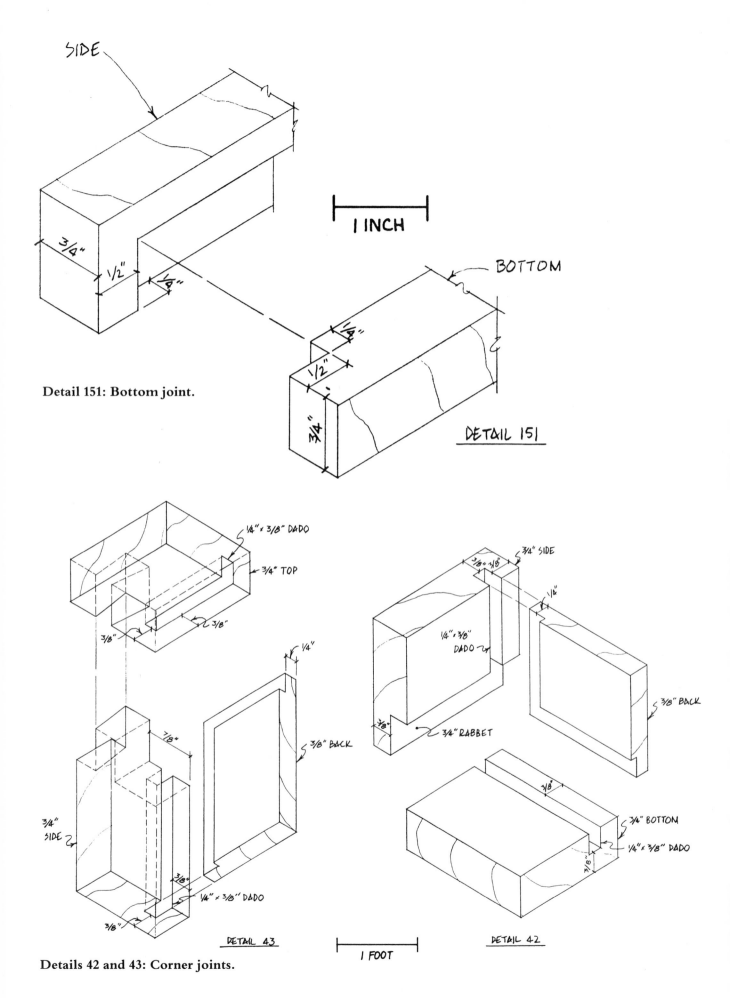

SIDE

3/4"

1/2"

1/8"

1 INCH

BOTTOM

1/4"

1/2"

3/4"

Detail 151: Bottom joint.

DETAIL 151

1/4" × 3/8" DADO

3/4" TOP

3/8"

3/8"

7/8"

1/4"

3/8" BACK

3/4"
SIDE

3/8"

1/4" × 3/8" DADO

DETAIL 43

3/8" 3/8"

3/4" SIDE

1/4"

1/4" × 3/8"
DADO

3/8"

3/4" RABBET

3/8" BACK

3/8"

3/4" BOTTOM

1/4" × 3/8" DADO

3/8"

DETAIL 42

1 FOOT

Details 42 and 43: Corner joints.

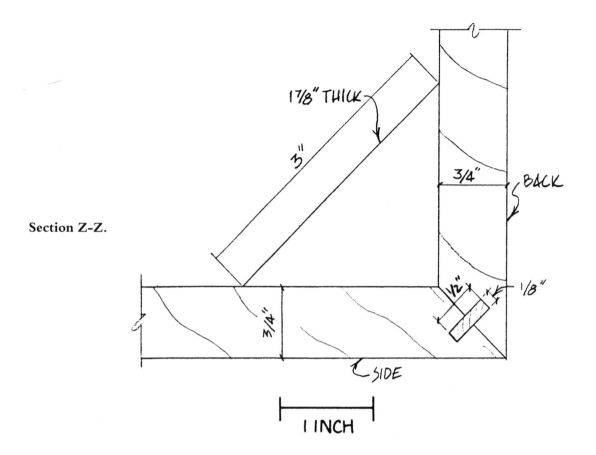

Section Z-Z.

1⅞" THICK

3"

3/4"

BACK

3/4"

½"

⅛"

SIDE

1 INCH

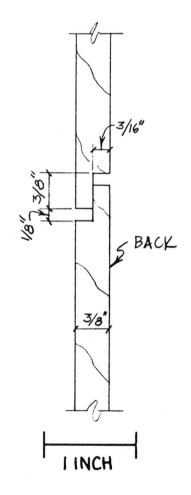

Detail 23: Case back.

3/16"

3/8"

⅛"

BACK

3/8"

1 INCH

File Cabinet (Two-Drawer)

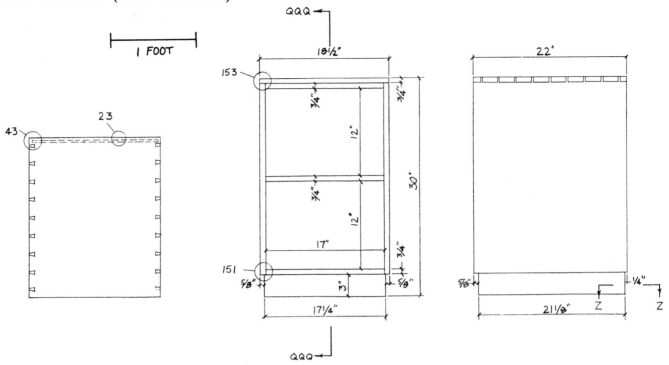

When less storage space is required, the two-drawer file cabinet with its 30-inch (76.2-cm) top doubles as a tabletop. Both of these file cabinets are designed to house legal-size documents.

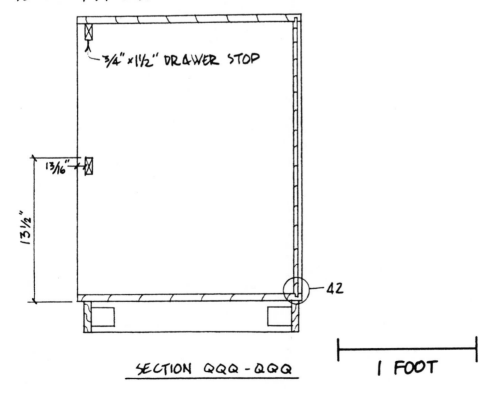

NOTES: 3/4" TOP, 3/4" BOTTOM, 3/8" BACK, 3/4" BASE

3/4" x 1½" DRAWER STOP

13/16"

13½"

42

SECTION QQQ-QQQ

1 FOOT

Section QQQ of the two-drawer file cabinet. For further details, see the four-drawer file cabinet (pages 284 to 286).

Étagère (Triangle)

The recessed incandescent light at the top of
this case projects through adjustable glass
shelves and gives an interesting glow to what
is displayed below. The triangular shape fits
almost anywhere in a room.

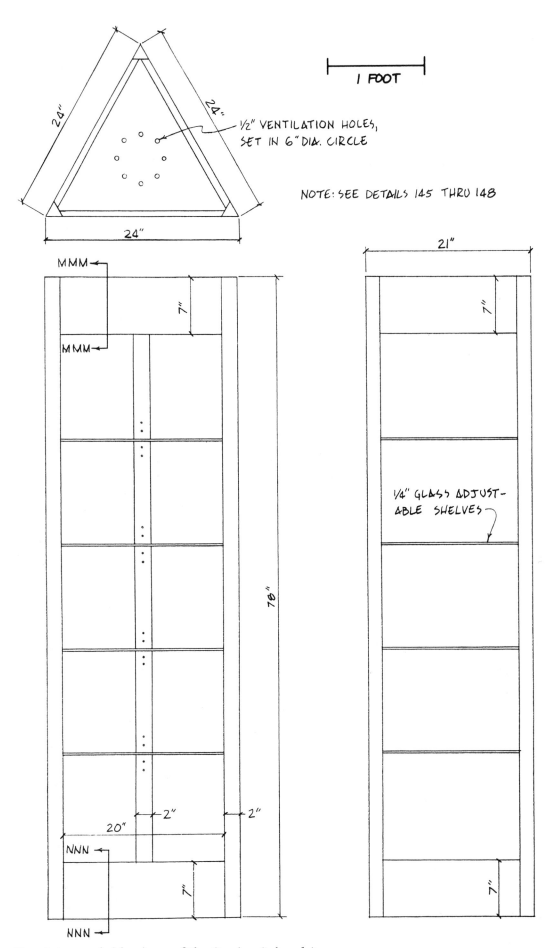

1 FOOT

½" VENTILATION HOLES,
SET IN 6" DIA. CIRCLE

NOTE: SEE DETAILS 145 THRU 148

24"

24"

24"

24"

MMM

MMM

7"

21"

7"

¼" GLASS ADJUST-
ABLE SHELVES

70"

2"

2"

20"

NNN

NNN

7"

7"

Front, top and side views of the étagère (triangle).

NOTE: TRIANGULAR POST-
SAME LOCATIONS

CORNER POST (RECTANGLE)

5/8" BEVEL

2"   2"

1/4"

DADO FOR
ELECTRICAL
WIRE"

1/4"
1/2"

1/2"

2"

— SECTION THROUGH CORNER
POST- TRIANGLE —

DETAIL 145

1 INCH

NOTE: HOLES 1/4"
DIA., 1/2" DEEP, 1"
O.C. APART

56 1/4"

43 1/2"

1/8"   1/2"
1/2"

1/4" × 1/4"
DADO FOR
ELECTRICAL
WIRE

1 3/4"

30 3/4"

18"

1 3/4"

— SECTION THROUGH
CORNER POST - RECTANGLE —

DETAIL 144

1 INCH

— HOLE LOCATIONS —

DETAIL 146

1 FOOT

Details 144, 145 and 146: Posts.

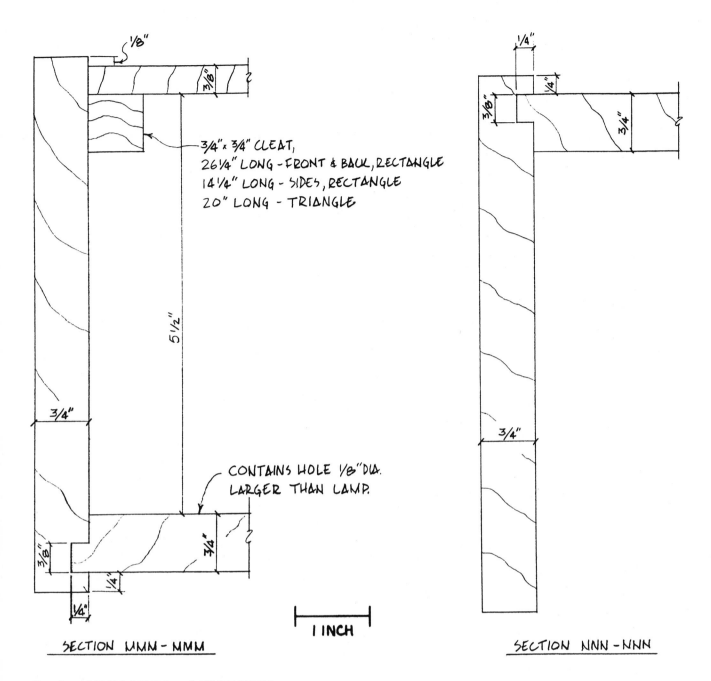

1/8"

3/8"

3/4" x 3/4" CLEAT,
26 1/4" LONG - FRONT & BACK, RECTANGLE
14 1/4" LONG - SIDES, RECTANGLE
20" LONG - TRIANGLE

5 1/2"

3/4"

CONTAINS HOLE 1/8" DIA.
LARGER THAN LAMP.

3/8"

3/4"

1/4"

1/4"

SECTION MMM-MMM

1 INCH

1/4"

3/8"

1/4"

3/4"

3/4"

3/4"

SECTION NNN-NNN

Sections MMM-MMM and NNN-NNN.

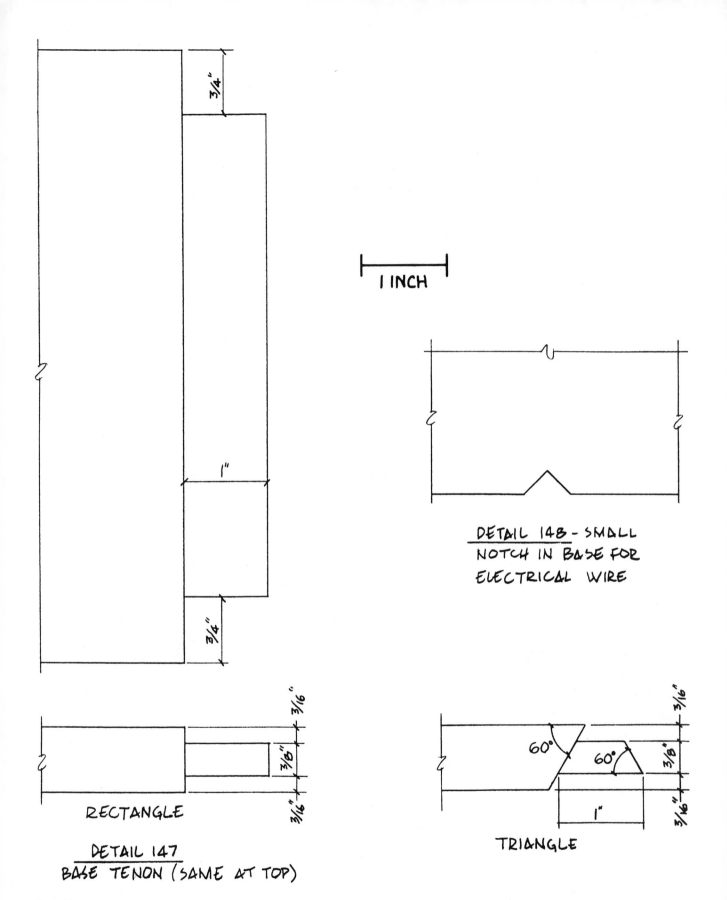

3/4"

1 INCH

1"

3/4"

DETAIL 148 - SMALL
NOTCH IN BASE FOR
ELECTRICAL WIRE

3/16"

3/8"

3/16"

RECTANGLE

DETAIL 147
BASE TENON (SAME AT TOP)

60°

60°

3/16"

3/8"

3/16"

1"

TRIANGLE

Details 147 and 148.

Étagère (Rectangle)

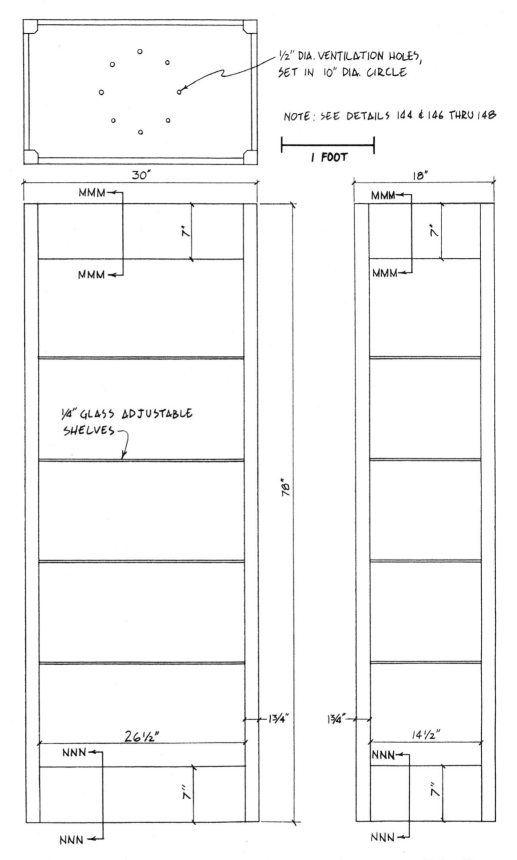

½" DIA. VENTILATION HOLES, SET IN 10" DIA. CIRCLE

NOTE: SEE DETAILS 144 & 146 THRU 148

1 FOOT

30"

MMM

7"

MMM

¼" GLASS ADJUSTABLE SHELVES

78"

1¾"

26½"

NNN

7"

NNN

18"

MMM

7"

MMM

1¾"

1¾"

14½"

NNN

7"

NNN

Less dramatic in its form is the four-sided rectangular étagère, which offers greater display space. Both the triangular and rectangular étagères can be used against a wall or corner, or standing free in the center of the room. Here are the front, top and side views of the rectangular étagère. For further details, see the triangular étagère (pages 290 to 292).

Stack Tables

These stack tables provide many functions and are easy to store.

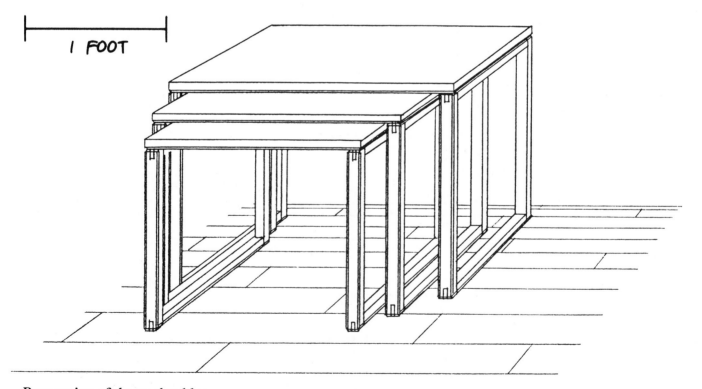

1 FOOT

Perspective of the stack tables.

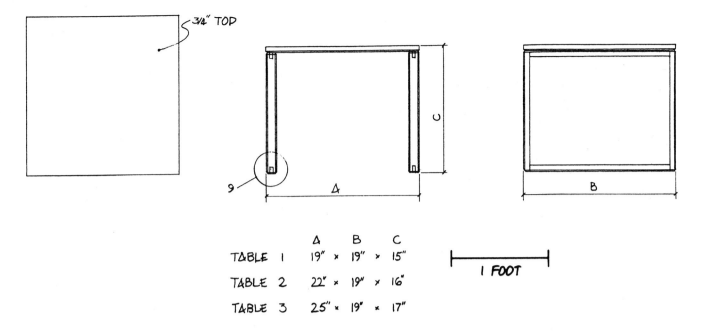

3/4" TOP

	A	B	C
TABLE 1	19"	× 19"	× 15"
TABLE 2	22"	× 19"	× 16"
TABLE 3	25"	× 19"	× 17"

1 FOOT

Front, side and top views of stack tables.

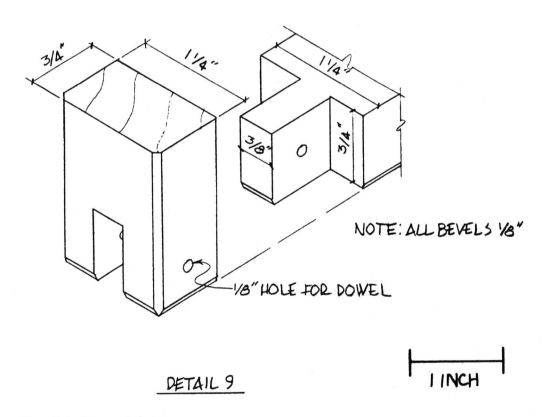

3/4"

1 1/4"

1 1/4"

3/8"

3/4"

NOTE: ALL BEVELS 1/8"

1/8" HOLE FOR DOWEL

DETAIL 9

1 INCH

Detail 9: Corner joint.

Bowfront Credenza

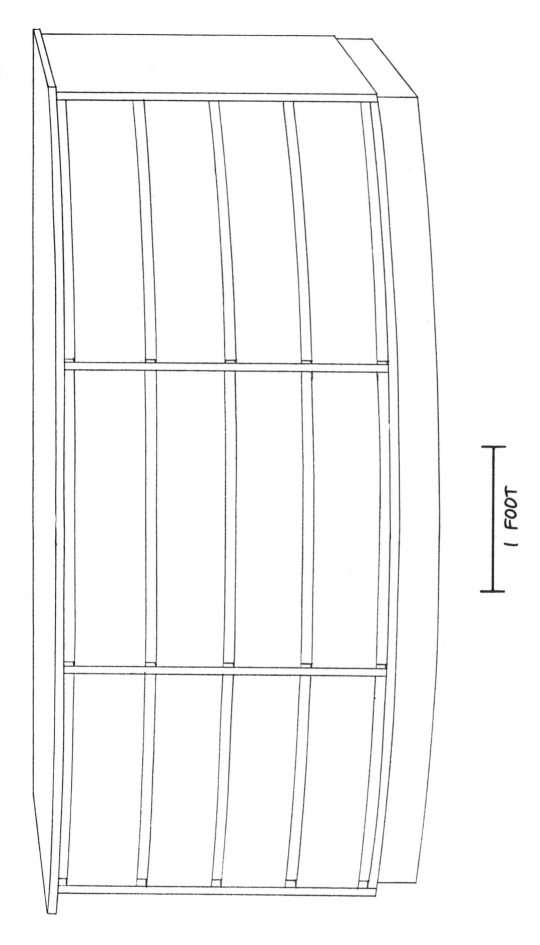

1 FOOT

Perspective of the bowfront credenza. See the following page for a
photograph.

The continuous curved front gives the bowfront credenza great visual appeal, but also makes its construction more difficult. This piece works equally well in an office or contemporary dining room. The back of this case, which is entirely paneled, extends its use as a room divider.

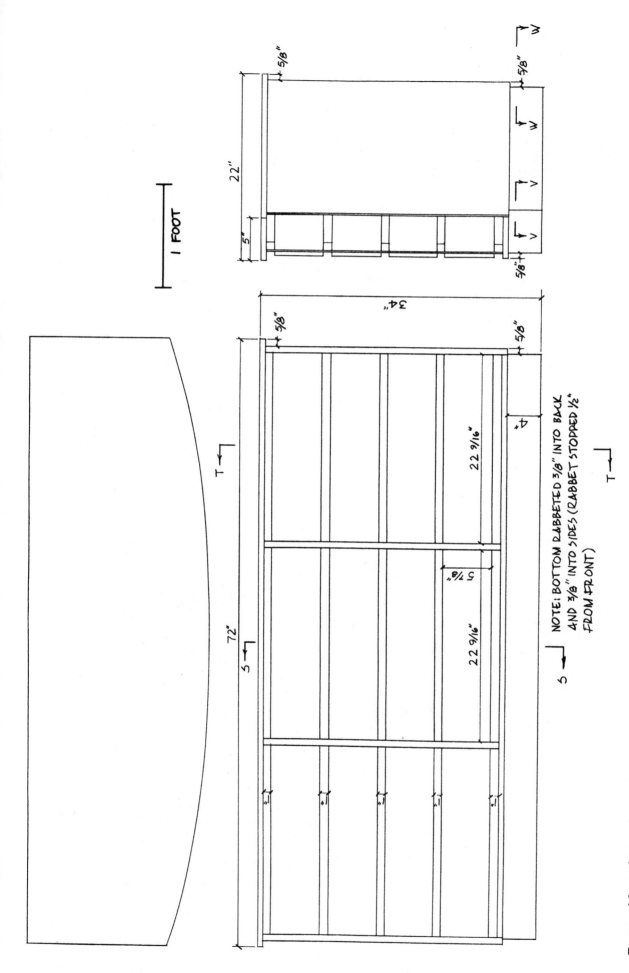

Front, side and top views of the bowfront credenza.

NOTE: BOTTOM RABBETED 3/8" INTO BACK AND 3/8" INTO SIDES (RABBET STOPPED 1/2" FROM FRONT)

1 FOOT

22"

5"

34"

72"

22 9/16"

22 9/16"

5 7/8"

5/8"

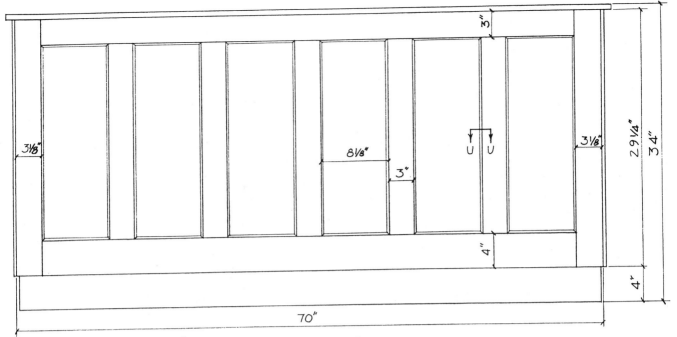

3"

29¼"

34"

3⅛"

8⅛"

3"

U U

3⅛"

4"

4"

70"

NOTE: BACK RABBETED
3/8" INTO SIDES

BACK VIEW

|——— 1 FOOT ———|

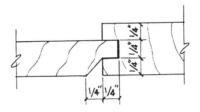

¼"

¼"

¼"

¼" ¼"

SECTION   U-U

|——— 1 INCH ———|

Back view and section U-U.

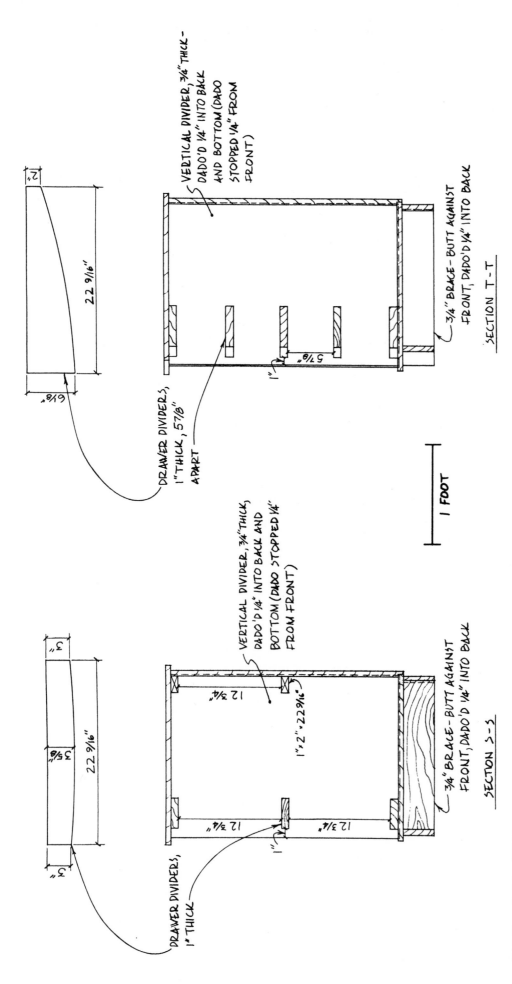

VERTICAL DIVIDER, 3/4" THICK – DADO'D 1/4" INTO BACK AND BOTTOM (DADO STOPPED 1/4" FROM FRONT)

3/4" BRACE – BUTT AGAINST FRONT, DADO'D 1/4" INTO BACK

SECTION T-T

12"

22 9/16"

6 1/8"

DRAWER DIVIDERS, 1" THICK, 5 7/8" APART

5 7/8"

1"

1 FOOT

VERTICAL DIVIDER, 3/4" THICK, DADO'D 1/4" INTO BACK AND BOTTOM (DADO STOPPED 1/4" FROM FRONT)

3/4" BRACE – BUTT AGAINST FRONT, DADO'D 1/4" INTO BACK

SECTION S-S

3"

22 9/16"

3 5/8"

3"

12 3/4"

1" × 2" × 22 9/16"

12 3/4"

12 3/4"

1"

1"

DRAWER DIVIDERS, 1" THICK

Sections S-S and T-T.

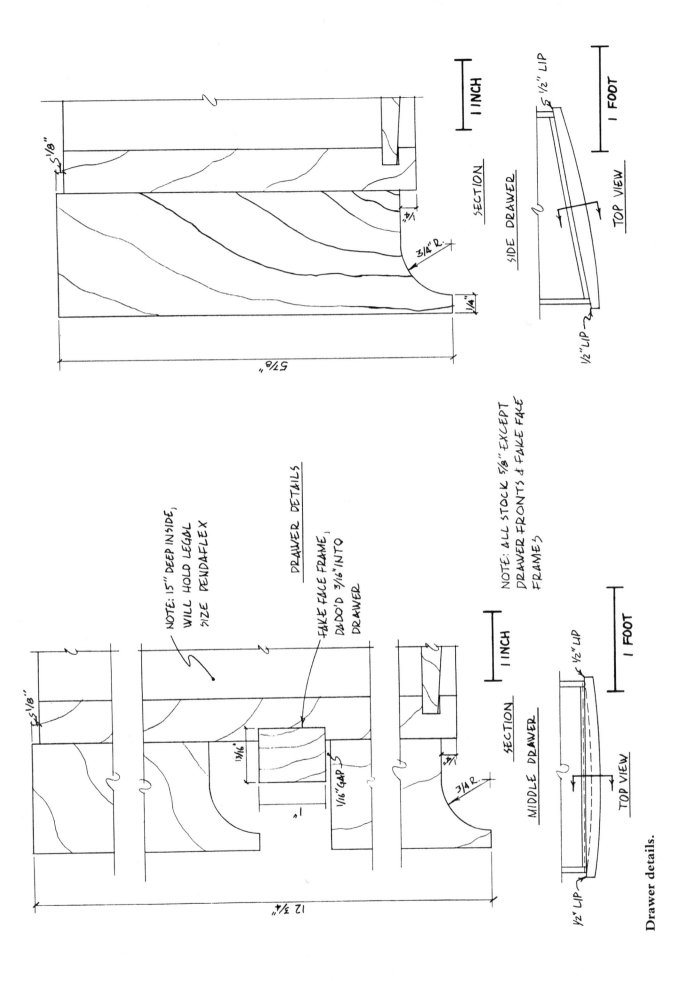

5⅛"

1"

SECTION

1 INCH

SIDE DRAWER

½" LIP

TOP VIEW

1 FOOT

½" LIP

3/4" R.

¼"

57⅛"

DRAWER DETAILS

NOTE: 15" DEEP INSIDE, WILL HOLD LEGAL SIZE PENDAFLEX

FAKE FACE FRAME, DADO'D 3/16" INTO DRAWER

NOTE: ALL STOCK ⅝" EXCEPT DRAWER FRONTS & FAKE FACE FRAMES

5⅛"

13/16"

1/16" GAP

1"

1"

3/4 R.

SECTION

1 INCH

MIDDLE DRAWER

½" LIP

TOP VIEW

1 FOOT

½" LIP

12 3/4"

Drawer details.

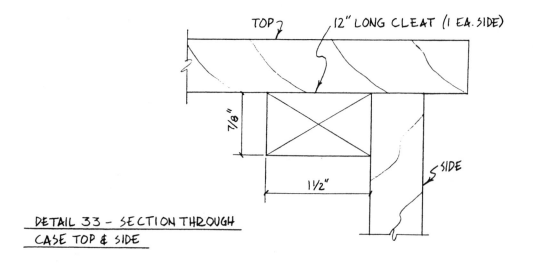

TOP

12" LONG CLEAT (1 EA. SIDE)

7/8"

1½"

SIDE

DETAIL 33 – SECTION THROUGH
CASE TOP & SIDE

Detail 33: Top. Detail 34: Finger joint used at all four corners of each
drawer. Curved drawer fronts are attached to boxes.

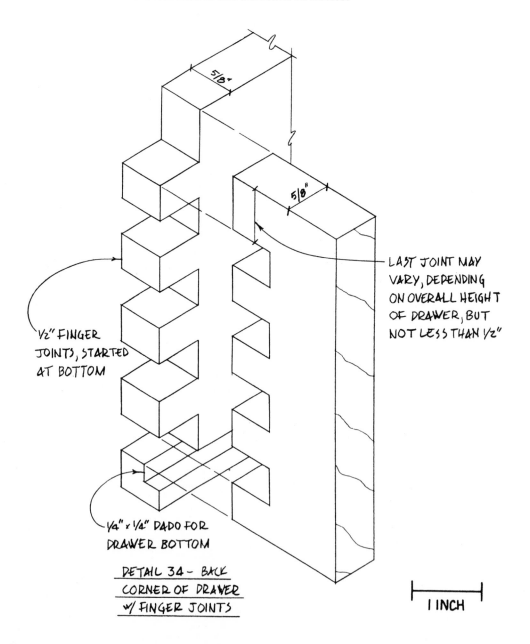

5/8"

5/8"

LAST JOINT MAY
VARY, DEPENDING
ON OVERALL HEIGHT
OF DRAWER, BUT
NOT LESS THAN ½"

½" FINGER
JOINTS, STARTED
AT BOTTOM

¼" x ¼" DADO FOR
DRAWER BOTTOM

DETAIL 34 – BACK
CORNER OF DRAWER
w/ FINGER JOINTS

1 INCH

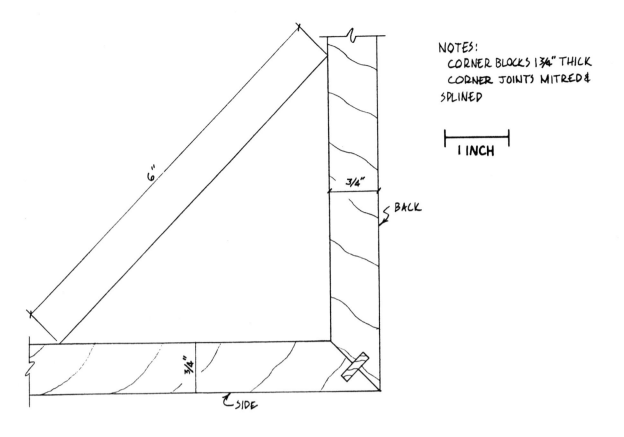

NOTES:
CORNER BLOCKS 1¾" THICK
CORNER JOINTS MITRED &
SPLINED

⊢———⊣ 1 INCH

6"

3/4"

BACK

3/4"

SIDE

SECTION W-W

Sections W-W and V-V.

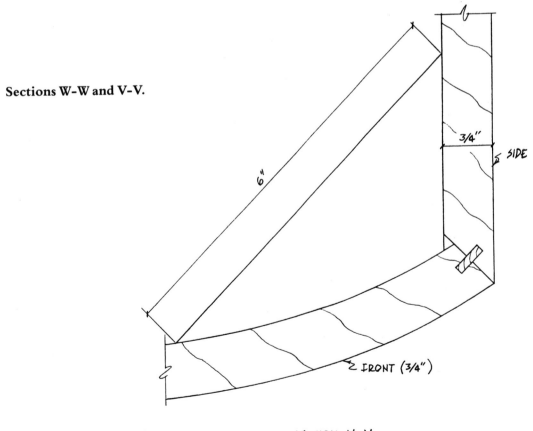

6"

3/4"

SIDE

FRONT (3/4")

SECTION V-V

Appendices

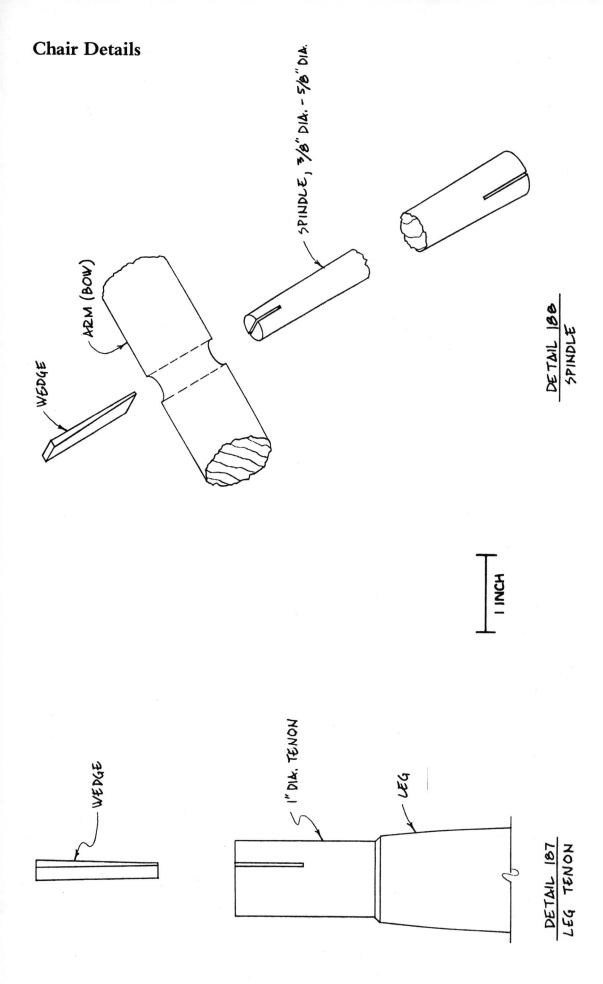

WEDGE

ARM (BOW)

SPINDLE, ³/₈" DIA. - ⁵/₈" DIA.

DETAIL 188
SPINDLE

1 INCH

WEDGE

1" DIA. TENON

LEG

DETAIL 187
LEG TENON

Detail 187: Leg tenon. Detail 188: Spindle.

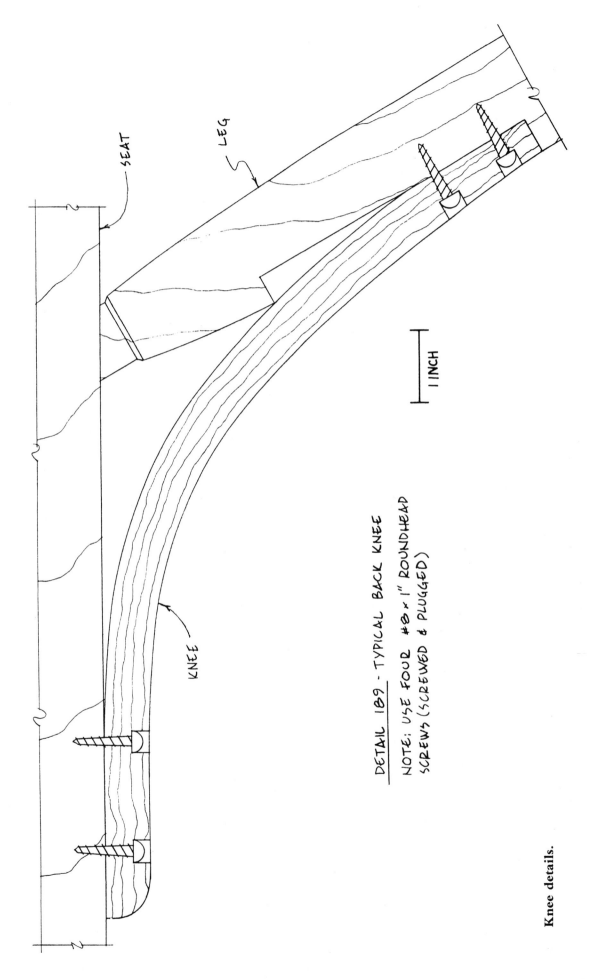

SEAT

LEG

KNEE

1 INCH

DETAIL 189 - TYPICAL BACK KNEE

NOTE: USE FOUR #8 × 1" ROUNDHEAD
SCREWS (SCREWED & PLUGGED)

Knee details.

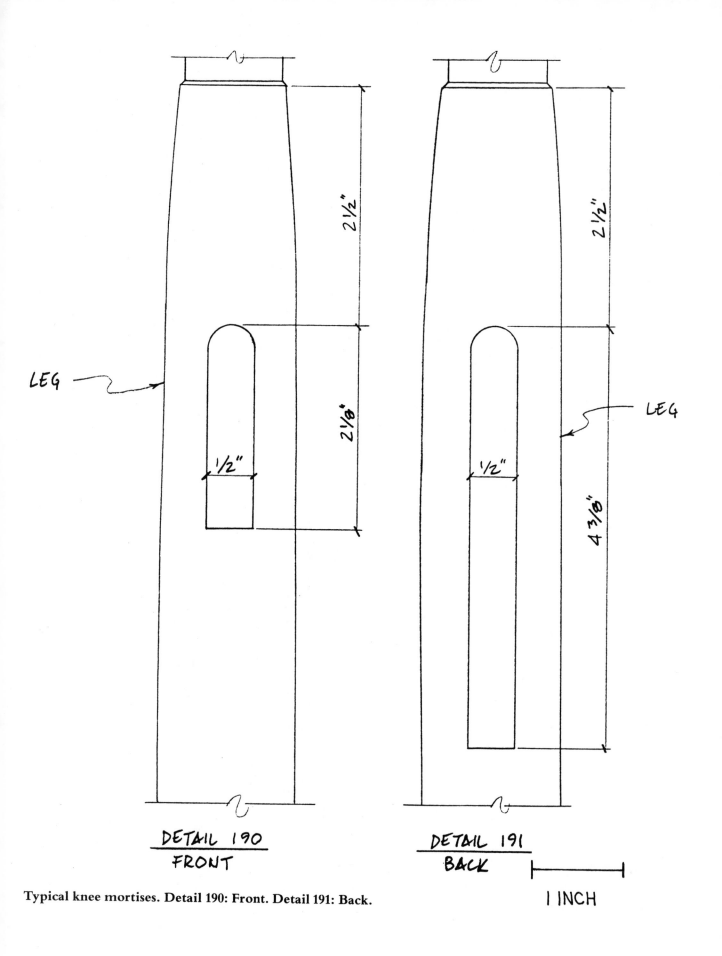

LEG

2½"

2⅛"

½"

DETAIL 190
FRONT

LEG

2½"

4⅜"

½"

DETAIL 191
BACK

1 INCH

Typical knee mortises. Detail 190: Front. Detail 191: Back.

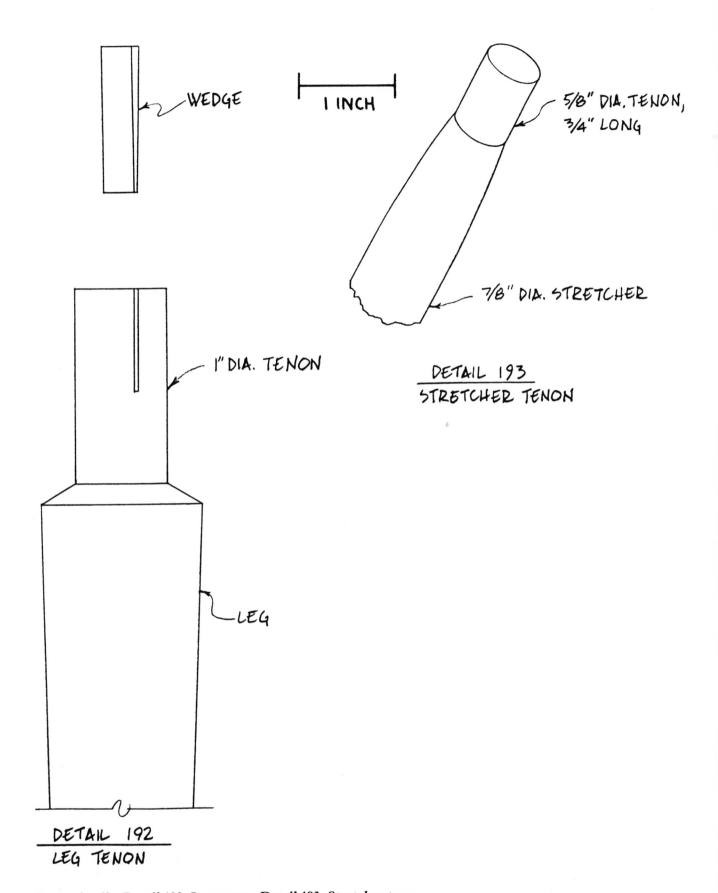

WEDGE

|⟵ 1 INCH ⟶|

5/8" DIA. TENON, 3/4" LONG

7/8" DIA. STRETCHER

DETAIL 193
STRETCHER TENON

1" DIA. TENON

LEG

DETAIL 192
LEG TENON

Tenon details. Detail 192: Leg tenon. Detail 193: Stretcher tenon.

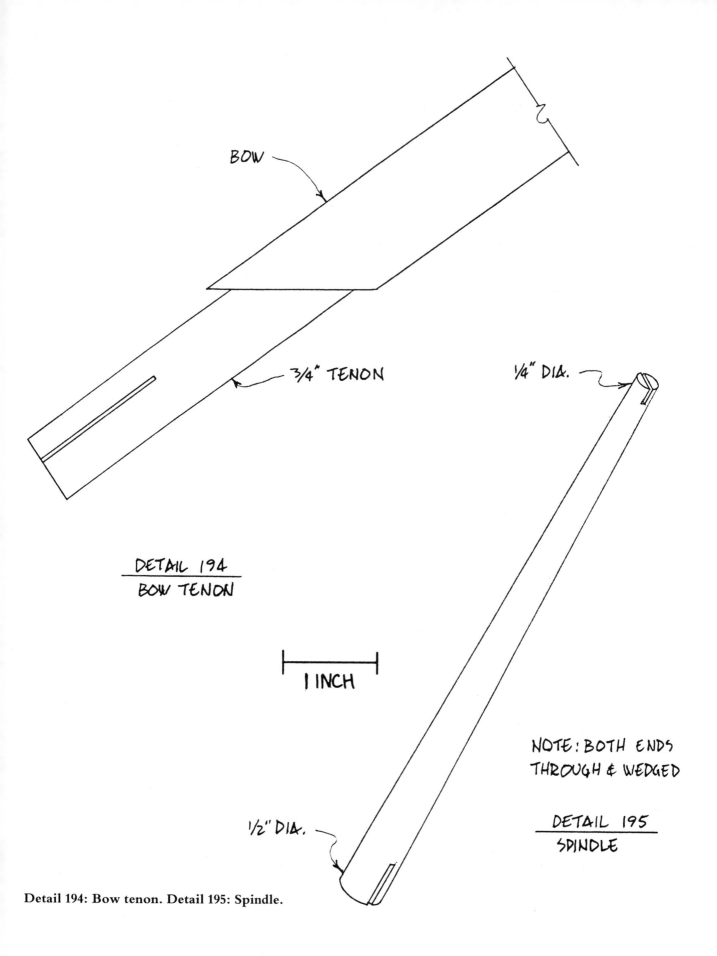

BOW

3/4" TENON

DETAIL 194
BOW TENON

1/4" DIA.

1 INCH

NOTE: BOTH ENDS
THROUGH & WEDGED

DETAIL 195
SPINDLE

1/2" DIA.

Detail 194: Bow tenon. Detail 195: Spindle.

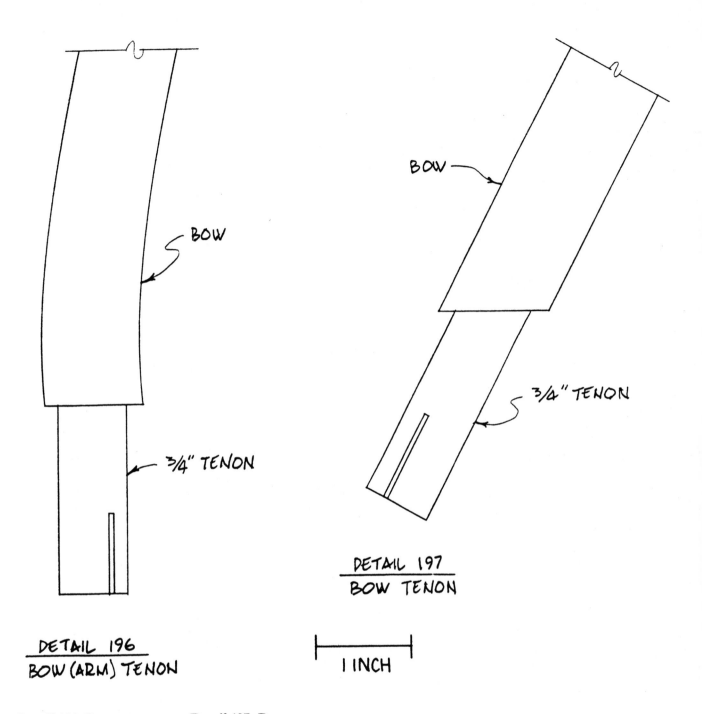

BOW

3/4" TENON

DETAIL 196
BOW (ARM) TENON

BOW

3/4" TENON

DETAIL 197
BOW TENON

1 INCH

Detail 196: Bow arm tenon. Detail 197: Bow tenon.

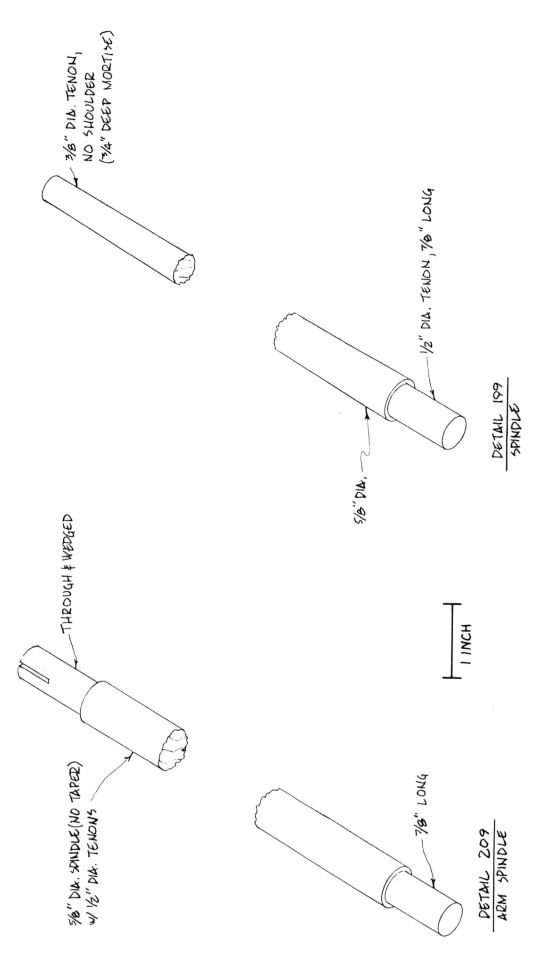

3/8" DIA. TENON, NO SHOULDER (3/4" DEEP MORTISE)

1/2" DIA. TENON, 7/8" LONG

5/8" DIA.

DETAIL 199
SPINDLE

THROUGH & WEDGED

1 INCH

5/8" DIA. SPINDLE (NO TAPER) w/ 1/2" DIA. TENONS

7/8" LONG

DETAIL 209
ARM SPINDLE

Detail 199: Spindle. Detail 209: Arm spindle.

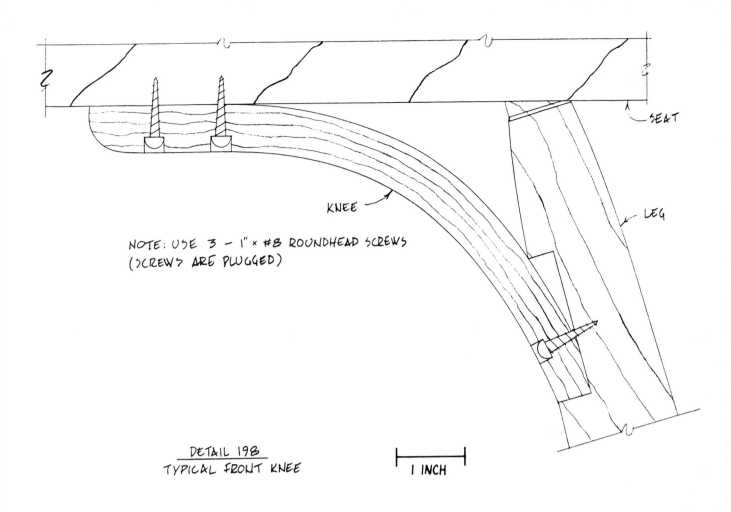

NOTE: USE 3 – 1" × #8 ROUNDHEAD SCREWS
(SCREWS ARE PLUGGED)

KNEE

SEAT

LEG

DETAIL 198
TYPICAL FRONT KNEE

1 INCH

Detail 198: Knee cross section.

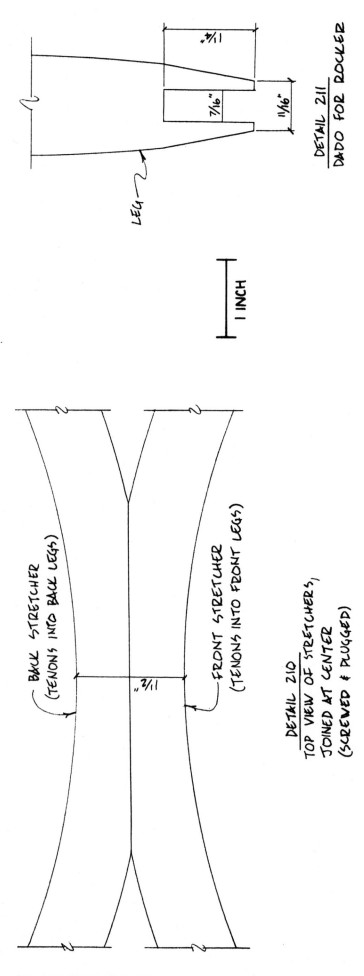

LEG

1 1/4"

7/16"

11/16"

DETAIL 211
DADO FOR ROCKER

1 INCH

BACK STRETCHER
(TENONS INTO BACK LEGS)

FRONT STRETCHER
(TENONS INTO FRONT LEGS)

1 1/2"

DETAIL 210
TOP VIEW OF STRETCHERS,
JOINED AT CENTER
(SCREWED & PLUGGED)

Detail 210: Front stretcher for inverted arm bench. Detail 211: Rocker dado.

Case Details

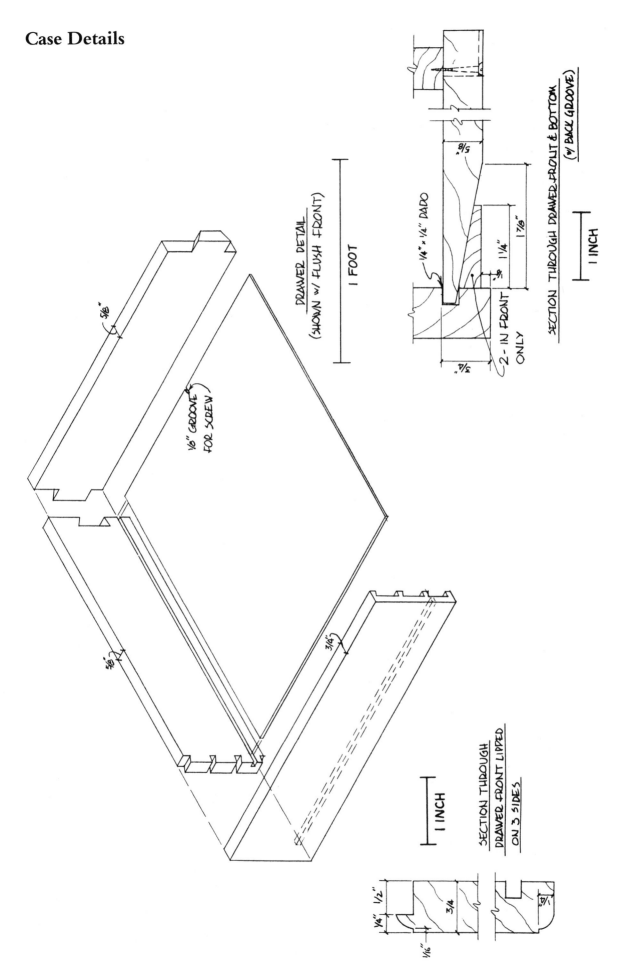

DRAWER DETAIL
(SHOWN w/ FLUSH FRONT)

1 FOOT

5/8"

1/16" GROOVE
FOR SCREW

5/8"

3/4"

SECTION THROUGH DRAWER FRONT & BOTTOM
(w/ BACK GROOVE)

1 INCH

5/8

1/4" x 1/4" DADO

1 1/4"

1 7/8"

2- IN FRONT
ONLY

3/4"

SECTION THROUGH
DRAWER FRONT LIPPED
ON 3 SIDES

1 INCH

1/2"

1/4"

3/4

1/16"

1/16"

Drawer details.

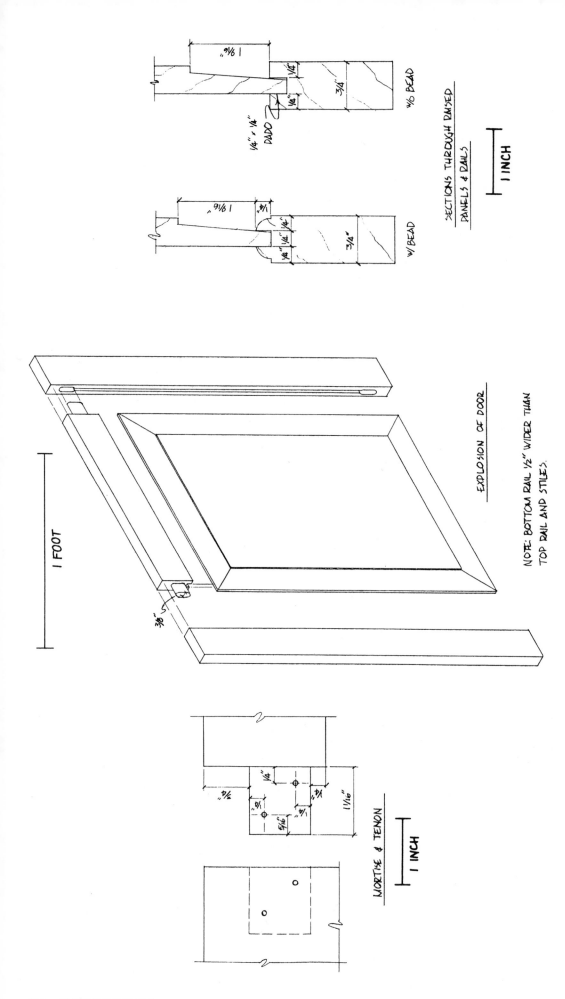

1 9/16"

1/4"

3/4"

W/O BEAD

1/4" x 1/4"
DADO

1 9/16"

1/4"

1/4" 1/4"

1/4"

3/4"

W/ BEAD

SECTIONS THROUGH RAISED
PANELS & RAILS

1 INCH

1 FOOT

3/8"

EXPLOSION OF DOOR

NOTE: BOTTOM RAIL 1/2" WIDER THAN
TOP RAIL AND STILES.

1/4"

1/4"

9/16"

5/16"

11/16"

MORTISE & TENON

1 INCH

Raised panel door details.

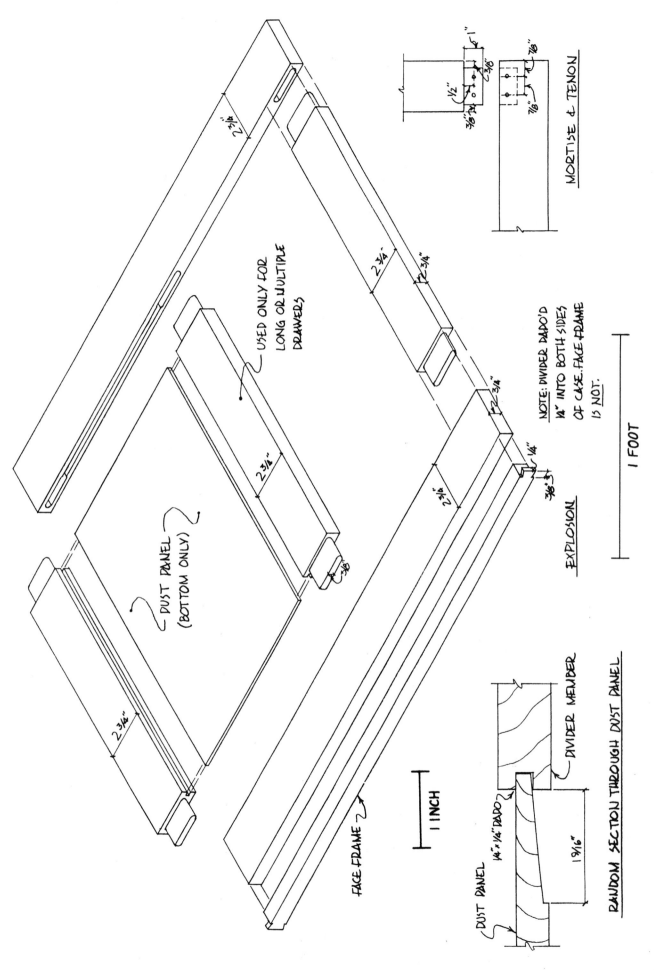

2 ¾"

USED ONLY FOR
LONG OR MULTIPLE
DRAWERS

2 ¾"

2 ¾"

2 ¾"

2 ¾"

3/8"

DUST PANEL
(BOTTOM ONLY)

NOTE: DIVIDER DADO'D
¼" INTO BOTH SIDES
OF CASE. FACE FRAME
IS NOT.

¼"

¼"

3/8"

EXPLOSION

1 FOOT

FACE FRAME

1 INCH

MORTISE & TENON

1"

3/8"

½"

3/8"

7/8"

7/8"

DUST PANEL

¼" x ¼" DADO

DIVIDER MEMBER

1 9/16"

RANDOM SECTION THROUGH DUST PANEL

Drawer divider.

CASE DETAILS 317

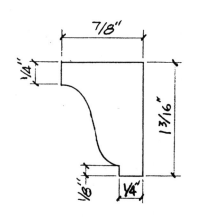

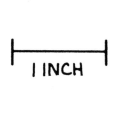

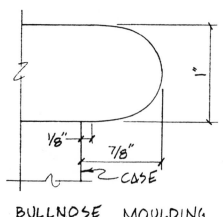

BULLNOSE MOULDING

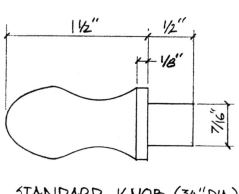

STANDARD KNOB (3/4" DIA.)

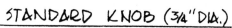

Knob and mouldings.

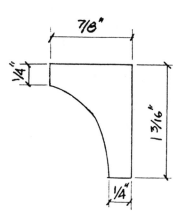

COVE MOULDING

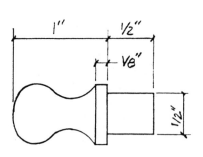

SMALL KNOB (5/8" DIA.)

METRIC EQUIVALENCY CHART

MM—MILLIMETRES   CM—CENTIMETRES

INCHES TO MILLIMETRES AND CENTIMETRES

INCHES	MM	CM	INCHES	CM	INCHES	CM
⅛	3	0.3	9	22.9	30	76.2
¼	6	0.6	10	25.4	31	78.7
⅜	10	1.0	11	27.9	32	81.3
½	13	1.3	12	30.5	33	83.8
⅝	16	1.6	13	33.0	34	86.4
¾	19	1.9	14	35.6	35	88.9
⅞	22	2.2	15	38.1	36	91.4
1	25	2.5	16	40.6	37	94.0
1¼	32	3.2	17	43.2	38	96.5
1½	38	3.8	18	45.7	39	99.1
1¾	44	4.4	19	48.3	40	101.6
2	51	5.1	20	50.8	41	104.1
2½	64	6.4	21	53.3	42	106.7
3	76	7.6	22	55.9	43	109.2
3½	89	8.9	23	58.4	44	111.8
4	102	10.2	24	61.0	45	114.3
4½	114	11.4	25	63.5	46	116.8
5	127	12.7	26	66.0	47	119.4
6	152	15.2	27	68.6	48	121.9
7	178	17.8	28	71.1	49	124.5
8	203	20.3	29	73.7	50	127.0

INDEX